7 Laws

OF WEALTH

SABEL
&
STONE

A Sabel and Stone Publication
LONDON & NEW YORK

7 Laws of Wealth

An Individual Stimulus Plan For Surviving In The New Economy

Ben Benson

7Laws of Wealth
An Individual Stimulus Plan for Surviving in the New Economy

ISBN: 978-0-9563898-9-3

A CIP catalogue record for this book is available from the British Library.

Printed and bound in Great Britain by TJ International Ltd, Padstow, Cornwall.

7 Laws
OF WEALTH

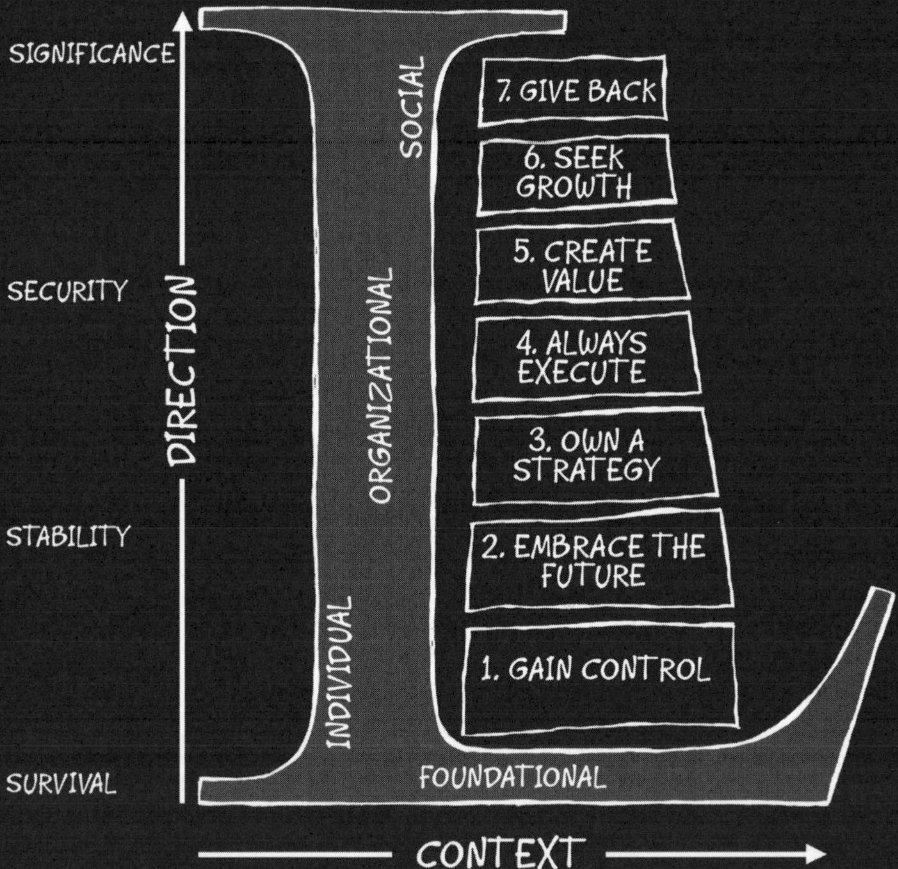

Wealth is inevitable for those who
understand the Natural Laws of its creation
Ben Benson

Contents

Acknowledgements

One component of Law 3; Own a Strategy, is that nothing worthwhile ever happens without the assistance of others and this book is no exception. I'd like to thank the following members of my team for their dedication to this project and willingness to put up with my often last minute demands. Their 'second-mile' commitment was truly inspiring. In no particular order: Joe Lawson who got me started over two decades ago and laid the foundation of today's achievements, M. Robert Rowe who's leadership and profound ability to communicate inspired me to be the best. Keith Wigglesworth for showing me that influence is something that is earned and not bestowed. Kurt Hanks for his willingness to make me think about how I think – you are truly an inspiration and the best interpretative designer on the planet. Bob Thiel, for teaching me that retired CEO's are often the best mentors – good advice. Dr Denis Waitley, for giving me six months of his life, inspiration and advice. Sir Richard Branson and over two hundred of the Times Rich List – greatful for your time and interviews. Richard Stockdale, Charlotte Mouncey and Nigel Reece. Dr Nido Qubein who is arguably one of the top speakers in the world. Alan Perlman for editing and advice in shaping the material. Stephen Brown who's marketing mind is truly one of a kind. James Leverage, for letting me into your network. Kai Maunel, my long time inspiration and friend. Craig Dalley who taught me how to turn a training event into a experience. Paul Horsley and David Platt for help and support in building my property companies. Andrew Hughes for your willingness to take my calls often late at night to make needed changes and adjustments in our businesses. Donald Angir, for his investment support and guidance. Sir Tom Hunter, Sir Philip Green, Felix Dennis and David Reiss. Jacquline Gold, Simon Woodroffe, Chris Evans and Tom Bloxham. John

Knight at the Knight Group, Mike Clare, Kevin Linfoot and Mayank Patel. Everyone at Sabel & Stone Publishing, thanks for your support. Capital Wealth International and my Venture Capital partners. My two fantastic assistants and anyone else that I may have forgotten, you know who you are...

To all of our the individuals, businesses and students current and past that have and are currently using the 7Laws methodology. All my mentees over the years and finally to my family who encouraged me to make this work a reality.

Thank you.

Introduction

It's only fair to warn you right up front that this book is not like the other books you may have read on creating wealth.

There are several reasons. #1: I am first and foremost a business person - long on experience and short on hype. As an entrepreneur, I have active business interests in real estate, finance, publishing and venture capital. I don't make my living writing books.

Difference #1: My Experience

There are thousands of books and seminars on how to become rich or financially independent. But most are written by authors or academics with little first-hand experience of wealth creation - but who hope that sales of their books or products will change all that.

Your local bookstore has an endless selection of titles on how to become a successful entrepreneur. Some are written by individuals who have achieved a noteworthy level of achievement. More likely, the authors are professors and writers who understand business theory, but have never built a business beyond marketing books, CD's and seminars. To know and not to do… is not to know.

Many of these books take the reader step-by-step through the stages of starting, growing and ultimately selling a business. Others provide information on how to take a company public, resolve growth and financing issues, and do other things that any self respecting, would-be entrepreneur needs to be able to do. A few include points of "how-to" information, but I've found most of them lack substance and 'real world' advice. Also, and more importantly, they too are written by people with little or no actual experience in building a business or creating sustainable wealth.

High Fives and Group Hugs

And then there is the endless choice of personal development and wealth creation courses to attend. Problem is, most of them are based on a lie or at best half-truths. Success gurus the world over are insisting on high fives and group hugs at every turn. Conference rooms and convention centers are packed to the rafters with desperate audiences, all hoping to be handed the quick, easy and fast "secret" to personal success.

But surely, you need to ask yourself, how many of these business success "experts" have made their money in the *business* world? How many of them fought their way to success in a volatile and unrelenting corporate environment? How many of them started from scratch and built a group of businesses worth tens of millions of dollars? Not many.

I, on the other hand, have built several businesses. I've made (and lost) a fortune. Thankfully, I lost a fortune only once, and what I have today I built from the ashes of that loss. I borrowed $10,000 from my sister and created a multi-million pound group of businesses in the UK and US.

Oh, and for the record, there wasn't a silver spoon within a hundred mile radius of my young life. I grew up moving from one public housing project to the next with my Father and younger sister. If my Father brought home a carton of freshly squeezed orange juice, *that* was a special occasion. There was always too much *month* left at the end of the money in our home. We never owned a car, and I had to leave school as soon as it was legally possible.

Difference #2: Experience of Truly Wealthy People

The second and more important reason this book is different is that over the past decade I have met and interviewed over 200 of the world's wealthiest individuals from *The Sunday Times* "Rich List" in the UK to *Forbes* in the

US. People like Sir Richard Branson, Sir Tom Hunter, James Caan, Sir Phillip Green, Felix Dennis, Jacqueline Gold, Warren Buffett, and many more.

My own experiences, combined with the invaluable insights offered by some of the wealthiest individuals on the planet, have been distilled for you here in the *7 Laws of Wealth*. This is the real-life, no-guts-no-glory, fly-on-the-wall expose of how wealth is really created - without the hype and hyperbole that so often accompany this topic.

The simple truth is that you have to learn about wealth creation from people who have actually created wealth. You wouldn't take relationship advice from a thrice divorced counselor or health advice from someone who eats burgers for breakfast, lunch and dinner or smokes a pack of cigarettes a day - so why would you take advice on wealth from someone who isn't wealthy?

There is no easy cookie-cutter formula for wealth creation. For every trust fund baby, there are another ten multi-millionaires who started their lives in public housing projects (or their British equivalent, council houses). There are countless examples of rich people frittering away a small fortune and those "less fortunate" creating a large one. Clearly, the circumstances of our birth and the experiences of our lives often have very little to do with wealth creation.

Meeting and interviewing people who have created vast fortunes *and* experiencing the process myself have allowed me to identify the common denominators of success. Wealth and success leave clues, and this book is dedicated to explaining those clues so you can solve the mystery of wealth that eludes so many.

Difference #3: Not What you Want to Hear

Which leads me to the third reason this book is different… it's not what you want to hear!

Think about when your girlfriend or wife says, "Does my backside look big in this?" Or your husband/boyfriend asks, "Do you think I'm getting a paunch?" The person asking the question already knows the truth. But you are faced with two options - you could agree and ruin any chance of an enjoyable evening, or you could lie. The lie might make the person you love feel better for a moment, but they already know their backside looks big or that they have gained a little beer belly - pretending you didn't notice isn't helping you or them.

It's the same with this subject matter. I could tell you what everyone else tells you, and it might make you feel better for a little while, but it's a lie, and it won't make you rich. It might make me richer, because that's the message that sells books, but it won't make you rich. And as I'm already rich, that seems like a complete waste of time.

Hard Truths about Wealth Creation

Wouldn't you rather know how to really create wealth, warts and all, so that at least you have an appreciation for what's involved, and you can either decide you want to take up the challenge - or grab another coke from the fridge and tune in to your favorite TV show.

And hey, if you choose option two - that's great; at least you can stop beating yourself up about what you "should be doing," accept your life as it is, and decide to be happy. So many of us waste so much precious time wishing we were somewhere else, doing something else or being someone else. If we can see our own situation through new eyes - even for a moment - and find a new appreciation for what we *do* have instead of what we don't have, then the world would be a better place.

I want this book to give you the facts about what it takes to create wealth. Wealth comes in all shapes and sizes. Being "wealthy" to one person could mean being your own boss, doing something you love on a daily basis, and making a good living from that. This book will help you do that.

Wealth is also about taking that idea further and creating significant equity from your ideas and activities. This book will help you with that too. I firmly believe that building wealth is nothing more than a by-product of doing what you are *supposed* to do and leaving customers better than you found them.

Success as Self-Expression

The most successful people on the planet are usually the people who have found a way to effectively express themselves through their products, businesses and services. Steve Jobs found a way to express himself through the Apple brand. Bill Gates has found a way to express himself through Microsoft. Sir Philip Green has found a way to express himself through his High Street empire. And my friend Sir Richard Branson has found a way to express himself through Virgin.

These individuals didn't set out to become billionaires - they set out to create something of value and make a difference. They took risks and were driven to express themselves and in that process became successful. The true road to wealth consists of finding out what that *something* is for you. And expressing it, in the best way you can.

There is no magic bullet or overnight process for wealth creation, but there are proven principles for creating, retaining and increasing your wealth. This book will walk you through those principles; explain their importance, and tell you why they work and perhaps most importantly, how to incorporate them into your life. There will be some laws that you resonate strongly with, while others will be less familiar. The differences are important because they will indicate areas that you may need to address if you are to harness the cumulative power of the 7 Laws of Wealth.

You may, for example, realize that Law 4 - Always Execute - is a natural strength, but you are not as confident with Law 1 - Gain Control, or Law 3 - Own a Strategy. This dynamic would almost certainly give you mixed results. This could mean that you are probably very active and busy, but because you have not Gained Control and fully taken responsibility for your results and because you don't Own a Strategy, your consistent execution and activity is wasted.

Self-Assessment

To help identify which Laws may be holding you back, you will be invited to conduct a short self assessment at the end of each Law. If you find it hard to self-assess, then ask someone you trust who has known you for a while. If you can check off five or more statements in column A as being mostly true for you, then you have a good handle on that particular Law. If you check three or more statements in column B, then you need to address your weakness in that Law if you are to succeed.

Remember, the world has changed and for the first time, big money is in the grasp of anyone with the determination to mould themselves to The 7 Laws of Wealth and succeed. But you need to embrace each and every Law. You can't pick and choose which ones you "like" or are already proficient in - it's all or nothing.

Welcome to *The 7 Laws of Wealth.* This is the beginning of your real wealth creation journey. And, remember, in the final analysis, what you become by traveling that journey will determine not only your destination - but who you are on arrival. *Enjoy the ride!*

Success always,
Ben Benson

Chapter 1

The New Distribution of Wealth

The Communist, seeing the rich man and his fine home says; '*No man should have as much.*' The Capitalist seeing the same thing responds with; '*All men should have as much.*'

The Capitalist system is the oldest in the world, and any system that has weathered the gales and chances of thousands of years must be sound and true. We believe in the right of man to himself, to his property and to his own destiny and his ability to profit from his own merits. We believe that government exists as the umpire of the game, not to come down and take the bat, but to see that all play the game according to the principles of fairness and justice.*

* *The 7 Laws of Wealth* philosophy is relevant to all regardless of gender, color or creed.

Chapter One
The New Distribution of Wealth

WE LIVE IN truly exciting times - times where your destination in life is determined not by the conditions of your birth but by the decisions of your life. And this is true whether you read this book today or a hundred years later. I can say that with absolute certainty because whether you realize it or not, we are in the midst of a new economy. And there is momentum in this wealth re-distribution that can't be halted or reversed.

The Changing Nature of Wealth: Industrial Revolution to Information Revolution and Beyond

Prior to the Industrial Revolution, wealth was held in land. The distribution of wealth was simple - those who owned land were wealthy, and those who did not were not.

In those times, either you were born into wealth and privilege, or you were not. If you were not, then there was very little, if anything, you could do to alter the hand fate dealt you.

If you were born into a "working class" family, you would be expected to live and die within a ten-mile radius of where you were born. As a boy, you would follow in your father's footsteps, regardless of interest or talent. If you were a girl, you would be married and having kids before you were out of your teens. The work was hard, the wages meager, and as for unions and fair treatment - forget it.

There was no social mobility. If you were born poor, you would die poor, and that was all there was to it.

Then the Industrial Revolution arrived. Industrialization of manual labor made it possible to exponentially increase output in mining, agriculture and manufacturing, and new systems of transportation opened up new markets. This was the first step toward globalization.

New opportunities created vast fortunes in new ways. Land ownership was no longer the only road to wealth, and the Industrial Revolution created a new age of prosperity in the Western world. In societies built on merit, such as the USA, UK and much of Europe, this period offered, at least in theory, the opportunity for more people to better themselves through hard work and ingenuity.

Unfortunately it didn't always pan out that way. Social mobility was still very much restricted by class. Although the Industrial Revolution opened up opportunity and markets, it also required a huge workforce to sustain it. Consequently, it wasn't in big business's interest to encourage ordinary people to tap into those opportunities.

Creating an Obedient Working Class

In his book *The Underground History of American Education*, author and former school teacher John Taylor Gatto explains how the formula for modern schooling, both in the US and in the UK, came out of the observations of a young Anglican chaplain, Andrew Bell.

Bell was stationed in India and had the opportunity to study the structure Hindus arranged for training the lower castes. Basically 5% of the Hindu population made up the "twice-born" groups - those at the top of the social pecking order. This 5% consisted of the industrial caste, the warrior and administrative caste, and those at the very top of the tree, the Brahmins. Brahmins are those individuals trained for law, medicine, teaching, and other professional occupations.

The remaining 95% of the population was divided into the menial caste and the "untouchables." You were born into a caste and you could rarely move up. Those at the top could move down if they did something to disgrace themselves, but other than that you lived and died in one caste.

At a time when the Industrial Revolution needed a vast workforce to sustain it, Bell recognized the merits of the caste system and its application in the UK. Here was an example of how a huge percentage of a population was conditioned to accept their lot without question. Ninety-five per cent of the Hindu population was never educated to better themselves. Instead their role was to serve the top 5%, and they never questioned their social inheritance.

The application of such a system in the UK was obvious because the wealthy elite cashing in on the Industrial Revolution didn't actually want to do the work themselves! This Indian system of training was therefore extremely attractive because it proposed a very efficient way of churning out individuals who would do what they were told in dirty, difficult, and poorly paying jobs.

Although the effect was not immediate, Bell's observations were irresistible to captains of industry. They eventually led to compulsory schooling as we know it today. What better way to ready a workforce to slot obediently into jobs that make other people rich than by limiting their information flow and making them think that they have a limited set of options?

"Schooled Ignorance"

Bell suggested that *"schooled ignorance was more useful than unschooled stupidity."* In other words if you took young children from their homes and got them used to long, boring monotonous "work," they would slip seamlessly into the mills, factories and workplaces of industrialized Britain.

But it wasn't just the UK. Across the Atlantic, industrialists and influential financiers were plowing more money into "education" than the government was. As late as 1915, Carnegie and Rockefeller, both financial titans even by today's standards, were individually spending more than the entire US government.

On the face of it, this sounds noble and philanthropic, and certainly there were good intentions as well as dubious ones. But consider the following excerpt from the first mission statement of Rockefeller's General Education Board in a document called "Occasional Letter Number One" (1906):

In our dreams...people yield themselves with perfect docility to our molding hands. The present educational conventions [intellectual and character education] fade from our minds, and unhampered by tradition we work our own good will upon a grateful and responsive folk. We shall not try to make these people or any of their children into philosophers or men of learning or men of science. We have not to raise up from among them authors, educators, poets or men of letters. We shall not search for embryo great artists, painters, musicians, nor lawyers, doctors, preachers, politicians, statesmen, of whom we have ample supply. The task we set before ourselves is very simple...we will organize children...and teach them to do in a perfect way the things their fathers and mothers are doing in an imperfect way.

In other words education was not about creating leaders, philosophers or "men of science." It was about creating an obedient army of workers who would learn to do what their parents did before them - only a little better.

The truth is the Carnegies and Rockefellers of the world needed and still need obedient brow-beaten individuals who will not question their "caste" and would get on with doing the jobs the bosses themselves don't want to do.

Whilst the Industrial Revolution offered new opportunity, the reality was that it was still the original wealthy that were able to capitalize on those opportunities. There were exceptions, and certainly ordinary people did rise out of poverty to seize a new-found wealth, but that was rare.

No Limits to Wealth

And here we are in the 21st Century, with no such limits to the wealth you can achieve. Today there is a new distribution of wealth, and it has nothing to do with land, manufacturing plants or buildings. This wealth is not built from concrete, steel or wood. It is not found in geographical areas such as lower Manhattan, Wall Street, or the financial district of London. The new distribution of wealth demands resourcefulness, not resources. It's about individuals taking control of their own situations and forging their own paths.

And this is possible only by the decision of the self-directed individual, who now has an unprecedented access to information and to advances in technology.

Do not follow where the path may lead.
Go, instead where there is no path and leave a trail.
Ralph Waldo Emerson

The reason schooled ignorance was so much more useful than uneducated stupidity was that those who wrote the curriculum or controlled the agenda could control the information. If you control the information, you control thinking, and if you control thinking, you control action. If you "educate" children not to expect too much from life, then they won't, and they will remain cogs in someone else's wheel. So what happened?

We entered the Information Age which enabled us to disseminate information on a scale never before seen. The information we now have access to is not limited to scholars, scientists and the textbooks we used in school.

A weekday edition of the New York Times contains more information than the average person was likely to come across in a lifetime in seventeenth-century England.
Rich Saul Wurman.

Much of the information we need to create wealth has always been around, but it has been concentrated in the hands of the few. The advent of technology - particularly computers and the Internet - has now changed all that. The Industrial Revolution presented opportunities for new wealth, but they were capital- and labor-intensive.

New Ways to Create Wealth

Today wealth is no longer restricted by birth, school or any other imaginary boundary. Wealth is no longer created only in mills and factories but in the mind - one idea at a time.

Remember Alex Tew from Wiltshire in England? He's the guy who came up with the idea to create a website and sell the pixels so he could fund his university education. His page contained a million pixels which he was selling for £1 each. The site launched on August 26, 2005 and became an Internet phenomenon. After frenzied bidding on eBay, the auction closed on January 11, 2006. Alex made $1,037,100 from one crazy idea in just 139 days.

And he's not alone. The Internet and the opportunity it presents has created thousands of millionaires. What is now possible and what *will be* possible is staggering, vast fortunes are being created almost daily. On the Internet, more than four hundred new companies are created every week. That's more than were created during the Dot-Com boom. Not all succeed, obviously. But the fittest do. In 2008, a new company went public every five days, making dozens of new millionaires in the process. We will see this number exceeded in the next decade.

The balance of power has shifted from the tangible to the intangible. Access to information and the dissemination of that information is transforming the way we live.

It's hard to believe, for example, that the Internet was invented as recently as 1990 and largely attributed to the work of Sir Tim Berners-Lee, an English engineer, computer scientist and MIT professor. Berners-Lee made a proposal for what would become the World Wide Web in March 1989. In December 1990, with the help of Robert Cailliau at CERN and a young student; Marc Andreessen, creator of the 'Mosaic' browser, made the proposal operational.

In 2007 Berners-Lee was ranked joint first alongside Albert Hofmann in *The Telegraph's* list of 100 greatest living geniuses. Since its inception, the Internet has transformed the way we, socialize, shop, communicate, conduct business and experience life.

For the first time in history, there is a level - or at least a leveled - playing field open to all business. Whether you are a "solopreuner" operating from your back bedroom in Northampton, England or a senior executive of a multi-national in Ypsilanti, Michigan, you can compete on a global platform and conduct your business from anywhere in the world.

A few clicks away

The Information Age and the Computer Age have worked hand in hand to make things that were previously impossible seem almost commonplace. Each of us is now a few clicks away from finding out all we need to know to invest in the stock market in real time, learn about property investing, view homes for sale via 360° virtual tours, and sign up to webinars or web based seminars from the comfort of our own home. You literally have the wisdom of generations at your fingertips.

These advances in technology have also had a dramatic effect on employment, as more and more people are able to work from home without the hassle of commuting for hours in rush hour traffic. More and more people are realizing that they don't have to be chained to a desk and that perhaps with a little ingenuity, they can pursue their own goals instead of the corporate ones.

In 2007, Daniel Pink wrote in *Fast Company* about the Free Agent Nation. At the time an estimated 25 million US residents had left their full time employment to become free agents - selling their services as self employed professionals and independent contractors in an increasingly outsourced corporate environment.

The article, which Pink later developed into a book, told the story of people like Deborah Risi, a forty-something marketing whiz who had spent her life successfully climbing the corporate ladder in some of America's most prestigious organizations. Then she quit and declared herself a free agent, landed her first client four days later, and hasn't looked back. Risi, like so many of the free agent solopreuners, operates out of a room in her home, and yet she consults to high-tech giants like Sun Microsystems, Oracle, and Cisco Systems, usually juggling four to six clients at a time and making a great deal more money than she ever did as an employee.

Technology has allowed this phenomenon to occur, and it is one that is sweeping all parts of the globe. It's no longer necessary to fly to the other side of the world for a meeting when you can easily set up a video link for a fraction of the time and expense. We have endless methods for cheap and efficient communication from Skype, SMS messages and networking sites.

Documents can be sent around the world in seconds. *Unleashing the Idea Virus* was an eBook written by Seth Godin and released free on the Internet in 2000. The book's central premise was to illustrate just how quickly the Internet could spread an idea - and the applications to marketing and brand development. Anyone who downloaded the book had permission to pass it on and email it to friends for free, and they did. The book is one of the most downloaded eBooks of all time, and it established Godin as a marketing legend.

Free Agent Nation

All of these factors and others have converged to change the nature of employment. There are those who join the Free Agent Nation through choice - seeing it for the opportunity it is. And there are those that have had it thrust upon them. Careers will come and go. Jobs will change - this is nothing new; it's just happening faster than ever before.

Greater efficiency has accelerated business, and there are inevitably fewer places to hide in a modern organization. In the next few years we will see less *than thirty percent* of the workforce in the industrialized world holding conventional full-time jobs. These *full-timers* will be the new minority.

Businesses need to be leaner and more efficient, and if they are not, then they will have to learn to be. Weak organizations are going to the wall - especially during economic downturns. But this is the nature of business; it is the nature of life itself. We must learn to evolve with the changes, grab the opportunities those changes present, and adapt to the new environment. If we do that, we grow and prosper. If we don't, we will go the way of the dinosaurs.

The days of 40 years' service and a nice gold watch are a distant memory. Today, most young people leaving school or university can expect to have two or three different careers, never mind jobs. Competition for those jobs is not always confined to a geographic location. A great many websites, for example, allow you to post your business requirements and have professionals from all over the world bid on your project. You could employ someone thousands of miles away (whom you will never meet) to do everything from draw cartoons to design websites to write marketing collateral for your business.

While all this may sound a little scary at times, it is incredibly exciting. The combination of these diverse influences has come together to create a melting pot of opportunity. Wealth is no longer simply held in land; it is not confined to corporate boardrooms and huge manufacturing plants. It is not just built from bricks and mortar or glass and steel, and it does not require millions to get off the ground. I built a multi-million-dollar company from a borrowed investment of just over $10,000. It didn't happen overnight, and it was hard work, but great things can and do come from small beginnings.

Wealth is now being created through the dissemination of ideas, thought, creativity and resourcefulness. A teenage girl in her bedroom in Massachusetts is as likely to make a fortune as a weather worn executive in his skyscraper corner office. Perhaps even more likely.

A Wealth of Ideas

No longer is there anything to stop you from achieving the wealth you desire. It doesn't matter where you were born: it doesn't matter who your parents are, or what school you went to. It doesn't matter what gender you are or what color your skin is, because we all have access to the information of generations - often at the touch of a button. We all have a brain capable of thinking, and we have the capacity to turn those ideas into action. We all have the unlimited ability to create wealth - and that has never been possible before.

For the first time in history, you and I are truly exercising the one thing that makes us human - choice. You don't have to be a farmer because your father was. You don't have to stay in a job you hate for 40 years because you don't think you can do anything else. You don't have to work for someone else in order to make money. You can exercise your free will and start taking conscious control of your future. *The message is clear; behave like you're in business for yourself.*

This New Economy is creating new terrain, fundamental truths about real wealth are more relevant than ever. These principles have been around for as long as I can remember, and yet you rarely ever see them written down anywhere. They are understood by the wealthy but never really discussed - not because of some desire to maintain a sacred secret, but because to the people who appreciate their wisdom, they are so obvious they don't warrant a mention.

For those that are not wealthy, they are surprisingly unknown. They hide in plain sight, yet they represent universal truths about how wealth is accumulated in today's world. They are often overlooked because they can be difficult to accept. But they remain true, regardless of whether we choose to accept them or not.

The 7 Distinctions of Wealth

These are simply rules that you must accept and get comfortable with if you are to make significant money. By "significant money," I mean millions, not thousands or even hundreds of thousands. I mean total financial freedom, so if you choose, you would never have to work another day in your life (although I don't know anyone who actually stops). The 7 Distinctions of Wealth are:

1. Being an employee will not lead to significant wealth. Wealth is created by equity in a series of transactions, not income.
2. Becoming wealthy involves borrowing significant amounts of money.
3. Overnight success takes about a decade.
4. Most serious wealth is tied up in assets.
5. You will not create significant wealth on your own.
6. Significant wealth is unlikely if you want a balanced life.
7. Self education is the shortest distance between poverty and abundance.

Let's discuss them one at a time.

1. Being an employee will not lead to significant wealth. Wealth is created by equity in a series of transactions, not income

I know you were told that you should do well in school, get good exam results, maybe go to college so you could get a good job and make good money. But if you want to be seriously wealthy, then you must realize that being an employee will never get you there. A job should be seen as a temporary inconvenience that generates cash flow for living expenses, while you build a business that not only provides cash flow but real equity.

Yes, there are some senior executives, CEOs or investment bankers who are extremely wealthy - but only while they show up for work. What happens if they choose not to? What happens if they can't?

A high paying job is only of real value if the individual has the foresight and common sense to use the income to invest in assets that appreciate over time. And this doesn't just mean property.

The difference between income and investments is that you have to swap personal effort for income; it's what you do to generate money. It's a personal exchange between your effort and the money you receive for that effort. Investments, on the other hand, are about getting your money to make money. You will *never* achieve extreme wealth until and unless, you can make money without swapping your time and effort for it. And that is true, whether you make $20,000 a year or $2 million a year.

The amount of income is irrelevant. It's still income and therefore it's still dependent on you. Real wealth is created through equity in a series transactions. In other words, real wealth is made when you own a company that makes money - whether you go to work or not. That business is therefore an asset and can be sold to create even more money.

There may be luck in getting a good job, but there's no luck in keeping it.
J. Ogden Armour

Real wealth is made when you own assets such as a share market portfolio, real estate, businesses and intellectual capital. These assets generate income or appreciate in value without your personal involvement and are critical in creating significant wealth.

Making your Money Work for You

Don't get me wrong - you still have to manage those investments and know what you are doing; otherwise, you risk losing everything you've accumulated. Learning how to make your money work for you to make more money is a fundamental aspect of wealth.

We all have 24 hours in the day; even if you charge $5,000 an hour, you still have a limit to what you can earn. But if you own assets that generate wealth, there is no limit to what you can accumulate.

Even the ancient Babylonians knew this truth - over 8,000 years ago. George S Clason mentions this Commandment in his classic little book *The Richest Man in Babylon*. He refers to it as "The Third Cure" to a lean purse, i.e., "*Put each coin to laboring that it may reproduce its kind even as the flocks of the field and help bring to thee income, a stream of wealth that shall flow constantly into thy purse.*"

The Babylonians were no slouches when it came to obscene wealth, despite very unfavourable surroundings. Situated beside the Euphrates River in a flat, dry valley, Babylon rose out of the desert like an opulent oasis. They were clearly an educated and resourceful people. Archaeological excavations found entire libraries containing hundreds of thousands of engraved clay tablets.

This written record shows that Babylonians were engineers, astronomers, mathematicians, financiers, and the first people known to have a written language. So far as we know, they were the first to come up with money as a means of exchange; they created promissory notes and used written titles of property. They knew how to accumulate wealth, and part of their charter was ensuring that their gold laboured to reproduce its own kind. If you want significant wealth, you have to do the same.

Interestingly, one of the central messages about how to create wealth that comes out of Babylon is the idea that you *must* "pay yourself first." In other words, you have to take a proportion of your income before anyone else gets a penny and put it aside for investment so you can make that money work for you.

As an employee, you never have the opportunity to pay yourself first because the government collects first from your wage. As an employee, you are taxed on your income first, that tax is removed from your wages or salary before you receive a penny. If you run a business or manage investments, this is not usually the case. You can enjoy the benefits of business ownership, offsetting expenses against income first, *then* paying all your business related tax on what's left.

There are significant tax advantages in employing others or from deriving your "income" from investments as opposed to income from work. Income from work is almost always taxed at a higher rate than income from property and investments.

As an employee, you will always be a cog in someone else's wheel - be it the government, your boss or shareholders. The other people are the ones that make the money. They are the ones that reap the benefit from your labor.

There is a misconception that wealth is all about how much money you make. But wealthy people appreciate that it's never about how much money you make - it's about what you do with what you make. To make your income work for you to accumulate more wealth. Income will pay the bills and put food on your table and clothe your kids, so it's extremely important, but income does not make you wealthy. It's having equity in a series of transactions that makes people rich.

Significant wealth comes from intelligent use of income to buy appreciating assets and investing wisely in places that will outstrip inflation and build long term prosperity.

2. Becoming wealthy involves borrowing significant amounts of money

Get comfortable with this one. The brutal truth of significant wealth is that it almost always involves borrowing significant amounts of cash. There are many examples of people who have bootstrapped their fortune. I actually started with a borrowed credit card from my sister, but in order to create the wealth I have today, it's been necessary to borrow huge sums of money, and that's been stomach churning at times.

There might be those reading this book who will say that the days of easy money are over and that the credit bonanza of the '90s and early '00s will never come again. They may be right - but regardless of how the global finance industry recalibrates, regardless of what boom and bust cycles emerge in the coming years, borrowing will remain a crucial building block of wealth, and a healthy economy.

There may be changes to regulations, but borrowing will continue because without it the global economy would grind to a halt - and we know that the laws of supply and demand will ensure that this doesn't happen.

Almost without exception, the super-wealthy people I've interviewed over the last few years have all had to use borrowed equity to finance the next move and advance to the next level.

3. Overnight success takes about a decade - Minimum

I know this isn't what you want to hear. I know that you want me to tell you that you can be a millionaire by this time next week, or at least this time next year. Again, I could lie to you and tell you that it's true and that all you have to do is believe, but it's nonsense, and you know it as well as I do.

In fact, most people overestimate what we can do in one year and vastly underestimate what we can do in ten. Remember ten years is nothing - it flies by in a blink of an eye. It is a fraction of your adult life.

I'm sorry to be the bearer of bad news, but unless you are six feet tall, have long blond hair, blue eyes, a Russian accent, and are willing to marry a little bald millionaire from Texas, then the only way to become a millionaire in a short space of time is to buy a lottery ticket or do something illegal. Both of which are not very clever.

But most people aren't very clever. In fact what's mind-blowing to me is that an estimated 70% of the UK adult population plays a National Lottery game regularly. According to Camelot's own figures, the total annual sales of National Lottery products are greater than the combined annual UK sales of Coca Cola, Warburton Bread, Walkers Crisps, Hovis Bread, Cadbury Dairy Milk, Nescafé, Andrex, Lucozade, Kingsmill Bread and Robinson's Soft Drinks combined. In 2008 lottery sales were just under £5 billion.

Clearly millions of people are sold the dream with catchy slogans such as, *"You have to be in it to win it."* But with odds of 13,983,816 to one, I certainly wouldn't recommend that you hold your breath.

The creation of wealth follows tried and tested laws. If you adhere to those laws, you will create wealth, but it won't happen overnight. It takes hard work, and anyone who thinks otherwise is delusional. So forget the get-rich-quick ideas - they seldom work. Read this book, understand what it really takes to create lasting wealth, and either decide to go for it, or accept that you are happy where you are.

But don't kid yourself and your loved ones that it's all going to be different next year if you are not prepared to do what needs to be done today in order to make it different in the next few years.

Astonishing Achievements

If you *are* prepared to put the effort in, turn all your focus to creating significant wealth for the next 5-10 years, you might be astonished at what you could achieve.

I vividly remember one of my mentors saying to me, *"Why don't you become a millionaire?"* At the time the idea was preposterous to me: I didn't see myself in those terms at that point in my life. I must say it had a nice ring to it. He also said something else that really stuck in my mind, *"...Not because of what you'll get but because of what you'll become."*

A mind once stretched by a new idea never
regains its original dimensions.
Oliver Wendell Holmes

I didn't really know what he meant at the time, but he was right. My own journey to becoming a multi-millionaire has stretched me into a different person. And that process rarely happens overnight.

4. Most serious wealth is tied up in assets

Various Rich Lists appear in major business publications around the world. In the UK it's the *Sunday Times* Rich List; in the US, it's the *Forbes* Rich list; and in Australia, it's the *BRW* List. Note: With a few exceptions, the wealth that these people have accumulated is not sitting in a bank account somewhere.

We have been led to believe that making money is about saving money and squirreling it away in a bank account. If we religiously save more than we earn, we will eventually be rich.

No, you won't.

Yes, you do need to spend less than you earn, but it's what you do with those savings that really matters. Even if you had a fantastic job and made a six- figure salary, you can't save enough money to make serious wealth. That is why you need to get comfortable with debt. Debt gives you leverage that isn't possible from savings alone.

To become rich, you need to acquire wealth-creating assets. In reality, about 60-80% of wealth is usually tied up in assets - either business stocks or real estate. In 2009, Bill Gates was at the top of the income pile, according to *Forbes* magazine, with an impressive $40 billion. But that doesn't mean he has that wealth sitting around the house or under the mattress. His wealth is not necessarily that liquid, and converting it to cash cannot be done quickly or easily.

And, by the way, if I own $50 million in assets but owe the bank $50 million I am not that rich.

5. You will not create significant wealth on your own

There are plenty of people who quit their job in a blaze of glory and decide that they are going to work for themselves. While this is often a great first step, wealth is never created on your own. There are thousands, probably millions of individuals, who have taken the plunge and are part of the

Free Agent Nation I mentioned earlier, but that is not the way to wealth either. You need to team up with other people.

You have to network and join forces with others to create something bigger than you can ever create on your own.

Andrew Carnegie didn't know much about the actual manufacturing of steel, but it didn't keep him from making a fortune. He hired experts who understood the industry, professionals who were familiar with the finer points of steel manufacturing. This reliance on expert advisors is foundational to all wealthy individuals.

During World War I, a Chicago newspaper published editorials which attacked Henry Ford, calling him, among other things, "an ignorant pacifist." Ford sued the newspaper and the case ended up in court.

The attorney for the paper tried to prove his client's point by asking Mr Ford a series of general knowledge questions designed to reveal his ignorance. Finally Ford became tired by the line of questioning and said, "*If I should really WANT to answer the foolish question you have just asked me or any of the other questions you have been asking me, let me remind you that I have a row of electric push-buttons on my desk and by pushing the right button I can summon to my aid men who can answer ANY question I desire to ask concerning the business to which I am devoting most if my efforts. Now, will you kindly tell me why I should clutter up my mind with general knowledge for the purpose of being able to answer questions when I have men around me who supply any knowledge I require.*"

Henry Ford had around him the very best minds in the automotive industry and they allowed him to create a fortune. He couldn't possibly have done it by himself, and he was intelligent enough to recognize that and surround himself with smart people.

The wealthy know that they can't do it all on their own and they don't want to, so they hire the best people they can to do it for them. Perhaps this is the reason that some of the smartest people all over the world die poor. They are using their knowledge and brain power on their own or are giving their brain power to someone else, who then cash in on it. This is not a sensible strategy. More on this subject in Law 3.

6. Significant wealth is not possible if you want a balanced life

You know that work/life balance that people talk about - time to spend with your family, time to chill out with your mates on a weekend, time to walk the dog and go fishing as well as making buckets of cash. Sounds fantastic, doesn't it?

It's another lie. Becoming extremely rich is not possible as part of a balanced life. It requires almost total focus and dedication. Making millions is a full-time endeavour. And by full-time, I don't mean 9-5 five days a week. I mean 18 hours a day, seven days a week.

Once you are on this path, you live and breathe business almost all the time. Everything you do is connected to building equity. It becomes an obsession - it needs to become an obsession; otherwise, you won't achieve your objective. You can only concentrate on one or two things at any one time, and if you want to achieve wealth, then those one or two things must include making money. It has to become a major priority.

The Implications

There are implications for this that I am loathe to get into, but I promised myself that this book would be a sugar-coating-free guide to getting rich. With that in mind, I think it's only fair to elaborate on what this idea of balance actually means.

It means that you won't see your friends as much as you'd perhaps like to. It means that you'll probably miss some important events - family gatherings, holidays, even kids' performances and birthdays.

It means that if you are in a relationship, acquiring wealth is really something that you both have to be committed to; otherwise, there may be trouble ahead. That is especially true if you have children. If you and your partner decide to go for it, then it may have repercussions for the kids. You might not see them as much as you like. If they are teenagers, that might be a real bonus, but if they are still very young, that may not be something you are prepared to miss out on. Only you can decide.

If you are in your early twenties, these sorts of choices are probably easier than when you are in your forties and you have dependents to consider. Although sometimes that extra pressure to achieve success because loved ones are counting on you…is often just what's needed to get you over the line.

Forget About Balance

Wherever you are in life, and whatever you want to achieve, there will always be a price. If you want to create wealth, then it *is* possible, but it can't be done without sacrifice. You can't become rich while still catching up with your weekly soaps, seeing all your friends, spending quality time with family, and holidaying three times a year. Something has to give - what that is, is up to you but "balance" is a fabrication, at least in those early years.

7. Self education is the shortest distance between poverty and wealth

The only way you can effectively create serious wealth is to get yourself educated. That doesn't mean qualifications and letters after your name.

Some of the richest people in the world never finished school and dropped out of college. Bill Gates; Sergey Brin and Larry Page from Google; Michael Dell - all famous examples of how little your academic qualifications have to do with making serious money. They were however brilliant in their respective fields and in most cases dropped out of school due to the success of their growing business.

You may not need to go back to school but you will need to be continually educated, and that doesn't necessarily mean attending a training course now and then. There is a huge difference between training and education. I often hear people using these two terms interchangeably, and we really shouldn't, because there is an important distinction that is often overlooked.

Difference Between Training and Education

Education is a process and training is an event. Training asks how and when, education asks what and why. We train elephants and seals but educate people. Training is about showing people what to do, and education is about teaching people how to think. If you teach people how to think, then they will work out what to do and may even find a better way in the process.

Education is a life-long process that *starts* for many when you leave school. The people I've met over the years who have achieved stellar success and made a fortune along the way often share one characteristic - curiosity. They are always learning. Their minds are always open to new ideas. They want to learn new things, even if it's relatively late in life.

If you want to be wealthy, you have to find other people who have become wealthy - and learn from them. Notice how they have incorporated the 7 Laws into their own lives. The following pages will be a great foundation as I will share my own experiences as well as those of some of the richest men and women in the world.

Never Again

Understanding the context of this New Distribution of Wealth means that you will never again have to march to someone else's drum. It means that you will never be downsized or passed over for promotion again. It means that you can choose to work hard and enrich yourself instead of someone else. Information and opportunity is all around you - you just have to grab it with both hands and implement it into your own life.

But there is one caveat... If you want to thrive and grow in this new economy, you will have to give up the story that some external cause is responsible for your current financial situation. Good or bad, the marketplace or the economy is not responsible.

It doesn't matter what the economy is doing - booms and busts are cyclical, and they will never be eradicated. In the downturn of 2008-09, there were people who lost billions from the financial fallout of the subprime debacle and the resulting credit crunch. According to *Forbes* magazine, there were 1,125 billionaires in the world in 2008. One year later there were only 793. By June 2011 that number increased to 1,210.

Staying On Top

Many of those 793 people saw the bigger picture. They realised that downturns are nothing more than a test - a rallying cry for increased resourcefulness, an opportunity to get more creative, not less. To seek out more opportunity, not expect less. The really wealthy know that there is no better time to make money than at the bottom of the market. They don't dwell on the loss of a few million because they understand the cycles and know that a downturn heralds an even greater opportunity to create even more ways to generate wealth. You have to be ready to do the same thing and think the same way.

Investors such as Warren Buffet, who specialize in buying under-valued shares, quietly move in when everyone panics and the market and stocks take a tumble. Even after disasters like 9/11, the smart money was picking up bargains at rock bottom prices, and yet markets around the world recovered relatively quickly.

Now it's Your Time

You can either accept the definition of how you should be living your life, which was handed down by your parents, the condition of your birth, and mass media expectations - or you can call a halt to that particular propaganda and choose a different path.

In the past, changing our business or social life was incremental, and a set of personal strategies was not required. Today, in the new economy, change is the only constant. We must embrace that change and grow continually, and that means that a set of personal and business strategies is now absolutely essential.

The following pages will give you those distinctions and strategies. This will assist you to secure your financial future and live the life you were supposed to live. The 7 Lws of Wealth are not easy, and they are not for the faint-hearted - but they work, period. Better yet, once they are internalized, once you really "get it," you will never again have to look to employment or to others for your security, fulfilment or happiness.

Chapter 2

Mastering the Context

He that will not understand, a bigot, that cannot understand, a fool and dares not understand, a slave.

When the wise men of antiquity wished to make their mark on the world, they first put their own state in proper order. Before putting their own state in proper order, they regulated their own families. Before regulating their own families, they intentionally governed themselves toward personal sovereignty. Personal sovereignty only emerges from sincere thought, access to truth and a willingness to see things exactly as they really are. They understood the nature of reality and Mastered the Context.

Chapter Two
Mastering the Context

YOUR FIRST STEP to wealth creation has everything and nothing to do with making money. You must begin by understanding yourself, "Mastering the Context" is about understanding what makes you do the things you do. It's about understanding that human beings are born into a natural state of disorientation - we are not ready to function effectively in the world. Who you are today is thus a consequence of a myriad of social, cultural and biological events - experiences, situations and influences that have woven together to create the person reading these words. By truly appreciating the implications of this truth, you inherit your birthright - personal sovereignty. The ability to preside over your life and create it any way you choose.

Perhaps this chapter, more than any other, is essential to your results, as it will lay the groundwork for your financial success. In fact, *unless you appreciate the impact of what follows and how it influences your actions and consequently your results, I can confidently predict you will* ***never*** *be wealthy - or at least you will never keep the wealth you make.*

Becoming rich is 80% psychology and 20% strategy. If you are serious about becoming wealthy and creating financial freedom for yourself, you first have to gain a level of self-awareness: why are you where you are right now? If you don't understand what makes you who you are, what motivates you, and what governs your decisions and the choices that you make, then you will forever be a slave to those motivations, decisions and choices. You might think you are making decisions and taking action based on rational thought, but most of the time you're not. In reality each of us is a walking reaction, until we recognize how we unconsciously process and understand information.

There is a well travelled, predictable path that connects feelings to outcome. That process is illustrated in the 7 Laws Model:

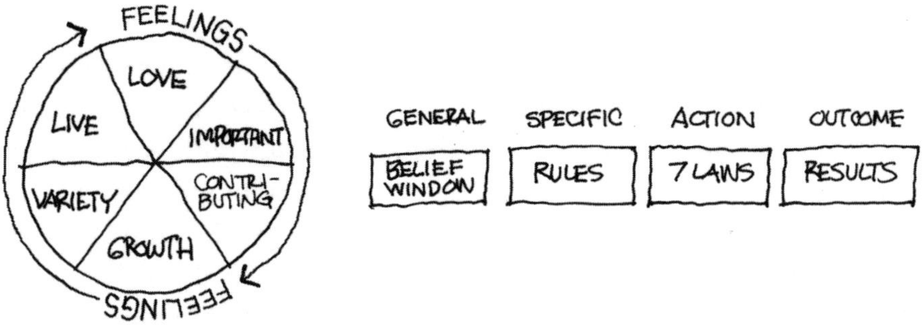

For an expanded version of this model please visit: www.7lawsofwealth.com/context-model

When your results or outcomes in life do not match your desires, we can almost always identify it somewhere in this process. By knowing the links and relationships between each part of the model and understanding how each is developed and plays out in the world, we can tell where the issues lie. This allows you to amend your errors in judgement and achieve your desired outcome. One that is consistant with your real needs and true desires.

Everything Begins with Feelings

Your results in life up to this point are not random. If you are not enjoying what you do or living the way you want to live, then the first step in *getting* to that state is to become aware of the results that you are producing. More particularly, the reason(s) why you might be producing them.

Everything you do you is for a reason. That reason isn't always conscious or obvious or even logical, but every decision you make, every action you take or don't take...is a result of the fact that you are seeking to meet a basic human need. Those needs ultimately translate into feelings. In other words, everything you do, every action you take is the result of trying to *feel* a certain way.

If you want to be a millionaire or multi-millionaire, it's unlikely that you want that money because you like the way money looks or because you plan to frame it or wallpaper your house with it. You want wealth because of the feelings you think it will give you. Chances are you want to be rich because you assume it will be fun and exciting. You feel sure that people will respect you more and listen to what you have to say. You might think that money will give you a sense of achievement and allow you to feel important. Or it might be the security that you are seeking - knowing that you'll never again have to worry about how you will pay the mortgage.

If you are overweight and want to lose a few pounds, then chances are you want that result because you think you will feel better. You want to be slim because you remember that when you were slim, you had more energy and vitality - life was more fun. Or you might want to lose weight because you're convinced that it will increase your self esteem and you'll be more confident - or attractive to your partner. You may even feel confident enough to go after that promotion you so desperately want. All of these feelings are normal and natural.

Note: Whatever it is you think you want is usually not the actual thing that you're after. Often the *feeling or emotion that is attached to the thing you want* is what you really seek. Everything we do is based on the anticipation of experiencing certain feelings, and our energy and effort are often spent trying to achieve this end. One way in which we ensure that we experience the feelings we want is by meeting the 6 Basic Human Needs.

Before you are ready to become truly wealthy, you must face certain realities about yourself. Understanding your human needs will help you to achieve that end.

The 6 Basic Human Needs

We are all motivated by 6 basic human needs. Everything we do is driven by our need to:

Live

Love and Be Loved

Feel Important

Experience Variety

Growth

Contribution

However, this list tells only part of the story. Jeremy Bentham, an English philosopher and legal and social reformer, was the first to recognize that we are fundamentally driven to avoid pain or seek pleasure. In 1789 he wrote (in his book *The Principles of Morals and Legislation)*:

Nature has placed mankind under the governance of two sovereign masters, pain and pleasure. It is for them alone to point out what we ought to do, as well as to determine what we shall do. On the one hand the standard of right and wrong, on the other the chain of causes and effects, are fastened to their throne. They govern us in all we do, in all we say, in all we think...

So while we are motivated toward the fulfillment of these basic human needs and the pleasure we associate with them, we are equally, if not more intensely, driven to avoid the pain of failing to fulfill them.

Live

The reason that we are often more motivated to avoid pain than to seek pleasure is probably due to our human inheritance. Our most basic need is survival. So we are more acutely tuned into things that could cause pain and ultimately threaten our survival than we are to those things that foster development.

The urge to survive is a powerful one and is dramatically demonstrated by extraordinary stories such as those of Joe Simpson or Aron Ralston. Simpson was the man made famous by the film *Touching the Void.* He and fellow climber Simon Yates were the first to ascend to the summit of Siula Grande in the Peruvian Andes. The descent, however, didn't go well, and Simpson broke his leg. Tied to him by a 300-ft. rope, Yates lowered Simpson down the mountain, but disaster struck again, and Yates was forced to cut the rope. Simpson dropped 100 ft. Miraculously, he survived and crawled into base camp three days later. His survival is considered one of the greatest in mountaineering history, and he has always strenuously defended Yates' actions, insisting that if Yates hadn't cut the rope, they would both have died.

In April 2003, Aron Ralston entered Utah's Bluejohn Canyon, but during his expedition, an 800-pound boulder crushed his right forearm, pinning him against the canyon wall. As he had never told anyone he was going and was there on his own, he faced certain death. After several days he ran out of water, and in an act that demonstrated our innate desire to survive, he snapped his radius and ulna bones and used a blunt penknife to cut off his lower arm. His story is depicted in the film '127 Hours' directed by the English filmmaker and producer Danny Boyle.

Luckily, most of us will never face these life-and-death decisions, but they prove just how strong our desire is to live - and they show what a human being will do to avoid death. A more mundane expression of our desire for life is our drive to be healthy and live a long life.

Similarly, our desire to live also drives our need for safety, security and certainty. We want to feel protected from the world and able to provide for our loved ones. Often the drive for wealth is related to our need to feel secure. We want to be able to take care of ourselves and those we love, provide a safe, secure home, and have enough money for the future.

We want to know what's coming so we can be sure of the outcome. That desire for safety creates our own personal "comfort zone." We feel safe and reassured when we know what to expect, when we can act in familiar ways and achieve predictable results - even when those expectations, behaviors and results are negative. This is often why people stay in abusive relationships. It's familiar. They stay because they assume it's *"better the devil you know"* than to plunge into the unknown, which *might* be even worse.

Love and be Loved

This is arguably the strongest drive; it relates to all sorts of human connections. It therefore includes parents, siblings, spouses, children, as well as friendships and other social connections. Being loved and loving others is what gives life meaning and richness. It is fulfillment around these important relationships that often determines whether we are happy and contented.

Just think about it for a moment - if you had all the money in the world but no friends to enjoy it with and no family to share it with, then the money wouldn't be much fun. It is love that makes the world go around, but don't forget that it's money that pays for the trip.

Although few people could admit it, the drive for wealth is often connected to this need. When a husband-and-wife team want to make money to ensure their children have everything they need, this feeling is often born of love. When an individual builds a large business because of the admiration he or she will receive from peers - that too is born out of a need to be loved and admired.

We all have a fundamental need to connect with others. We are social creatures that work best in small groups. No one likes feeling lonely and unloved.

The lack of love is devastating to human development. Orphans in impersonal institutions suffer physical and mental harm from the lack of connection and love. Even in hygienic orphanages, the mortality rates are far lower than in those with love and care. Although this care need not always come from a parent, it's not possible for us to thrive without it.

Often institutionalized infants fail to develop even the most basic social and mental skills. They become extremely susceptible to infections and disease and frequently the damage done in those formative years is never repaired, even if the children are adopted into loving homes. Our need for love and affection is vital to our mental health, physical health and well-being.

The drive to avoid loneliness is therefore, very strong. The life-enhancing power of connection may help explain why, when one member of an older couple dies, the other often dies soon after.

To love and be loved includes our drive for acceptance and approval from people that matter to us. We crave that connection, as everyone needs to feel needed and appreciated.

Feel Important

Everyone wants to feel important. We want to feel that what we do is meaningful and that we have made our mark on the world. We want to feel listened to and respected.

Each of us meets this need in a slightly different way. Some get to feel important through the accumulation of qualifications and letters after their names. Others use their career or livelihood to make themselves feel important. We seek positions of authority, either in work, in clubs, or organizations where we want to influence others. Some feel important because of the number of friends they have or the number of hours they work. And some derive their sense of significance from money.

In fact, a great many people use money to feel important. You've probably come across these characters - they will look down the right-hand side of a wine list just to find the most expensive bottle of wine. They have no appreciation for whether that wine is a good bottle or not; they're simply showing off and using their wealth to feel important. We may not always like it, but wealth is a universally accepted way of keeping score in a capitalist society, and some people use it as a measure of how important they are - and how well they're measuring up against others.

That is not to say that you are important only if you make money - far from it. But it is true that there are people in this world who use that yardstick as a measure, not just of net worth, but of self-worth. No one likes to feel unimportant. It's often low self-worth and a sense of irrelevance that can drive individuals to make something of themselves.

Feeling important is really about having a purpose - about feeling that we are here to do a specific thing and that it is our job to do that thing and do it well. This drive gives our life meaning and allows us to feel part of something useful and vital. We want to know that what we do makes a difference.

In the end, *we are all motivated to do or not do certain things because we are trying to satisfy unmet needs* and feel the feelings we assume those needs will give us.

Looking at my own life, I see that one of the strongest themes in my childhood was a constant lack of money. I remember being embarrassed because we didn't have a car and lived in public housing. I always remember how the other kids had so much more than me and lived in the nicer neighborhoods in the city. Perhaps that was my greatest motivation to become rich. I didn't want to live that way all my life and was determined to change it. I was seriously motivated to avoid the pain of poverty and the feelings I associated with it. After all, it's very difficult to feel safety, importance, variety, growth or altruism when you have no money. I always felt loved, but life itself was always tough.

Interestingly, many of the very wealthy individuals I've met in my life have shared similar stories - starting with less than nothing and using that pain to propel them out of their situation. Perhaps this is why there are so many "rags to riches" stories (although I personally dislike the term). Perhaps people brought up in moderate comfort simply don't have that drive to escape because their lives just didn't require it.

Experience Variety

Human beings are dichotomous creatures. On one hand, we want security and certainty. We like to know what's coming so there are no surprises, so we can remain confident in our abilities and expectations. Yet if we get too confident in what to expect, we experience boredom.

While too much variety can sometimes impinge on our need for security, we all crave variety. Isn't variety really the spice of life? Variety comes in many forms. It's around every corner if you look for it. You could choose to join a local club and meet new people. You could decide to visit a new place or go to a new town. You could take a holiday in a different culture. Or you could start a new project or learn a new skill.

The challenge with all these ways to explore variety is that you will often confront some of your other needs and issues. Meeting new people, for example, can be confrontational for some people. They may be afraid that they won't be liked or that they won't get along with someone. This creates uncertainty and can activate a primal need for safety that keeps us in our comfort zone. So instead of reaching out for new experiences to meet our need for variety, we procrastinate and decide not to bother.

Money has the capacity to meet our need for variety in an infinite number of ways. With money we can pursue all sorts of activities and adventures that would be off-limits for us otherwise. This prospect can drive us forward and offers us endless opportunities to alleviate boredom. It is, however, often a false god - money may give you more options, but it's surprising how quickly people can become bored with even the most extravagant toys.

Entertainment is, in fact, the biggest cause of
boredom in the modern world.
The more man is entertained, the more bored he grows.
Anthony Daniels

Growth

American psychotherapist Carl Rogers found evidence for the basic need for self-actualization or growth. He described the characteristics of a fully functioning person: a good life of constant change and development.

He says, "*This process of the good life is not, I am convinced, a life for the faint-hearted. It involves the stretching and growing of becoming more and more of one's potentialities. It involves the courage to be. It means launching oneself fully into the stream of life.*"

I think he's right; growth is an important human need. We need to feel as though we are improving and getting better in some way. All of us are either growing or dying; there really is no middle ground. There are those that try to hang on to that middle ground. They complain about how much has changed and feel sadness for days long gone. And there are those that embrace change and constant growth as an adventure that keeps them young - regardless of age.

This drive - to be better tomorrow than you are today - is often prominent in the very wealthy. They want to build something because they have an innate desire to improve, develop and grow. Growth and a drive for betterment are about self expression and achievement as much as making money.

Contribution

We all want to make a difference. We all want to feel valued and to know that our existence on the planet mattered. This includes adding value and knowing that what we do is important - at least to someone. We all have a drive to feel useful and valued. That something of value may be as simple as a conversation in which we find that we are able to help a friend by providing information, ideas, companionship, services, skills or abilities. Knowing we brought something special to another's life is important to all of us.

One of the things I've noticed about some of the wealthy is their drive to expand their contribution beyond their circle. There really is only so much you can buy, only so many toys and trinkets before the drive for contribution kicks in. Thus, the first three of *the 7 Laws of Wealth* are dedicated to personal action, while the last four involve others working together and giving back. That is the way wealth works.

Once the wealthy have satisfied their own needs, bought the toys, experienced the variety and reached the inevitable plateau, they come full circle and want to use that wealth to help others.

That drive to contribute is first evident in their personal lives and allows them to achieve a respectable level of success. Then it is directed outward, as the wealthy seek to Give Back to the society that assisted in their growth. Many of the really wealthy people in the world are driven to make a significant contribution to areas of special interest.

Andrew Carnegie, the American industrialist who made a fortune in steel, famously spent the first half of his life making that fortune and the second half giving it all away. In modern times, Bill Gates and Warren Buffet, at writing, the richest and second richest men in the world, are already giving their amassed wealth away and doing a great deal of good in the process. Gates and his wife are now distributing a huge slice of their fortune through the Bill and Melinda Gates Foundation. In 2006 billionaire investor and

CEO of Berkshire Hathaway Warren Buffet pledged to give 85% of his fortune away - most of which, some $30 billion, to the Gates Foundation.

So why are some people more driven toward love while others just want to feel important? Why are some dedicated to contribution while others just want their lives to be filled with variety? Why do we make the choices we make and do what we do? The individual that you are now - how was that person created? And why do you do what you do? This brings us to the subject of your...

Belief Window

Each of us lives in our own unique world based on a "Belief Window," a mental construct that is effectively strapped to our forehead. Imagine a sweat band around your head. Hanging from the sweatband directly in front of your eyes is a window that sits permanently in front of your face. It cannot be taken off, moved, or ignored. It doesn't matter where you turn your head - the window goes with you. Everything you see is accepted and understood through this window. Your entire world view is constructed based on your ability to make sense of everything you "*see*" through its frame.

Your Belief Window is invisible and weightless, so you have no idea that it's even there. And yet by the time you reach adulthood, you literally have thousands upon thousands of beliefs or rules written on your window: "*I am*

good at math," "*Organic is better,*" "*I am successful,*" "*BMWs last,*" "*I'm a good parent*" "*Making money is hard,*" "*I should speak up,*" "*Peas taste better than carrots,*" etc.

Not only do you look out at the world through your Belief Window and draw conclusions, but you also make assumptions and decisions based on what's already written on it. All the data we experience from the outside world is filtered through our window. Our Belief Window can act as a barrier against information we don't want to acknowledge.

There is nothing that is too obvious of an absurdity to be firmly planted in the human head as long as you begin to instill before the age of five by constantly repeating it with an air of great seriousness.
Arthur Schopenhauer

As a result you are not seeing reality - you are interpreting the world through your Belief Window filter system.

This means that reality is a purely subjective experience based on the Belief Window that we accept as an adult. If you doubt this, ask any police officer who has taken witness statements at the scene of a crime. Five people will see the exact same event, at the exact same time from exactly the same location, and the police officer will hear five different accounts of the event.

There may indeed be some similarities, but invariably there will be more differences, because each of those people is seeing the outside world through a separate frame of reference, or Belief Window.

One person may notice that one of the suspects was wearing a particular T-shirt, because his brother owns the same T-shirt, so it was easy to remember. The other four may not have noticed the T-Shirt but rather the suspect's expressions or actions. Another person might think that one suspect looked like her Uncle Albert; she ends up identifying the suspect on that basis, because the immediate similarity clouded her objective ability to describe the scene. We see and react to things based on what's written on our Belief Window and not necessarily on what is really happening.

As no two people have had the exact same upbringing and experiences, no two people will have the exact same Belief Window. Everyone will view the world in a slightly different way. Your version of "reality" thus depends on your own Belief Window. However, when groups of individuals are brought together for a common purpose, good or bad, you will often see a "group Belief Window" manifest itself; we see these in countries, companies, religions and governments. Whether we like it or not, our Belief Window will influence our every thought, decision and action. And they are most definitely here to stay.

In a simple experiment conducted in the 1960s, volunteers were given goggles that they had to wear for two weeks. The goggles had two colors in the lenses. If the subject looked to the right, the world would look yellow, and if the subject looked left, the world would look blue. As the volunteers went about their daily business over the course of those two weeks, they eventually stopped seeing the colors. They didn't even register the difference in color when they looked from right to left.

This experiment suggests that it's not the eyes that see at all - it's the mind. The subjects effectively replaced "reality" with a memory and began to see what they wanted to see. They didn't notice the yellow or the blue. We are the same way - we don't notice all the beliefs that unconsciously direct our life.

So what's on your Belief Window and how did it all get there?

Conditioning

From the moment we take our first breath, we are being conditioned by external influences. We are conditioned by our parents or major care givers. What they tell us is taken as fact, and their beliefs and attitudes become ours. Those facts, whether true or not, are scribbled on our Belief Window with invisible ink.

We are also conditioned by the media, the environment and the culture we are born into. We are conditioned by the language we speak and the customs we adhere to. We learn what is right, what is wrong, what will gain praise and punishment, what will hurt us and make us happy, all by the process of conditioning. We decide what is normal by seeing what those people in our immediate environment are doing. Most of this conditioning occurs below our conscious awareness.

The reason conditioning is so important has to do with the natural state of disorientation I mentioned at the start of the chapter. Human beings are not born "ready." We are born with unfinished brains, and the conditioning process allows the brain to develop into adulthood. When you were born, your brain was relatively small. If it wasn't, then your mother wouldn't have been very thrilled, and collectively the species would have died out. By the time you become an adult, your little brain is 300% larger, and yet the vast majority of its growth has occurred between birth and age five.

During those early years, your brain is given the finishing touches through the information and education you received after birth. When a sea turtle is born, it instinctively knows to scramble to the sea. It doesn't need its parents to give directions, tell it to be careful, and wave it goodbye. The turtle is born ready to go, as fully developed as it needs to be.

Humans, on the other hand, need that extra tuition and training in order to be ready for the world and learn how to fit into their society. This "finishing touches" process is, however, far from an exact science. The good news is that what you pick up during these early years is innate and effortless. As a small child, you were a breathing sponge, capable of taking in vast amounts of information from the environment and classifying it without conscious effort or even awareness.

The downside is that those classifications are not always accurate, and it is this early education that plays such a crucial, yet unconscious role in the creation of your Belief Window. The assumptions, beliefs, ideas, customs, facts, religious ideals, cultural expectations, values and environment into which you were born have all had a profound effect on your life and how you view the world.

The evolution of the brain not only overshot the needs of prehistoric man, it is the only example of evolution providing a species with an organ which it does not know how to use.
Arthur Koestler

The disastrous consequences of this process can be seen in cults all around the world. Remember the terrible tragedy at Waco, Texas in 1993? David Koresh, or Vernon Wayne Howell as he was born, was the self professed leader of a Branch Davidian religious sect. In his mind, he was the final prophet of God. A raid by US officials led to a subsequent siege by the FBI, which ended in the cult's torching the ranch, killing Koresh, 54 adults and 21 children. DNA tests later proved that some of those children were his own, with mothers as young as 12 years old.

Or what about, "The End of The World" cult located in a remote corner of New Mexico called Strong City? Their leader, Wayne Bent, is known to his followers as Michael Travesser. He also thought he was the Messiah. UK Filmmaker Ben Anthony was allowed inside the group in the lead-up to the "End of the World," which was predicted, by Travesser, to be midnight on October 31, 2007. Clearly, it didn't pan out.

What's fascinating, however, is that no one questioned this, even though some of his devotees had been patiently waiting to die for almost 20 years! Travesser's hold over the group was so complete that he simply changed the date and carried on - even after the 67-year-old was sentenced to 18 years in prison in December 2008 for his inappropriate relations with minors.

Thousands of people are lost to cults every year, and sadly, it's possible because human beings will accept just about anything if the indoctrination is begun early and repeated constantly and with conviction. That process is called conditioning.

Pavlov's Dogs

You've probably heard of Pavlov and his famous dogs. Ivan Pavlov was the Soviet scientist who explored conditioning and demonstrated how inexact it can be as a learning mechanism. Through a process of repetition, he was able to get his dogs to associate the sound of a bell to being fed. This conditioned reflex became so strong that eventually Pavlov only needed to ring a bell and the dogs would salivate. Yet there is no logical and sensible reason why a bell should be connected to salivation, and that's the challenge. This process of associative conditioning is fantastic for classifying huge amounts of data, but it doesn't always connect the right dots.

As we gather new bits of information from our peers, parents, environment and culture, we log that information in our brain, so that in the future we don't need to classify it again. That's how we can make faster assessments of the situation and remain safe.

There are two main ways that conditioning works. The first, exemplified by Pavlov's dogs, is repetition. If you are told something over and over again, you will come to believe that it is true and inscribe it onto your Belief Window. Even the most loving parents are guilty of saying things without realizing the impact of their words.

As a consequence, most of us have some unhelpful inscriptions on our Belief Window. As we age, teachers, friends, siblings and enemies add to the collage. If you were told that you can "*do anything you want in life*," that "*you just have to put your heart and soul into something,*" then you will believe that and act accordingly. If, on the other hand, you were repeatedly told that you are stupid and "*will amount to nothing,*" then you may believe that and act accordingly, bringing about that very result.

Immediate Conditioning

Conditioning can also be immediate. There are certain things that you don't have to keep learning. The day you first burned your hand on matches or touched a hot stove was so painful you didn't need to keep doing it. The association of pain and fire was immediate, and it was effectively seared into your subconscious memory banks. So when there is a high emotional content - when you are really excited or scared - then the learning you gain in those moments can happen very quickly. But again, it isn't always accurate.

For example; Emily goes to the zoo for the first time. She is just five years old, and while she's outside the elephant enclosure, the elephant trumpets suddenly, and a nearby dog panics and bites Emily. Needless to say, Emily is in a flood of pain and tears and is very distressed. Emily's brain immediately scans the environment to classify the experience so that she can be protected from similar situations later. The brain logs everything, but for simplicity's sake, suppose it logs - "zoo," "elephant," "noise," "dog," "sunny," "barking," "ice cream." All this is done in a flash without Emily's consent or awareness.

Fast-forward thirty years. Emily is talking to her eight-year-old nephew Scott and asking him what he would like to do for his upcoming birthday. His eyes light up, and he says he wants to go to the zoo. For some reason, Emily's heart sinks. She feels uncomfortable, but because Scott is so excited, she puts her feelings aside and goes to the zoo.

They arrive at the zoo and are walking around when Emily sees a dog. The presence of these two elements associated with a long forgotten memory, are enough to trigger anxiety, possibly to the point that Emily makes some excuse and is forced to abandon the zoo expedition. She has no idea what happened and feels guilty because Scott is now upset.

The information logged by Emily's brain when she was just five was still influencing her feelings and actions thirty years later. At the zoo with Scott, Emily's brain cross- referenced the new experience with past experiences to "decide" how to react. Once a few similar triggers were flagged in the new situation, Emily's fight-or-flight response was also triggered, and she left the zoo.

Unhelpful Connections

When the brain associates burned fingers, pain, and matches - it's at least a useful association, because if you let a match burn too long, it will burn your fingers and cause pain, and that association is helpful to future protection. When the brain connects dog, zoo and pain, it's not accurate or even helpful.

The fact that the dog bit Emily when she was five had nothing to do with the fact they were at the zoo or in front of the elephant enclosure or that it was a sunny day or even that she'd just had an ice cream. It didn't mean that every time she was going to visit a zoo in the future she would be bitten by a dog. Yet that's effectively what her five-year-old brain deduced.

This is an incredibly efficient way of learning, and it is at least part of the reason we're able to take in such vast amounts of information. However as we can see in the example above, it's not always accurate and can lead to faulty thinking. This process is essentially how habits are formed and phobias created.

Every time we do something or learn something new, there are new neural connections made in the brain. If that connection is repeated over and over or occurs under extreme circumstances in a significant emotional event, then the neural connection becomes stronger. This is known as Hebb's Law, after Donald Hebb, the Canadian psychologist who proposed the theory. Hebb suggested that "cells that fire together, wire together." (Wikipedia). If Emily always gets anxious at zoos, the neural connections will fire over and over again at the mere mention of visiting the zoo and form a stronger connection. Eventually, the mere idea of a zoo will make her feel sick.

A Walking Bundle of Reactions

When I said you are a walking reaction, I wasn't being flippant. Your responses and decisions are not triggered by rational, logical consideration but by long forgotten memories or conditioned reflexes.

Most of us have experienced this phenomenon before. Someone says something to you - and in a nano-second you get upset. You yell at the person and storm off. Several moments later, when the red mist subsides, you are confused about your inappropriate response. What you don't know is that *your brain filtered the incoming information through your Belief Window*. It was instantly cross-referenced against possibly thousands of past experiences. Part of that information was recognized as being sufficiently similar to an earlier event in your life as to initiate a "fight" response, and you flew off the handle.

You try to pacify yourself by saying you made a decision to be "assertive." You didn't make any decision at all - it was a reaction. Your brain reacted to previously classified data and made a knee-jerk response. That is what most of us consider "thinking."

We learn almost exclusively by association and have millions of these associations by the time we are adults. This effectively means that as you emerge into adulthood, you see the world through your own unique, personally distorted "Belief Window."

These beliefs represent the truths that you deduced about yourself, your worth, and your future potential based on those people around you. They are a consequence of your conditioning and exert a massive influence, whether positive or negative, on your life.

The will to believe is perhaps the most powerful and certainly the most dangerous attribute.
John P. Grier

You've heard that "What you don't know can't hurt you." I disagree. You are not consciously aware of beliefs that sometimes *do* hurt you. They limit your potential, as well as what you believe about yourself and what you are prepared to do and not do. They influence your actions, your behavior - everything about who you are. If you believe that rich people were inherently bad or that money corrupts everyone eventually, then do you think you will consequently move toward wealth? Or will you have one foot on the accelerator and the other on the brake?

Rules

As you move through the process from needs to results, you will discover that each belief has a number of "rules" attached to it. These rules are the requirements that have to occur for you to experience the feeling that you seek. Again, the rules are unconsciously constructed but can be made explicit by asking yourself, "What has to happen for me to feel X?"

Your rules effectively tell you the circumstances under which you give yourself permission to feel a certain feeling. And although that seems sensible. it's fraught with problems.

For example, let's say you had a belief of "I am tidy" on your Belief Window. Being tidy is something your mother appreciated, so you got to feel loved and connected through this belief. Over the years, however, you will construct rules about how this belief plays out in real life. So what has to happen for you to feel good about being tidy?

Your rules might include:

- Everything in my home must be in the perfect place
- All clothes must be hung up at night
- I must do my laundry every two days
- I have to dust my home every day
- I must clean behind the fridge every week
- I must dust the blinds every week

Imagine that you have children. How likely is it that you are going to get to feel good about being tidy? Never.

And that's the problem: *we create complicated and intricate rules that make it extremely easy to feel bad and very difficult to feel good.*

How your rules can rule your life

Suppose a young man is really close to his family. His family is religious, so he has unconsciously inherited some beliefs about money that were inscribed on his Belief Window. They might include beliefs such as "*money is the root of all evil,*" that it's "*better to give than to receive,*" and that there's "*something noble about poverty.*" He grew up in an environment where people he loved assured him that all rich people were greedy, self obsessed sinners who would burn in hell!

He would, over time, construct a series of rules around these beliefs to help him decide when he could feel certain feelings. Those rules might include *"I have to agree with my family to feel loved by them." "Everyone who drives a nice car has obviously done something dishonest to get that car." "I have to give at least $500 to charity every year."*

What does this have to do with becoming rich? We all create (often arbitrary) rules around beliefs, and I've written about 27 of the beliefs that are most toxic to financial health in my first book, *The New Rules of Wealth - Dispelling the 27 Myths of Personal Prosperity.*

The big problem with beliefs and rules is that ultimately they affect behavior. If the young man in my example came to the conclusion in later life that he really doesn't enjoy his hand-to-mouth existence and would like to make some changes to his financial circumstances, his inaccurate beliefs and rules about money are going to make change very hard for him.

On one hand, he wants more money because he wants to be more secure and own his own home. He also wants some variety in his life and he thinks money will help enable him to travel and take up new and exciting hobbies. However if he did become wealthy, he would risk rejection by his family. That prospect would distress him, and ultimately his fear would influence his choices.

Because of his negative beliefs and rules about money, he will actively avoid people who have money. He will make judgments about individuals based on what car they drive and where they live. He will not take an active interest in his financial well-being, and he will see no reason to familiarize himself with financial language. All those little choices, actions and inactions will come together to actively keep him poor.

It is these types of conflicts that can cause us to sabotage our own success. It is our beliefs and rules that determine our thinking, and it is our thinking that determines our action. Our beliefs and rules are crucial to wealth creation because they influence our behavior and the actions we take (or don't take). Since our actions, inactions, attitude, and expectations determine our results, you can see why I say that wealth is 80% psychology and 20% strategy.

If you don't understand the power and influence that these unconscious aspects of your nature have over your life, then you will be a slave to them. If you do, then you can regain control of your results. If wealth is what you seek, then all you need to do is ensure that your behavior is aligned with the natural laws that govern all success in business and life.

Approach-Avoidance

It's worth noting that self-sabotage can also result from what psychologists call "approach-avoidance."

Kurt Lewin, widely recognized as the founder of social psychology, was the first to identify the forces that are either driving or blocking movement toward a goal. This quandary is something I experienced myself, and it's worth noting in case you discover it in yourself.

I set a goal: to be wealthy. At the time I created that desire, I was not wealthy, and the idea of being a millionaire seemed genuinely preposterous. I was driven to achieve that wealth and was willing to do whatever I needed to do to make it a reality, but what I was not ready for was my own experience of approach-avoidance.

The more I moved toward my goal of wealth and the more I actually started to create money in my life, the more uncomfortable I felt. Luckily I had read about approach-avoidance through the training I was involved in, and that awareness helped me to manage the process. Essentially approach-avoidance occurs when an individual gets closer to his goal and the negative consequences of achieving that goal "push back" with a force that can derail even the very best effort. In other words, as you get closer to the desired outcome, fear kicks in, and you sabotage your own efforts, so you don't achieve the desired result.

I was driven to create wealth, but as it became a reality, I was flooded with irrational fears and concerns about what that would mean for me. Would my friends and family still love me? How will I know if people like me for me or just the money? Will people try to take it away from me? The negative beliefs that I had picked up over the years about money, what it meant and what people who had money were like - they had all come home to roost.

Every Goal contains Positives and Negatives

Being rich isn't all great news. There are many downsides to wealth - you have to manage it, you have to put in the time and effort to understand how to make it grow and invest it wisely, you have to pay much more in taxes, and people will judge you because of it. You will be viewed as mean if you don't give big tips, and everyone will have certain expectations about you.

If you want to climb Everest and that's your passion, fine. Go for it. It may be exhilarating, but the negatives are considerable. You'll have to train extremely hard, you'll have to fit that training in with your current commitments, which may mean a 5:00 a.m. training session, six days a week. In winter that's going to be extra tough. You will be away from loved ones for a long time, and your project will cost a great deal of money.

If you want to lose 40 pounds, you may be looking forward to feeling great and looking fabulous - but there are other consequences. You won't be able to eat your favorite foods anymore, and if most of your socializing is done over dinner with friends, you may have to miss out on those evenings. You will have to buy new clothes, but perhaps you don't have the spare cash.

Everything has pros and cons. Lewin points out that as you get closer to your goal, the negative realities of that goal come into full view, causing you to alter your behavior and to actively *avoid* the goal.

In the quest for wealth, people are driven to do all the right things, and they start to make more money. Then they panic at the negative aspects of the goal and stop doing what made them the money in the first place - and consequently lose it. They make the journey from wealth to poverty into a round trip! When wealth is in the distance, you're motivated and passionate. As the goal becomes touchable, you jam your foot on the brake. As soon as the goal becomes distant again, you apply the accelerator - and so the approach-avoidance dance begins again.

That is why it's so important to understand your beliefs and to carefully examine the pros and cons of your chosen outcome. Everything in life has advantages and disadvantages. Being aware of the whole picture, not just the desirable part, will help you to manage the psychological curve ball of approach-avoidance.

Natural Laws

In the 7 Laws context model on page 27 you will notice that the space between the six human needs and action is largely controlled by thinking, or your Belief Window and your rules. However, the space between action and outcome is always controlled by Natural Laws.

As human beings we have the power of choice and the capacity for self awareness. We can make plans and implement those plans in pursuit of a goal. Significantly it is our ability to align ourselves to the universal natural laws that ultimately governs outcome. While we have the choice to make a decision or take certain actions, we do not always have a choice in how things turn out.

In all efforts a strict cause-and-effect relationship is in play. For example, if I choose to jump off a 20-story building, the law of gravity will ensure that I can confidently expect to end up squashed on the pavement below. I have the choice as to whether or not I jump, but once I've made that choice, I don't get to decide what the outcome will be. Natural Law decides. The consequences of my actions are predictable: Cause - I jump. Effect - I land, with an impact.

If I choose not to invest for my future or to take my financial situation seriously, then I can confidently (or unconfidently) expect that I'll live and die poor. I have a choice as to whether I take my finances seriously and live the *7 Laws of Wealth* - or live by neglect and take the "ho hum" approach.

Each decision will have an inevitable consequence, as sure as the impact of hard concrete would have on my body. I can choose and determine what my decision will be, but natural law will always determine the outcome.

If you are unfit, there's usually a reason. You can tell yourself that it's a hormone imbalance or that you've tried everything, but we both know you haven't tried *everything* - because if you'd tried everything, you wouldn't be unfit! If you want to be healthy but prefer to watch daytime TV with a jumbo bag of tortilla chips and three packs of Oreos, then you will see the effect of that choice when you look in the mirror.

I can choose whether or not to jump off the building, but I can't choose what the consequences of that choice will be. I can choose to eat an unbalanced diet every day and convince myself that searching for the TV remote constitutes exercise, but I can't control the consequences of those decisions.

There are thousands of these cause/effect relationships that govern our lives and our results every day. If you are successful, chances are you are probably living in harmony with these natural laws. If you're not as successful as you think you deserve to be or not experiencing the results you hope for, then chances are you are not living in accordance with these laws.

The cause/effect relationship will play out, come what may. All you can do is adapt your approach and work *with* them, as opposed to wasting your time trying to change them. You could sit and meditate on top of that 20-story building for five years and visualize yourself floating to the pavement like a feather on a summer breeze - but once you step off, gravity will do what gravity does, and you will hit the pavement with a fatal thud.

For the record, ignorance of these universal laws does not mean they won't work. Remember some things are true whether we believe them or not. Ignorance of gravity wouldn't keep your fall from killing you. It's the same in court - ignorance of the law is no defense.

A natural law is something that simply can't be repealed. It can't be revoked, rescinded, annulled, negotiated with, or ignored. Ultimately our acceptance or rejection of these laws will have little influence, as they are constantly and consistently working in our lives. We will never break a natural law; we can only illustrate it.

The *7 Laws* are Immutable

This is a really important distinction to make, because even if you manage to take charge of your beliefs and write some new rules that will support your quest for wealth, you still have to know what sort of behaviour is required.

These behaviours are *7 Laws of Wealth*. They have proven time and time again to be the reasons why individuals and companies prosper, why they can create and maintain wealth, while others live lives of quiet desperation.

THE *7 LAWS OF WEALTH* ARE:

1. Gain Control
2. Embrace the Future
3. Own a Strategy
4. Always Execute
5. Create Value
6. Seek Growth
7. Give Back

Each of the 7 laws relates to either an 'individual characteristic' or 'cooperative characteristic'. Laws 1-3 are primarily concerned with the 'individual' because these are laws that *you* must put in motion yourself. Laws 5, 6 and 7 are related with the cooperative elements of the model as they are chiefly concerned with what you do with and for *others*. Law 4 includes both individual and cooperative characteristics providing cohesiveness and the fusing together of all 7 laws. They follow an ordered arrangement that provide a stable foundation for each new law in the sequence. In a similar way that understanding of the law of aerodynamics will supersede an understanding of the law of gravity. The effectiveness of one is incomplete without the knowledge of the other.

Action is vital in the wealth creation process, but right action, in accordance with the *7 Laws of Wealth*, is the only thing that will deliver the desired result. You can learn to align your behavior with those laws so that you achieve the desired outcome - or you can ignore them and continue to reject what is proven and that which we know works. These laws are incontrovertible, malice may attack and indifference may ignore, but in the end... they are here to stay. Simple, but by no means is it simplistic.

If a picture paints a thousand words, then an outcome tells a thousand truths. If you want to know what you truly believe about money, look at your results. If you have money, then you probably have a positive set of constructive beliefs about money, and those beliefs translate into right action in accordance with the *7 Laws*. Your results are therefore the application of a correct belief, and your actions accurately reflect the natural laws outlined in this book.

Shallow men believe in luck. Strong men believe in cause and effect.
Ralph Waldo Emerson

Actions (and Results) ALWAYS Speak Louder Than Words

If your results are not delivering what you want, then you can be assured that something is missing somewhere between the "needs" and "results" ends of the 7 Laws Context Model. If you have no money, then you may have a problem at the "Belief Window/Rules" and/or the Action stage of the process. It's not luck, and you really can't blame anyone else for your current predicament. However, you can change things in a number of different ways.

The first way to break the conditioning created by negative beliefs and rules is to find new information. If you have no money in your life, then I can guarantee that in some way you are actively pushing it away by your beliefs, actions and behaviors. Or that it's simply not important enough to you. But considering that you are reading a book on how to become wealthy, we have to assume that you are interested in improving your situation.

Sometimes when we get new information that opposes an old belief, we experience what psychologists call "cognitive dissonance." This is the inner conflict caused when two or more opposing beliefs on your Belief Window try to occupy the same space. You can't believe money is the root of all evil and also believe that money is a powerful force for good. These are opposing beliefs, and the mind will seek resolution. A choice between the two beliefs is necessary to restore harmony. Knowing how your beliefs have been created and how new information may now be available can help that process.

For example, if that religious young man who is conflicted about wealth decided to actually read the Bible, he would realize that it doesn't actually state that money is the root of all evil. What it actually says is that "The love of money is the root of all evil." An entirely different meaning.

Later he may meet someone and come to know that person as a sincere and kind individual - then find out that they are also actually rich. This new information can create: cognitive dissonance, and the young man will have to start the process of change to restore harmony.

This is why this chapter is so important: it identifies valuable information about how you have become the person you are so you can actively take conscious control over that process in the future.

Trying to alter beliefs and track down the rules that govern your behavior can be time consuming and unpredictable. It's often a lot less hassle to just…

Align Yourself to the *7 Laws of Wealth*

Change for change sake is time consuming because it requires you to re-invent the wheel. Try a new approach, see what happens, monitor the results and repeat until successful. It can take time and effort to get it right.

There are two ways to make change successfully.

- Change your mind - make new choices.
- Change your behaviour - take different action.

Change Your Mind - Make New Choices

You really can decide to change your mind. If you can appreciate the fact that you have a Belief Window and unconscious rules that govern your life, you are immediately, at least in part, liberated from these limitations, because then you can exercise the thing that makes us uniquely human - choice. I believe it is choice, not random luck or circumstance, that makes us who we are. It is the decisions - not the conditions - of our life that determines our destination.

You are a product of choice - albeit often unconscious choice. You are not a captive to your past.

My earliest memory was of my mother sitting me down in the front room and saying, "Mummy's leaving home - who do you want to live with?" I was five years old. Naturally this news came as a major shock to me, and I ran out the house in tears. My father eventually found me about an hour or so later, and I returned to the house. My mother had left, and I never saw her again.

In many ways I was lucky because although it was difficult for me to come to terms with losing my mother, there was still a great deal of love in my home. Although we didn't have much money, I always knew my father wanted the best for me. I was also lucky enough to get an education - although not through school. I didn't like school, and it didn't like me much either. I left at 16.

After a brief sojourn at the Little Chef, a fast-food outlet near a freeway exit, I was offered a job with a network marketing company, as a sales trainer. The salary wasn't much better than at the Little Chef, but I was taught how to communicate to groups of people and train others. I was taught how to speak in front of people and deliver information on how to build a successful business. I was taught about motivation and, perhaps most beneficial of all, psychology. I learned how to *master my context* and *that* changed my life.

I discovered that we are not a product of our past, and the past does not dictate the future. We are a product of what we decide. I remember vividly the cognitive dissonance I felt when my mentor at the time suggested, "You could be a real success." The idea was so far outside my frame of reference and belief system that I was physically uncomfortable. I liked the idea but it didn't feel "me." But regardless, I set about altering my behaviour to align it with the *7 Laws of Wealth* (although I didn't know what they were at the time).

Left unattended, your Belief Window and the rules you construct will determine what you think, and your actions and behaviour will *always* determine your results. The only way you can change things is to take conscious control, master your context, and craft the life you want. To do this, you must first understand all the factors that influence you - and become conscious of their effects in your life.

Change Your Behaviour - Take Different Action

The second way you can effectively change is to change your behaviour and take different action.

Suppose Emily had realized that her fear of dogs and her discomfort at zoos or at seeing an elephant on TV was based on a long forgotten erroneous connection her brain made to save her time and theoretically protect her. At that moment she has new choices. Even if she never makes those connections but simply decides to do something different and go to the zoo and have fun with her nephew regardless of what she feels, then her new behaviour breaks the old conditioning.

I remember watching *The Andrew Marr Show* in the UK one Sunday morning. Shirley Williams, one of the breakaway "gang of four" who created the Social Democratic Party in British politics, was being interviewed about her career and recent biography. In a trip back to the UK from the US during the second world war, she was very nearly the victim of a gang rape.

Quite naturally, the power of conditioning the emotional scars of this event ran deep, and she became scared of all men that she didn't know. This reaction was so pronounced that she didn't even like being alone in a room with her own father. But she did recognize that her feelings could be a major problem for her if she was going to go into the male dominated world of politics, not to mention the consequences for her personal life.

So she dealt with it by going for long walks on the Thames River Embankment with her dog. She knew she would come in contact with unfamiliar men, but through constant practice, she got over her fear of them. She said, *"The Blitz didn't worry me at all. What worried me was unfamiliar men on the Embankment. I confronted my fear directly in that way and ceased to be scared."* She didn't have to spend thousands in therapy working out why she was scared of men. All she needed to do was make a different choice. She faced her fears and broke the chain. She had learned to *Master the Context.*

It was high counsel that I once heard given to a young person.
"Always do what you are afraid to do."
Ralph Waldo Emerson

In so doing she ensured that she was not a slave to whatever context was unconsciously created, and she did not allow her past to dictate her future. By having enough self awareness that something wasn't right, she was able to face her own fear and exercise self awareness and choice.

Our ability to choose is controlled by the frontal lobe in the neocortex of the brain. It is the capacity of the frontal lobe which separates us from the animal kingdom. The neocortex typically accounts for between 10-40% of total brain mass in mammals and about 50% in the most primitive primates. In humans it's even higher, at 80%.

The evolution of human frontal lobe bestowed on humans a focused,
intentional, creative, willful, decisive, purposeful mind,
if we will only put it to use.
Joe Dispenza

The frontal lobe is considered the seat of intention, conscious awareness, free will and choice. It is the part of our brain that accounts for such distinctively human traits as focus, creativity, making conscious decisions, coming up with plans, and carrying them out. It gives us the power to regulate our behavior rather than being a slave to instinct.

Doing Versus Thinking

At the beginning of the 20th century, influential people began to recognize the potency of choice and self determinism. The New Thought movement swept through America.

New Thought doesn't have a single origin but was created by a convergence of thinkers and philosophers of the day - James Allen (*As a Man Thinketh*), Robert Collier (*The Secret of Ages*), Emile Coue (*Self Mastery through Conscious Autosuggestion*), Wallace Wattles (*The Science of Getting Rich*), and others. The eminent American psychologist William James called the movement the 'mind-cure movement;' He described it as *"a deliberately optimistic scheme of life, with both a speculative and a practical side."*

But the practical side was nowhere near as desirable as the speculative side. The all-time personal development classic is Napoleon Hill's *Think and Grow Rich*. The title of that book changed the world. An entire industry quickly emerged as enterprising people recognized the sales possibilities of convincing others that all that was required for wealth was "right thinking."

But if you actually read the book, you find that thinking is actually just a small part of the puzzle. Between thinking and growing rich, there is *doing*.

Still, this was a great time in human development, because people were beginning to wake up to the possibility that thinking was an important factor in outcome. We were not cast onto the ocean of fate. We have a lot more control over a lot more things than we had previously been led to believe.

Your thought processes, your ability to handle change, to expand your awareness and gain greater self awareness - these are all crucial. The personal development industry did great things by putting the importance of right thinking on the map, but it played down the importance of the remaining crucial elements of success. Thinking *per se* will not make you rich. Even if you have empowering beliefs on your Belief Window, they won't automatically translate into wealth and success.

Yes, you have to really want what you are aiming for; yes, you have to believe that it's possible for you, and you have to confidently expect it. You have to direct your focus and have the right attitude. If you want to visualize yourself having achieved your goals, then feel free.

However if you think that's all it takes, then you're missing a huge point. You can make all the goal-envisioning bulletin boards you want, with cut-out pictures of the Lexus you will drive and the 10 bedroom country home where you'll live. You can laminate them all and stick them on the ceiling of your bedroom so they're the first thing you see in the morning and the last thing at night. You can recite positive affirmations in the shower till the cows come home - but this alone will not make you rich. Right thinking is only part of the process. It is necessary but not sufficient.

The missing element - the understanding that is consistently trivialized by personal development gurus because it doesn't sell product or seminar tickets - is *action*. You have to *do* something. And that's what the *7 Laws of Wealth* methodology is about. The 7 Laws are all introduced as verbs. Each one will require action on your part.

Wealth may indeed be 80% psychology. It's true that you need to appreciate that you have a Belief Window and rules that give you permission to feel certain feelings, but without the other 20%, you will still be no closer to creating wealth. Bottom line: Your success in business, finance, or life is a function of the degree to which you have aligned your actions to the *7 Laws of Wealth*. This is the *real* secret.

So let's begin laying the foundation of wealth with *Law 1 - Gain Control.*

Law 1

Gain Control

Promote Self Leadership & Initiative
Reputation, Distinction & Power will Result

When you decide to do something great, you must see it to the end. Never shrink from the responsibility of a once-made decision. No life ever grows great until it is controlled, focused and resolute. You must hold yourself accountable to a higher standard than anybody else expects. No excuses. To become outstanding, you must literarily stand out. The price of greatness is responsibility.

Chapter Three
Law 1 - Gain Control

AT THE TIME of his death in 1972, Herman C. Krannert was a successful businessman, entrepreneur and philanthropist from the American Midwest. He made his fortune in corrugated fiber products and is known for his generous contributions to education, health care, and the arts. There are 11 buildings in Illinois and Indiana that bear his name, including the prestigious Krannert School of Management at Purdue University.

Krannert's true colors were plain to see even in his twenties. After graduating from Crane Technical High School, he spent two years saving enough money to attend the University of Illinois. Working his way through college, he not only financed his own education, but he also sent extra money home to support his widowed mother.

He graduated in 1914 with a degree in mechanical engineering and began work for the Sefton Manufacturing Company, a Chicago-based firm that made paper boxes. Just 30 years old, he was transferred to Anderson, Indiana, where he became the youngest Sefton employee to be promoted to plant manager.

A Stunning Offer...with One Condition

During his successful tenure at Anderson, he was summoned to Chicago by the President of the company, but he had no idea why. He sat down for lunch with the President at the Athletic Club in Chicago. No one knows the exact conversation that took place that day, but essentially Krannert was told that the President was going to make an announcement to the company that would greatly impact Krannert's life. He was going to promote him to Senior Vice President of Sales and put him on the Board of Directors. Krannert was a hard working, motivated and successful manager, so we can only guess at his excitement at this new position, for which he didn't even know he was being considered.

The President no doubt told him of the high salary he could expect and the increased opportunity and responsibility that would come with the role. Krannert probably couldn't wait to tell his wife Ellnora.

Krannert, needless to say, responded enthusiastically. He told the President how grateful he was for the opportunity. He vowed he would be the most loyal employee Sefton had ever had, and he would dedicate his life to making the company one of the finest in America.

But the President made it quite clear that the promotion came with one condition - as a Director on the Board, Krannert would always have to vote as the President voted.

Talk about taking the wind out of someone's sails! Krannert sat in silence, slowly eating his soup, getting more and more annoyed about what he was hearing, until finally he stood up and said something like "I'm sorry, Mr. President, I can't accept a promotion on these terms. You are asking me to be a puppet on a Board of Directors - to behave unprofessionally and unethically. And, more importantly, I will not subject my own integrity and my team's integrity to this kind of behavior!" With that response, he left the Athletic Club and the company.

In one afternoon, Krannert was offered his dream position - more money, more responsibility, more opportunity - and was just as quickly out of a job. Some might say he was mad to turn it down, but Krannert was a man who was in control. He was a man who knew what he stood for and was willing to hold himself to a far higher standard than most other people.

So what happened to him?

Out of work, Krannert was surprised to find that six other employees of Sefton who had heard what happened were so inspired by his decision they also left the business, and together the seven started a new business called the Inland Container Corporation.

Controlling Your Destiny

All this was possible because Krannert was not willing to be a victim and accept whatever circumstances were given to him. He could have accepted the job; after all, it was more kudos, more money, and no one need ever have known that he was being told how to vote. But *he* would have known. This was a man who prided himself on hard work, integrity, loyalty and responsibility. This is a man who saved for two years to put himself through college, worked the entire time, and supported his widowed mother. Had he compromised, he would probably have become a bitter and twisted old man. But he didn't - because he had been living Law 1 in his life.

Krannert was familiar with the notion of personal responsibility and being in control of his own destiny. He took a stand for what he believed in, for who he was as a person, and he chose to live by his own code of conduct and forge a new and better path. Today the Inland Container Corporation is known as Temple-Inland, and it is one of the most successful and profitable corporations in America.

"Gain Control" is The First Law of Wealth, and it requires the fundamental need to recognize that the only thing we have true control over in this world is ourselves. Yet that is all we need in order to build the foundation for and actually create the wealth and life to which we're committed.

You can't escape the responsibility of tomorrow by evading it today.
Abraham Lincoln

It's easy to hear Krannert's story and come up with a ton of reasons why he could have taken that promotion, even why he *should* have taken that promotion. He could have rationalized his acceptance quite easily. He could have decided that taking the position was the right thing to do for his family. He could have thought that anything other than acceptance would have been disloyal to an employer, who up until that moment he admired and respected. He could have argued to himself that perhaps once he got into the position, he would have been able to change those terms. It's likely that he had all of these thoughts as he quietly ate his soup that day in the Athletic Club.

YOU are Responsible

But Krannert knew something that not everyone really truly understands. He knew that in the final analysis, he was responsible for his life, for the results he achieved, for the choices he made, and for the consequences of those choices. Krannert was a man who had truly mastered the First Law of Wealth. In that moment of personal power when he turned his back on that promotion, he set a course to become one of the wealthiest and most influential businessmen of all time.

Gaining Control is not always easy, and it can be a pivotal moment when we are called upon to do so. When I was 24 years old, I sold my first business for $3.5 million. If I'd been smart and invested that money wisely, I'd never have had to work another day in my life. But I wasn't that smart. Within 18 months, I had lost it all, including my home.

After I'd lost everything, I sat around for months, waiting for something to happen. Nothing did, and the result was one of the hardest lessons I ever learned in business. Eventually I realized that if I was to make money and achieve success again, then I had to make it happen. I had to become a better person. Reluctantly, I realized the Cavalry *wasn't* coming.

No one was going to get my money back for me. No one was going to fix the situation but me. If things were to change, I was going to have to change - before I could expect to see any change in my situation.

Make no mistake: it was a bitter pill. After all, why should I change? I'd become a multi-millionaire in my early 20s - I must have been doing something right. But the simple truth is that I just wasn't good enough to keep it. I realized that if I wanted this to change, I was going to have to change and if I wanted things to be better, I was going to have to be better.

You might make money, but you will never hold on to it and make it grow until you become the person that can handle the changes that money can often bring. I wasn't. I made bad investment choices that I wasn't committed to and was much too interested in cars and toys that were distractions, and investments that I didn't understand.

Wealth Depends on Your Ability to Take Personal Responsibility

I'm here to tell you point-blank - no one else is going to make you rich. It doesn't matter what school you went to, what qualifications you have, what sort of job your parents did raising you, or even if they did raise you. It doesn't matter if you struggled up the ladder or were given everything you ever wanted as a child - all that matters is what you decide to make those circumstances mean for you in your life. All that matters is the person you become. All that matters is your ability to take responsibility over your life and make choices that support you.

Man must cease attributing his problems to his environment, and learn again to exercise his will - personal responsibility.
Albert Schweitzer

We do not get what we want, and we don't always get what we expect or what we think about all day long - in life we *get* what we *are*. Life is a mirror. Who we are and how we behave is mirrored back to us through the experiences we have and the people we meet. If you are always angry, don't be surprised to find that your life is full of other angry people.

Consider this story: A wise old monk was tending his fields one day when a traveller passed by. The traveller beckoned the monk and said, "I have been in the village in the mountains and am travelling to the village at the bottom of the valley. Can you tell me what the people are like in that village?" The monk replied, "I can, but first I am curious. Can you tell me what the people in the mountain village were like?" "Oh" the traveller exclaimed, "They were dreadful. That is actually why I have decided to leave. The people in the mountain village were always bickering; they were mean spirited and cold. No one welcomed me in all the time I was there."

The monk hung his head. "Well I'm sorry to tell you, son, but you will find the people in the village in the valley to be much the same." "That's terrible news," snarled the traveller as he walked off.

Forty minutes later another traveller walked the path between the mountain village and the valley village. He too spotted the monk tending his crops. "Excuse me, sir, I am travelling to the village at the bottom of the valley, and I wondered if you could tell me what the people are like there?

The monk looked up and smiled, "I can, but first, I am curious. Can you tell me what the people in the mountain village were like?" "Oh," said the young man, "They were lovely; in fact, I am so sorry to leave, but I am committed to continuing my journey. The people were warm and generous and welcomed me like a long lost brother. They even threw me a farewell feast, and we ate and drank together until dawn - it was such a special evening."

The wise old monk smiled and said, "Well then, I am happy to tell you that you will find the people in the village at the bottom of the valley to be just the same."

The young man beamed with happiness and travelled on.

A Reflection of Yourself

We attract people that are like us. The first traveller saw other people only as unfriendly and cold - and didn't realize that it was he who was unfriendly and cold. The second traveller will only see people as warm and friendly because that's how he is. I'm not saying that the two travellers necessarily even met different people, just that they are different people, and as such they perceive a different reality. One focused on the negative things that happened and ignored the small kindnesses, while the other focused on the positive things and ignored the small cruelties.

When we constantly find the same types of people in new places, it's life's way of letting us see ourselves as others see us. That can either be a reward or a warning.

We do not see things as they are, we see things as we are.
The Talmud

When it's not what you want, it's supposed to be a wake-up call, an invitation to change and move on - not an excuse to become angrier, more unfriendly and indifferent.

This may not be easy to hear, but the results you've achieved up to this point are a direct consequence of the decisions and actions you've taken, or perhaps more to the point, *not taken*. Results don't lie; they are a reflection of the choices you've made. If you are not wealthy or where you want to be in your life right now, then the only person to blame for that situation is you. If it's not working, then you might not be working it as hard as you could be.

Remember the laws we talked about in the last chapter? There is a cause-and-effect relationship between who you are, what you do, what you choose and what you experience.

We are all free to choose our actions. But we are not free to choose the consequences of those actions. Consequences are governed by natural law. We can decide to step in front of a fast-moving train, but we cannot decide what will happen when the train hits us.

We can decide to be dishonest in our business dealings. But those choices have consequences, regardless of whether or not you are caught. Our behavior is governed by laws. The 7 Laws of Wealth are no different: living in harmony with them delivers inevitable wealth; violating them brings inevitable poverty and negative consequences.

Your results to date are a clear reflection of what you have done, not done - and, perhaps more importantly, who you have become.

New Age Nonsense

One of my biggest gripes against the personal development industry is the perpetuation of the notion that all you have to do is set a goal, be positive, expect the best, and think your way to success. The "philosophy" espoused by "The Secret"style literature is that you get what you think about. Thought manifests into reality.

Yes, you have to be confident and to expect the best. You have to dream big, aim for a target, create a plan and visualize the realization of an ideal. It is important to think positively, and optimism is a more enjoyable way to live than expecting disaster around every corner. However these things alone will not deliver your prize. They are at best only a partial solution.

I know hundreds of people who sit around pontificating about what they want to have in life, and five or ten years later, they are still sitting around pontificating about what they want to have in life. The only difference is they are also wondering why they don't have it. You can go for a walk in a thunderstorm and tell yourself, "It's not raining, it's not raining, it's not raining." You can visualize a warm sunny day, and imagine the feel of sand between your toes all you want, but it won't keep you from getting wet. Someone once said, "Affirmation without discipline is the beginning of delusion."

Tuning thought into action and executing that action - come what may - is what translates thought into reality. The self-help advisors have been so keen to provide you with an "easy" solution that they have happily played down the need for action. Consequently there are now millions of people around the world who are even more distressed that they can't create the life or business results that they dream of because they wrongly believe that positive thinking is all that is required to manifest that outcome.

I'm sorry if this comes as a shock, but you will have to get off your backside and do something. If you're serious, you will have to become a better person and you *will* have to get into action.

Gaining Control is about learning to own your life and everything in it. It's about owning your past results and taking responsibility for your future outcomes. Accept that your results speak for themselves - if you are currently not getting the results you desire, then you will have to change your behavior. It's not the economy or your parents, it's not because your mother dropped you when you were five, it's not because you didn't finish school or because you missed the train. *You* and *only you* are responsible for your results.

Tap Into Your True Potential

The truth is, we all have a far greater capacity than we ever dreamed possible. And I'm not just talking about money. There are plenty of examples of people pushed to extraordinary lengths in difficult situations that did superhuman things to save someone they love.

On April 9, 1982, Angela Cavallo's teenage son Tony was fixing his 1964 Chevy Impala when the jack slipped and pinned him underneath the car; he was knocked out. In a superhuman attempt to save her son, Angela, who was at the time in her late 50s, lifted enough of the car off him for five full minutes while a neighbor ran for help and someone was able to reinsert the jack and pull Tony to safety.

In an article in the *Journal of Applied Physiology*, scientists Michio Ikai and Arthur H Steinhaus demonstrated that human strength could be increased by up to 31% under certain conditions. They concluded from their research that what we think we are capable of is nothing more than "Pavlovian procedures." The authors concluded that it was the conditioned responses that we explored in the last chapter - and not real potential - that inhibit results. We're all capable of feats beyond what is considered "normal," but it often takes a crisis for us to actually tap into that capacity. We all have the strength of Angela Cavallo; it's just that most of us never create the situations that demand we use it.

We all have six cylinders under the hood, but we just don't realize it, so we amble along using two or three. We never tap into that power because (a) we don't know it's there, (b) we don't want anything badly enough to activate it, or (c) we simply don't know how.

What are You Prepared to Do?

I often ask the audience in seminars, "Who here would like more money?" Without exception ALL the hands shoot up. And I say, "That's the problem - you'd *'like'* it. Truth is, if you *had to have it*, you'd have it. You'd find a way." To demonstrate this idea further, I call someone up to the stage for the "I-beam test." Imagine one of those huge 50-ft. construction beams. They're called I-beams because if you cut one in half, the cross section is shaped like the letter I.

So in the training I say to my volunteer, "Imagine there is an I-beam on the floor here. You are at one end and I am at the other. If I offered you $100 to cross the beam, would you cross it?" The answer is always a "Yes."

Then I raise the stakes. I get the volunteer to imagine that the I-beam is raised to straddle two buildings 50 stories high. The volunteer is to imagine him or herself at the end of the beam. Again I offer the same amount to cross the beam. I ask them if they would still cross the beam. This time the answer is always a resounding "No."

So I raise the stakes a little more. "Would you come for $250,000?" The answer is still usually no, but there is certainly more hesitation. As I increase the reward for crossing the beam, eventually I'll arrive at a figure - often around $2 million - for which the volunteer would be willing to cross that beam.

Then I raise the stakes again. I tell the person that the wind speed has increased significantly and it's started to rain. The beam is slippery - would they come for $2 million? Most people decide the risk is too high and would refuse to cross.

Finally I say to the volunteer, "I'm not a nice person anymore, and I've got your four-year-old daughter. I'm doing a *'Michael Jackson'* and dangling her over the side of the building. If you don't cross the I-beam, I'm going to drop her - would you come?

The answer is always an overwhelming, "Absolutely!"

What we are talking about here is the need to create a desired result. We will do whatever it takes if our desire for that reward is great enough. As you can see, love is always much more powerful than money. It would be a rare parent who would not do anything to protect their own child - even risk their own life - because they have to succeed. Most parents would prefer to die trying than do nothing.

Would you like more money or do you *have to have* more money? You have to decide what you want - and, more importantly, what you're prepared to do or *not* prepared to do to get it. When the President of the Sefton Manufacturing Corporation asked Herman Krannert to join the Board of Directors and become his puppet, the risk-reward ratio was insufficient for Krannert.

He was simply not able to accept the position without going against his own values and losing his own self respect, which was simply too high a price. So he took a stand for what he believed was right, took control of the situation and his future, and created a new template for himself, illustrating the essence of Law 1.

You have to do what you have to do,
before you can do what you want to do.
Ben Benson

The Control Continuum

When I talk about this subject in seminars, there are always one or two people full of reasons why this isn't true. They'll say, "Yeah, but he was probably independently wealthy and could afford to make that choice." Or "Yeah, but he had an education; he would have known that he could get another job." Or "Yeah, but that was almost 100 years ago. The world is a different place now."

Everything in the world can be split into two categories - the things we can control or influence and the things we can't.

To demonstrate this point, I often run a little experiment in my presentations. The right-hand side wall of the room represents things over which we have "Low/No Control." The left side wall represents things over which we have "High/Total Control." I ask the audience for examples of things in our lives over which we have low or no control. People will shout out things like "the weather," "other people," "the economy," etc.

Then I move to the left side of the room and ask for suggestions of things that we have high or total control over. Again the audience members will shout out various answers such as "our thoughts," "our free time," "what we eat," "how our house is decorated."

When split up like this, it becomes quite obvious that all the things over which you exercise high or total control are things relating to you or your life. They are things over which you have some direct influence.

Yet where do most people spend most of their time and energy? They worry about the weather. If it's raining, they automatically feel depressed. They worry about the fact that their friend didn't return their call and imagine a hundred and one explanations for this (all of which are bad). They worry about whether or not their boss is happy with their work. What is the point of getting upset about things over which you have absolutely no control or at best a tiny amount of control?

The only appropriate response to this stuff is to roll with it. Adapt to the new circumstances and focus your time and attention on the things you can control.

The truth of the matter is that there are things that we think we can't control that we actually can - and there are things we think we can control that we actually can't. Some people in Herman Krannert's position would have assumed they didn't have a choice and would have accepted the condition, even if it made them angry inside. Krannert didn't, because he appreciated that he *did* have a choice - and he exercised it. Gaining Control is about getting a very clear appreciation of the difference between the things we do have influence over and the things we don't - and spending all your time and energy on the right side of that equation.

Grant me the serenity to accept the things I cannot change;
courage to change the things I can;
and wisdom to know the difference.
Serenity Prayer

We all have problems. It doesn't matter who you are or where you live or how much money you have in the bank - we all have problems. Why exacerbate those by worrying about things you can't have any impact on? It's crazy, and you're wasting valuable time and resources on a fruitless struggle. In fact, most of the things we worry about have either already happened, in which case we cannot change them, or are future-based and almost never occur.

If instead you turned your attention away from the things you can't influence and you focused on all the things you do have control over, you may be surprised at how unimportant those other things become. Where you focus your time and energy on the control continuum will give you some insight into your current degree of control and self leadership.

Control and Responsibility

Remember Aron Ralston in the last chapter? What you may not know about Ralston is that he escaped because he managed to accept responsibility for his self inflicted situation.

In an interview with the *National Geographic*, he was asked how he finally decided to cut off his own arm. He said, "After having enough sleep deprived, meandering thoughts about how I arrived in the canyon, I realized that my situation was the result of decisions that I had made. I chose to go out there by myself. I chose not to tell anyone where I was going. I chose not to go with two climbers I had met in the canyon on the first day. But I also realized that I had made all of the choices up to that point that had helped me survive. I took responsibility for all of my decisions, which helped me take on the responsibility of getting myself out."

Hopefully, we won't ever have to cut off our arm with a blunt knife. But sooner or later we all have to accept responsibility for where we are - even if it is a terrible predicament - and learn to Gain Control. We all have to take responsibility for our situation - and, more importantly, figure out what we are going to do about it.

The dictionary definition of *responsibility* speaks of "being the primary cause for." There is an implication of future direction: When you take responsibility for yourself, you are drawing a line in the sand and saying that regardless of what happens, you will find a way around, over or through those situations in a relentless march toward your future. There is no room for complaining or blame. If you can't change something, then don't waste your time or energy thinking about it. Instead you turn all your focus on what you can change and you take complete and total control over those things.

Responsibility is married to accountability. The dictionary says that if you are accountable, you have governance or liability for something. This implies past and future direction that in this example are inextricably linked.

First you must accept that you are accountable for everything that has happened in your life (you might not be to blame for it, but you have to be able to accept it) and then move on.

These issues arise in the Madoff scandal. Former financier and Chairman of the NASDAQ stock exchange Bernie Madoff appeared beyond reproach. Unfortunately for thousands of his investors, he was also the operator of the largest fraud ever committed by a single person. He was arrested after his sons told authorities that their father had confessed to them. In June 2009, he was sentenced to 150 years in prison.

Effectively he'd been running a "Ponzi scheme," in which returns were paid to investors from their own money or subsequent investors' money rather than actual profits. Madoff took his investors' money and put it in his Chase Manhattan Bank account. He was able to pay returns from this money and from additional money that new investors gave him because of his growing reputation for high returns.

Perhaps the biggest beneficiary was his bank, estimated to have made $483 million in fees from his account. What Madoff did was wrong, and thousands of people lost billions. There were reports of suicides and the disaster sent a shock wave through the financial world.

Madoff was fully accountable for his actions and is now paying the price. When professional investors get taken for large sums of money, they naturally get angry, upset and quickly look for somebody to blame. But each investor or fund (or at least their auditors) that invested were also responsible for their due diligence obligation in the transaction. A successful con job requires two parties. The bilked investors, sad as their situation is, must also take some personal accountability for getting involved with him in the first place, the repercussions of which will go on for some time.

Concerns about Madoff's business surfaced in 1999, when financial analyst Harry Markopolos informed the SEC that he believed it was mathematically impossible to achieve the returns that Madoff was claiming to deliver. But the investors never thought to look too deeply into what Madoff did with their money, as long as it kept increasing. A difficult decision when every chart is 'up and to the right'.

Let It Go

We all have to come to a point where we accept our own mistakes and even take responsibility for those made by others. This is the essence of Law 1. We may not like it, and we may think it unfair, but this is an inevitable reality of life. At times we will all make bad decisions, sometimes other people will make them for us. Bad decisions, personal or inflicted, usually precede good judgment. In the end, regardless of who makes them, mistakes will be inevitable. What is important is how you tackle these situations, and what you personally do to take responsibility for yourself by navigating the situations that your decisions may create. We can't always control other people, but we always have the ability to choose what their behavior is going to mean for us.

So let it go - whatever it is. Forget the past; forget the "mistakes" you've made or the mistakes others have made. Learn from them, take responsibility for them, but don't waste your energy stewing over them. They are gone - they belong in the domain of things you can't control, and any effort to change that will be futile. We can't recall them, we can't undo them, and we can't control the consequences.

You must learn from the mistakes of others.
You can't possibly live long enough to make them all yourself.
Sam Levenson

As human beings we have the capacity for self-awareness. We have imagination - the ability to create in our minds a reality beyond our present reality. Also we have independent will - the ability to act based on our self-awareness, free of all other influences.

Even the most intelligent animals may have some of these human traits. All animals have a form of intelligence. However they can't consciously change or direct or question their lives, even if they are aware of them. What makes us different is that we can become aware of the conditioning that has programmed us, and we can choose a different response and therefore produce a different outcome. In short, we can write new programs for ourselves, totally apart from our conditioning and training. It is this ability that empowers us to fulfil our uniquely human potential.

Our freedom of choice, our free will is our greatest asset. It is within each of us, just waiting for us to Gain Control, so we can begin to use it for whatever we want to achieve.

The mind is its own place, and in itself can make
heaven of hell, a hell of heaven
John Milton

How to Master Law 1 and Gain Control:

- Accept Personal Responsibility
- Set a New Standard
- Be Proactive, NOT re-active
- Concentrate on Your Resourcefulness, *not* Your Resources

Accept Personal Responsibility

While we may not be able to control all that happens to us,
we can control what happens inside us.
Benjamin Franklin

Gaining Control is the first and the most personal Law of Wealth. You can't skip it or go round it, and you can't decide to come back to it later. Consequently, like all important things in life, the journey toward its recognition isn't always easy. The need for personal responsibility is often a continuous process that mirrors what is known as the Kubler-Ross Grief Curve.

Developed by Swiss-born psychiatrist Elizabeth Kubler-Ross and explained in her ground-breaking book *On Death and Dying,* the Kubler-Ross grief process involves five stages that people pass through when faced with grief or tragedy. Whether or not Kubler-Ross is accurate about her stages (there is considerable dissent and rebuttal), we see the same five stages as people travel the path to self determinism and personal responsibility. I believe we could find them in any situation where human beings confront the inevitable.

The five stages are:

Denial

Anger

Bargaining

Depression

Acceptance

Denial

If you are in denial, then you simply don't see how you could possibly be responsible for your current situation. You are just a victim - an innocent bystander at your own financial disaster zone. As far as you are concerned, it's always someone else's fault. If you lose your job, it's your boss's fault for being a bad manager. If your wife leaves you, it's because she was at fault. If you are up to your back teeth in crippling debt, it's the credit card company's fault for lending you the money. Besides, why shouldn't you have a six-foot High Definition TV with Surround Sound?

Some things are true whether we choose to accept them or not.
Ben Benson

If you are in denial, then it's never your responsibility. As far as you are concerned, you are simply a victim of circumstance. Nothing changes in denial.

Anger

The second stage is anger. If you are experiencing this stage, you probably feel frustrated about your situation. Why isn't anything working? Why aren't you rich already? Clearly something is wrong, but you have no idea what that might be. You may be confused about what to do and how to solve the problem, and that's what's causing your anger. You still can't see what responsibility has to do with anything and are quite happy blaming anything and everything in your vicinity on your current predicament.

When a man is wrong and won't admit it, he always gets angry.
Thomas C. Haliburton

Usually if you are angry about the lack of money, and are resentful of those who are wealthy, you might try and pacify yourself by thinking *"money is the root of all evil"* and other such misquoted nonsense, but it still doesn't make you feel better. Nothing worthwhile changes in anger.

Bargaining

Once the red mist clears, you might be nudged into stage three. If you are in the bargaining stage, you may begin to recognize that maybe you have had a hand in creating your current problems. But you don't want to accept full responsibility for what's happened. So you bargain. You want to be able to pick and choose what you are accountable for. The reason you do this is that you probably confuse responsibility with blame. What has happened to you in your life may not always have been your fault, but you still have to accept responsibility for how you choose to deal with it.

All blame does is keep you locked into a victim mentality, and it's very hard to move from that position. You can't undo what has happened in the past, but you can choose a different reaction and choose a different outcome for the future as a result. Nothing changes in bargaining.

Depression

The next stage is depression. You feel that the little responsibility you have reluctantly assumed should be enough, and yet things are not changing. If you are depressed, you've probably spent thousands of dollars on wealth creation seminars and self help books and logged countless hours in seminars hugging complete strangers and high fiving about the future, only to find that nothing changes. You may have irritated your friends and family for a couple of weeks afterwards, but that's the extent of the alterations.

This is the "what's the use?" stage of sadness and withdrawal as you resign yourself to poverty and a life half-lived. Nothing changes in depression.

Acceptance

Finally there is stage five - acceptance. Acceptance is the Holy Grail of transformation and the beginning of a whole new life in which you fully accept (albeit reluctantly at first) that where you are right now is because of you - and only you can make the needed changes. Only then can you really create what you want. Law 1 is the golden law - without it, none of the others will work.

When you can fully appreciate that you and your choices, decisions, actions, and inactions have brought you to this place, you reclaim your personal power. This is the beginning of a new way of being, the emergence of a new, better, stronger and happier person. Everything changes with acceptance.

Seek your own liberation with diligence.
Buddha

I have thought on many occasions that it would do us good to see the Statue of Liberty in New York supplemented by a Statue of Responsibility on the West Coast. We have come to confuse our liberty and freedom with a lack of responsibility. The notion that we are free when we can do what we want, when we want…is false. True freedom is a consequence of disciplined effort. Freedom is the flip side of responsibility. They are the two sides of the same coin; you can't enjoy one without the other.

Set a New Standard

One of the things that I found most interesting about my interviews with over 200 people from the Rich List was that they all had a personal standard. It wasn't always something they were conscious of or would talk about in those terms, but every one of them had a code of conduct or ethics that determined everything they did in life. There were no half measures - everything was calculated to achieve a result.

Consider the following three levels of operation in life; the third is the "new standard" to which you need to aspire to:

Haphazard

Disciplined

Purposeful

My estimate is that more than 80% of the population lives in a haphazard state. Sometimes they do what they say they will do and follow through, and sometimes they don't. Sometimes they are driven toward a goal, and sometimes they are not. Their actions are determined not by a proactive goal or choice; instead, their behavior is a reactive compromise.

What is necessary to change a person is to
change his awareness of himself.
Abraham H Maslow

"Disciplined" is the goal level at which someone has transcended the haphazard lifestyle and is aiming toward a particular goal or target. This is definitely an improvement and will always yield better results than the previous level. You can live a good, happy and fulfilled life in a disciplined way.

But if you want real wealth, then you must elevate your operating style to a purposeful way of life. Almost all the people I have been fortunate enough to meet and interview have been purposeful. It's rarely about the money; their pursuits are often a reflection of who they are as people.

Proactive, Not Reactive

While the word *Proactive* is now fairly common in management literature, you won't find it in every dictionary. It means more than merely 'taking initiative.' It means 'being responsible' for the outcomes you desire. Look at the word *responsibility* - in effect, "response-ability" - the ability to choose your response. Highly proactive people recognize their ability to respond. They do not blame circumstances, conditions, or conditioning for their behavior.

Their behavior is a product of their own conscious choice, based on their beliefs and values, rather than a product of their genetics, upbringing, environment or mood.

Reactive people, on the other hand, are buffeted from pillar to post by their physical environment, what others say and do, and other circumstances that they can't control. If the weather is good, they feel good. If it isn't, it affects their attitude and their performance. Proactive people carry their own weather with them. Whether it rains or shines makes no difference to them. They are values-driven, and if their value is to produce good quality work, it isn't a function of whether atmospheric conditions are conducive to it or not. Quality work is just what they do.

Reactive people are also affected by their social environment, by the "social weather." When people treat them well, they feel well; when people don't, they become defensive or protective. Reactive people build their emotional lives around the behavior of others. They use language like "There's nothing I can do" "That's just the way I am." "He makes me so mad." "They won't allow that." "I have to do that. I can't. I must. If only..." They are driven by feelings, circumstances, conditioning and by their environment.

Proactive people are driven by values - carefully thought about, selected and internalized. Proactive people are still influenced by external stimuli, whether physical, social, or psychological. But their response to the stimuli, conscious or unconscious, is a value-based choice or response. As Eleanor Roosevelt observed, *"No one can hurt you without your consent."* In the words of Gandhi, *"They cannot take away our self respect if we do not give it to them."* It is our willing permission, our consent to what happens to us, that hurts us far more than what happens to us in the first place.

Proactive people use language like "Let's look at our alternatives." "I can choose a different approach." "I control my own feelings." "I can create an effective presentation." "I will choose an appropriate response. I choose. I prefer. I will."

What it takes to become wealthy can be extremely hard to accept emotionally, especially if you have experienced years and years of rationalizing misery and doubt in terms of circumstance or someone else's behavior. It's not what happens to us that matters; it's what we decide those things mean.

Of course, things can hurt us physically or economically and can cause sorrow. But our character, our basic identity, does not have to be hurt at all. In fact, our most difficult experiences often act as the foundation of our character. We become a better, stronger person through adversity - not by avoiding it.

The finest steel goes through the hottest fire.
Richard Nixon

We have all known individuals who have surmounted great odds, perhaps with a serious illness or a severe physical handicap, who maintain magnificent emotional strength. How inspired we are by their integrity. Nothing has a greater, longer lasting impression upon other people than the awareness that you have transcended suffering, have transcended circumstance, and are expressing yourself and inspiring others.

Concentrate Your Resourcefulness, *Not* Your Resources

Everything you need for change is already inside you. You have the capacity to use your creativity, your ingenuity, your ideas and thoughts to create a better future. It doesn't matter what resources you have in terms of money to invest or even time to invest it. What matters first is your willingness to be resourceful with whatever you currently have.

Over the years, I have frequently counseled people who wanted better jobs to show more initiative - to take an interest in their profession, take aptitude tests, study the industry, even the specific problems the organization is facing, then develop an effective presentation showing how their abilities can help solve the organization's problem. It's called "solution selling," a key paradigm in personal and business success.

One must learn by doing the thing, for though you think you know it,
you have no certainty until you try.
Aristotle

A friend of mine once saw an advertised position that was her "dream job." She applied for the job. In the meantime she started to write up a proposal for all the things she wanted to do in the role, all the ideas and possibilities that could be developed for additional income streams. Ideas for the online side of the business, prospects for what could be achieved over 3-5 years. A few weeks later she still hadn't heard anything, so she sent her complete proposal to the firm. She was called within five minutes of its hitting the fax. She got the job because she had engaged in solution selling, although she wasn't aware of it. She just wanted that job and went the extra mile to demonstrate what she would bring to the role.

When I counsel people about solution selling, they invariably see the advantages. It's not rocket science, after all. Going the extra mile actually only requires you to go an extra inch or so - because most people won't even do that. The accepted wisdom is that "I'll do more when I'm paid more." Most people who are happy to settle for mediocrity expect to *get* before they have *given*, but Law 1 doesn't work that way.

You have to give yourself, your ideas, your time, your energy, your commitment, your dedication, your resourcefulness - before you can ever expect to receive the same or better in return.

So even though people can see how attractive that approach would be to a prospective employer, they typically fail to take the initiative, to make it happen. Instead I hear things like, "I don't know where to go to take the aptitude test." "How do I study the industry and the organization's problems?" "No one will help me."

Too many people wait for something to happen or someone to take care of them. But people who end up with the good opportunities are the ones who take the initiative - the ones that are proactive and provide solutions instead of becoming a problem. My friend could have sat at home whining about not hearing back from the company - or badgered them to make a decision. Instead she took the time to demonstrate her suitability for the role and explained what she felt she could bring to the business. She gave the company ideas they had never even thought about - all before she even knew if she had an interview.

Our basic nature is to act, and not to be acted upon. If we act, we give ourselves the opportunity to respond to particular circumstances, since we are thus empowered to create opportunities where none previously existed. Taking the initiative does not mean being pushy, obnoxious, or aggressive. It means recognizing that if we want to make something happen, we must do everything in our power to make that happen.

It was awise man that said: "As I grow older I pay less attention to what men say. I just watch what they do."
Wilfred A. Peterson

The difference between people who exercise initiative and those who don't is literally the difference between night and day. I don't mean a small difference in results; I'm talking about significant difference, particularly if the proactive people are also smart, aware, and sensitive to others.

It takes initiative to live the 7 Laws of Wealth. As you study the other six laws, you will see that each depends on the development of your proactive muscles. Each puts the responsibility on you to act. Each builds on the last, until you arrive at your chosen destination a stronger, happier, wealthier and more fulfilled person.

What To Expect If You Fail To Gain Control

- Exactly what you've already got

Exactly What You've Always Got!

One definition of insanity is doing the same thing over and over again and expecting a different result. It's a cliché - and for good reason. If you continue to do what you've always done, you indeed will continue to get what you've always got. If you don't believe that taking responsibility for yourself will make any difference and you are emotionally attached to blame and recrimination, then I can only assume this book has been given to you as an intervention by someone who cares about you. There is no way you would have bought it yourself.

The difficult part is that if you read this book, you won't be able to hide from the truth anymore. There will be a part of you - even a quiet, reluctant part - that is forced to accept that what I'm saying is true. And guess what? Now you can't escape. You now know something that you can't un-know. You can't hide behind circumstance. You can't blame others or situations for your current situation anymore. At least you can't if you are genuinely interested in changing it.

Take charge and create the business you want instead of living a life full of regret. Jungian Psychologist James Hillman said, *"You have to give up the life you have to get to the life that's waiting for you."* He was right.

To be in hell is to drift; to be in heaven is to steer.
George Bernard Shaw

Law 1 is imperative to achieving what you want. You won't succeed without it. Even if you don't want billions or even millions - even if you just want to make a good living and do what you love, you can't achieve that without first taking complete responsibility for your life.

What You Can Confidently Expect If You Gain Control

- Increased reputation, credibility and distinction
- Power - enhanced self leadership and initiative
- The ability to create of opportunity
- Less dissatisfaction, more peace

Increased Reputation, Credibility and Distinction

People who achieve what they set out to achieve are inspirational - whether by climbing Kilimanjaro or making a million. We admire those that battle against the odds and achieve their desired outcomes - not the ones who come up with excuse after excuse. We admire those that take a stand for what they believe in and take responsibility for their actions.

Just as an apple will fall to the ground because of the Law of Gravity, Gaining Control and taking personal responsibility for your past, present and future will lead to increased reputation, credibility and distinction. There is a new-found level of self-respect and confidence that comes from doing what you say you will do. Others will gravitate to you. And the sense of control and self-mastery you will experience will become clear.

Power - Enhanced Self Leadership and Initiative

Individuals who have mastered themselves usually find that other people look to them for leadership and guidance. When you can stand tall, shoulders back, and say with absolute honesty that you take responsibility for yourself, then nothing can pull you off course. When you accept that you and you alone are in charge of how your business life turns out - regardless of what circumstances you meet along the way - then you have true personal power. To paraphrase the British poet William Ernest Henley from his famous poem *Invictus - "then you will be master of your fate and captain of your soul."*

Creator of Opportunity

To Gain Control, you don't sit around waiting for someone to direct you or for some great idea to fall out the sky and hit you on the head. You go out into the world and make things happen. If you want to be fit, then you don't sit at home visualizing what you'll look like when you're lean and healthy - you go to the gym or join the local kick-boxing club. You take action to make what you see in your head…real in your world. If you want more money, you will come up with a way to create value, and you work that plan until the objective is reached. It's up to you to make what you want a reality.

Less Dissatisfaction, More Peace

This is simply a happier way to live. You appreciate that other people can't hurt you unless you allow them to. You can't control what others do or say, but you can control what you decide those things mean. If someone is rude to you, you can choose to let that upset you all day, perhaps for weeks. Or you can choose not to. It really is that simple. I'm not saying it's always easy, but it is simple. If the thoughts you are creating around a situation are making you unhappy, and you can't change the situation, then a place to begin is to change the meaning.

The Cavalry is Not Coming

Law 1 is first and foremost about recognizing, as my grandmother used to say, "The Cavalry is *not* coming." There is no one waiting in the wings to sweep in on a white horse and save the day. There is no magic carpet ride to financial freedom and no fairy godmother to turn pumpkins into Princes or Princesses. And no, your numbers probably *won't* come up on the Lottery.

Even though we all know this in our heart, there is still a childlike hope that maybe, just maybe it will all miraculously fall in our lap. The unspoken assumption is that wealth and prosperity is nothing more than a lucky accident that befalls the chosen few.

I've done the calculation and your chances of winning the lottery are identical whether you play or not.
Fran Lebowitz

Wealth and prosperity are the result of time honored laws that if applied with consistent persistence will yield their fruit. There truly is nothing magical about money.

A stream is often crooked because it follows the path of least resistance. As it meanders along on its journey, it does not find the straightest path; it simply goes where it is easiest to flow. Most of us live our lives in the same way. We don't want to surmount obstacles, we don't want to deal with the resistance we experience in life, and instead of forging forward and finding new paths, we change our plans and scale back our aspirations.

And yet nothing of worth is achieved in life without effort, focus and determination. If you refuse to plan for your future, then your future will arrive one day and it won't look anything like what you hoped it to be. Resolve to do whatever it takes to make it a reality. There *is* a formula for wealth creation - these pages will give you that formula, and if you have the strength and determination to implement it without fail, without excuse or without shrinking from your tasks, then you will create wealth in your life.

About the only thing that comes to us without effort is old age.
Gloria Pitzer

All the really wealthy people I've met during the last few years have all had a high personal standard. They have the ability to do what needs to be done regardless of whether they want to do it or not.

Knowing what to do is one thing, and it's important information. But doing what you know is quite another, and it is this quality that separates the wealthy from the rest. Doing what you know you should do and doing it regardless of what alternative emerges or what you feel like - is the hallmark of brilliance in any field. People who achieve great things do so because they have the self-control and determination to do what most people will not.

Muhammad Ali, one of the greatest boxers of all time said, "I hated every minute of training, but I said, 'Don't quit. Suffer now and live the rest of your life as a champion.'"

There must have been thousands of times when he'd rather have been doing anything else but training. However he did what he needed to do to become a champion. Not just any champion - Ali is and always will be a boxing legend. If you want things to be better, you need to be better. Be assured of one thing. If wealth is seriously important to you, then you *can* achieve it. If you want *serious* wealth, then you need to be serious *about* wealth, and that means being harder on yourself than perhaps you've ever been in the past. This is the foundational truth of Law 1.

Are You Aligned to Law 1 - Have you Gained Control?

On the next page there are 7 sets of two statements - 1A/1B through 7A/7B. Read each pair of statements and check off the statement that's mostly true for you. That means, on balance, which more accurately reflects your situation, view on life and opinions? It won't always be easy, but choose the one that best matches you. And check either A *or* B for each of the seven pairs.

Be honest - no one need see this. If you don't want to write in the book or want to keep your selections private, then make the selections in a separate notebook. Don't check what you wish you were like or hope to be like in the future. Answer as you are right now. If you are unsure, then ask someone you know, and trust to give you feedback.

	A	B
1	☐ If I look back on my life, I can usually see what I did wrong or could have done differently for a better result.	If I look back on my life, I can usually see what others did wrong or could have done differently for a better result. ☐
2	☐ I rarely blame others when things don't go well. I prefer to focus on finding a solution.	I usually blame other people when things don't go well and will spend a great deal of time complaining about it. ☐
3	☐ I think voting is very important because if you are not happy with the government, you have to do something to change it.	I think voting is a complete waste of time. Individuals can't change anything. ☐
4	☐ If I do something wrong or upset someone, I will apologize. I appreciate that it's not always about being right or wrong. *Sorry* is one of the most powerful words in the English language.	I hardly ever say "sorry" even when I know I'm in the wrong. To do so is a sign of weakness. ☐
5	☐ I don't get upset at others very often.	I have a quick temper, and I spend a lot of the time being upset with others. ☐
6	☐ If things don't work out the way I want, then I'll see how I can change my approach and try again.	If things don't work out the way I want, I will usually just give up after one or two attempts. ☐
7	☐ I think I deserve wealth because I'm a hard worker and I'm willing to do whatever it takes to achieve business success.	I think I deserve wealth because I'm smart, so it's just a matter of time before I achieve business success. ☐

If you checked five or more of the statements in the A Column, then you already have a good grasp of Law 1. If you checked three or more statements in the B Column, then we suggest you read the supplementary guidebook; ***Law1 - Gain Control: Applications and Insights.*** This companion guide will give you further information about Law 1, together with practical techniques, ideas and insights into how you can successfully align yourself to this law and harness its power.

Law 2

Embrace the Future

Develop a Clear Outcome, Aim & Intentions But be Discerning & Responsive in Approach

Your circumstances may be unfavorable, but they can change significantly if you can perceive an ideal and strive to reach it. You must endeavour to unveil your innate bounty, by cultivating expertise in your own field while being alert to new ideas from any source of inspiration. Many valuable ideas at first seemed strange and awkward, even impossible, but were ultimately accepted as the best and only way. The longer our imagination retains the new idea, the clearer and more attainable it becomes.

Chapter Four
Law 2 - Embrace the Future

IN PRESENTATIONS I often tell the story of Howard Hill, unofficially known as the "World's Greatest Archer," partly because he's the only person to win 196 archery field tournaments in succession. He would perform trick shots like shooting an apple or even a prune off someone's head from sixty feet away, although I wouldn't have fancied being that person! He could shoot a flipping coin. He's the archer responsible for the "splitting arrow" scene in the 1938 movie *The Adventures of Robin Hood* staring Errol Flynn. In the movie Hill fires at the target and splits another arrow already in the bulls-eye - clean in two from neck to tip. Suffice it to say Howard Hill was good - exceptionally good.

But what would happen if I blindfold him, spun him around ten times and asked him to split an arrow? Clearly he wouldn't be able to do it. Chances are he wouldn't even be able to fire the arrow and hit a target with any precision.

And that's what this chapter is all about - regardless of your competence, you can't hit a target you cannot see. Embracing the Future is getting clear about your target.

One of the reasons that businesses owners fail is because they lack a clear target. They meander from one idea or initiative to the next, never really having a clear picture of the desired outcome. I have found that people consistently over-estimate what they can do in a year and under-estimate what they can do in a decade. They set steep goals to be achieved in a year, such as "to become a millionaire," when all they currently have is a mountain of debt and a part-time job. Such an outcome seems virtually impossible, and the individual becomes despondent and gives up. With disappointing one-year results, the idea of planning for five or ten years seems futile.

Yet a year is a relatively short period in the context of a lifetime. Expecting miracles in 365 days causes pressure and stress. Refusing to plan five, ten, or twenty years in the future, however, will cause you even more of the same.

Do you think the millions of pensioners struggling to survive on Social Security every month planned to be almost destitute when they reached retirement? Do you think that the twety percent plus of those pensioners who still have a mortgage in their old age anticipated that things would turn out that way?

No one thinks he or she is planning to fail, but failing to plan guarantees it. Just think back on your own life. Do you remember the bullet-proof confidence of your late teens and early twenties? Do you remember when you were convinced that you would be nothing like your parents when you grew up? Do you remember the conviction that you felt about how you were going to make your fortune one way or another? Do you remember the posters on your wall of the car you were going to drive when you were loaded? So what happened?

If you're reading this book, then I'm guessing it didn't pan out quite as you expected. Why not? My guess is that life got in the way. You got a job, and you decided that you'd get your financial house in order when you made that next promotion. Or perhaps you were going to make your fortune when the kids were older? Or perhaps you were going to start your own business when you'd paid off the mortgage? Only you didn't. Whatever it was, the reason life was able to pull you away from your intentions was that you didn't have a clear enough target, and beyond daydreaming, you had absolutely no plan of action as to how you would reach that outcome.

How to Master Law 2 and Embrace the Future:

- Identify Your Natural Talents and Abilities
- Identify Where You are Now and what Wealth Means to You
- Establish a Clear Outcome

Identify your Natural Talents and Abilities

If **Law 2** is about establishing your target, then there is a process you have to recognise before you can do that successfully. The first part is to identify your natural talents and abilities. That means learning how to decipher some personal clues to highlight potential natural gifts and best avenues for exploration.

There is one thing that we all must do. If we do everything else but that one thing, we are lost. And if we do nothing else but that one thing, we will have lived a glorious life.
Rumi

But before we do that, I want to cover one of the most toxic personal development mantras - *"Do what you love and the money will follow."*

The idea is that we are all have unique talents and abilities and all we need to do is uncover those talents, use them, and the money will miraculously arrive in our lives. Sounds great, but let's get clear on the principle. I agree that we each have certain abilities that mean we can do certain things better than other people and that those things hold clues to our natural talents and most fulfilling career paths.

However...

a) Natural talent is often not that obvious or easy to uncover

b) A talent may not be commercially viable

For example, you uncovered a love of croqueting. It may be a fulfilling hobby, but no matter how good you are at it, it's unlikely to hold the key to untold wealth and prosperity.

In addition, *"do what you love and the money will follow"* implies that there is one specific talent or ability that we are meant to uncover, and if we don't, our life will be only half-lived. That's enormous pressure! It's like being convinced that out there among the seven billion plus people that populate this planet there is *"The One"* - a special person perfectly suited to you and no other - your soulmate. Seriously, how likely is that? Isn't it more likely that there are quite a few "soulmates," and who you choose depends as much on timing as on some magical, unique chemistry?

The personal development approach is far too specific and thus causes unnecessary pressure and extra stress as we try to work out what we are good at and what makes us fulfilled.

So instead of trying to find the proverbial needle in a million haystacks, focus on the bigger picture and give yourself a chance.

Discovering your natural talents isn't always easy, largely because they were probably ignored; unappreciated or discounted when they were first observed. Part of the reason is due to our schooling system. Unless your particular talents and abilities fell neatly into the strict boundaries of the curriculum, then it's highly likely that they'll remain an absolute mystery to you.

Everyone who has ever gone to school has, to some extent, been conditioned into believing that the only intelligence worth having must fall neatly into one of a small number of buckets - say, math, language, art, or science. If your skill set lay outside those boundaries, then you were probably led to believe that your usefulness was limited. And yet nothing could be further from the truth.

Different Types of Intelligence

One individual who has made great strides in trying to rectify this imbalance is Dr. Howard Gardner, Hobbs Professor of Cognition and Education at Harvard Graduate School of Education. Gardner believed that the traditional I.Q. is far too limited as a measure of intelligence. In 1983 he developed the theory of multiple intelligences and proposed eight different intelligences to account for the broad range of potential in children and adults: Verbal-Linguistic Intelligence (word smart), Logical-Mathematical Intelligence (numbers smart), Visual-Spatial Intelligence (picture smart), Bodily-Kinesthetic Intelligence (body smart), Musical Intelligence (music smart), Interpersonal Intelligence (people smart), Intrapersonal Intelligence (self smart), Naturalistic Intelligence (Nature smart).

Dr. Gardner's work clearly demonstrates that there is a far greater range of talents and abilities than we traditionally recognize. In his work with very young children, he has observed these various intelligences at work - for example, the little girl who instinctively knew which class members would able to naturally get along. This type of intelligence is completely ignored in modern schooling, and yet if the girl had been helped to become aware of and develop that innate skill, she might find fulfilment from being a match-maker or recruitment consultant; or perhaps she would have a bright future as a producer, agent, casting director or talent coordinator.

How to Uncover Your Natural Talents

If you are serious about making money, then you have to create something in return for that wealth. So what are *you* going to do? What *value* are you going to add? What *contribution* can you exchange for wealth? Uncovering your natural talents will help answer those questions.

First, you need to step back and reflect on what you are good at. It may also help you to consider the following seven questions:

1. What would you do even if you were not paid for it?
2. What are you better at than most people?
3. What are you doing when people complement your effort or ability?
4. Where do you add value?
5. If you were financially free, what would you do with your time?
6. What TV programs do you enjoy - is there a consistent theme?
7. If you knew you could not fail - what would you do?

Ask your parents what you wanted to do when you grew up. Try and find out what your first-ever career ambition was; sometimes this can hold a clue to your natural abilities. Over time we are conditioned to ignore these little personal quirks - yet they often hold the key as to how best to make money.

And before you write anything off, consider the story of Michael Flatley. He grew up in Chicago of Irish parents, loved Irish dancing and was good at it. But watching dancers who didn't move their upper body was hardly an obvious money spinner. Yet he shot to fame as part of the intermission act in the 1994 Eurovision Song Contest.

Flatley has since been in the *Guinness Book of World Records*, in 1998 for achieving 35 taps per second in his dancing and in 1999 for being the world's highest paid dancer, earning $1,600,000 per week. Not bad money for a discovering a personal skill like Irish dancing.

The other point to remember is that even though things sometimes don't pan out the way we want, there are often many more ways to use a skill than you might initially appreciate.

I heard the story of an individual who was passionate about music. He was a brilliant guitarist and played in a band in the style of Bon Jovi. He even toured in the US at one point and was on the cusp of making it into the big time. However it all came to nothing. He spent the next ten years in quietly living in a cottage at the edge of his mother's garden. His dream was dead, and he turned his attention, albeit reluctantly, to the IT industry.

A few years later, he met a friend of mine who suggested that there was more than one way to tap into his talent and love of music. Today he owns his own recording studio. It wasn't his initial dream, but he is still using his unique talents. He's good at what he does, enjoys it, and makes a great living.

Focus on the "How," not the "What"

Sometimes trying to uncover your special talents can be daunting, especially if this is genuinely a new idea for you. So instead of getting too hung up on the "what," focus on the "how."

Do you like working with people or do you prefer tasks and things that don't talk back? Do you like being on your own, or are you happiest when you are working with a group of people? Do you like to work on a wide range of projects so that you have variety, or do you like a routine that enables you to get better and better at particular skills? All of these insights can help to narrow down the areas to consider, so that you are more likely to find something you really enjoy.

For example, if you think back on your life and realize that you were happiest when you were on your own working on a project, then it's unlikely that sales is going to ring your bells. If you realize that you love the start of projects but soon get bored when you have to implement systems, then clearly an administration role would drive you quietly insane. Working out *"how"* you work best and when you are happiest can help you find the *"what."*

To help with this process, I've created the Wealth Quadrant (see page 106) which explores these different aspects of wealth creation.

When people think about the rich, they invariably think of the "classic entrepreneur," people like Oprah or Sir Richard Branson.

The classic entrepreneur is usually flamboyant, full of life, vivacious, driven and quite ruthless. However there's more than one way to crack the wealth creation code. Part of Law 2 is appreciating where *you* sit in the Wealth Quadrant that follows, so that you can be realistic about what you can achieve. And I don't just mean realistic in terms of wealth created; but realistic in terms of what you can do.

If a man can actually make machines better than anyone else, let us, in the name of common sense, keep him on the job of making machines.
William Feather

We are all different. You and I are unique individuals with our own strengths and vulnerabilities. If you prefer to work alone, then there is no point choosing a wealth path that will require you to work constantly with people. If you love being with people, but decide to shut yourself in your basement until you invent something useful, then you're not going to be happy or productive. You may be able to force yourself to go against your innate nature through sheer will power, but after a while, you will be unhappy, and that's just crazy. Building your business should be compelling. Ask yourself how do you prefer to deploy your talents? Can you tolerate (and thrive in) the politics and pressure of a large organization? Would you rather be in a small, tight-knit company? Or can you simply not bear to have a boss or work in teams? You need to find something that you are going to enjoy and that you have a natural affinity for.

Identify Where You are Now and What Wealth Means to You

The conventional wisdom is "To know where you are going, you have to know where you've been." I'd add: You have to know where you currently are. The **2nd Law of Wealth** - requires a clear path to where you are heading and a knowledge of how you are going to get there. To do that, you have to acknowledge your current position, because that will determine the route and length of your journey.

If you want to go to New York, then how you get there depends very much on where you are right now. Clearly, the trip is going to be longer and involve more stages if you are in England than if you are in Washington DC. If you are in England you first need to get yourself to London; you'll need a train into London and a subway to Heathrow. You then need to board a plane for New York, and once in the US, get a taxi to your final destination. All in all, you may use four or five different forms of transportation over a number of stages in the journey. If you are already in the US - and especially if you are already in a major city like Washington - it may only take one or two methods of transportation to reach your destination, and it's likely to be quicker because of the distance covered. The same is true of any successful business.

Regardless of what you have or where you are right now, you will progress through subsequent stages of the following financial continuum.

Financial Survival

Financial survival means a hand-to-mouth existence; you may require government support to keep your head above water. Sadly, there are still far too many people struggling every week just to put food on the table and keep warm in winter. Financial Survival occurs between point 1 and 2 on the wealth continuum but is unlikely to affect anyone reading this book. It would be extremely improbable to be at the survival level and choose to spend your precious cash on a book rather than a loaf of bread and some milk. It's fair to say that survival is not much fun, and is a primary source of concern.

Financial Stability

Financial stability occurs at points 3, 4 and 5 on the financial continuum and represents varying degrees of stability. At this stage you are running to stand still, you must prioritize, not only on want but on need. There is rarely much room for maneuver. Certainly, toward the bottom end of financial stability, there is a constant juggle of priorities. Often credit plays a large role in this area of the continuum, as people borrow from one credit account to pay another, this can quickly escalate into serious difficulties.

Again, this is no fun, I clearly remember my early life in a home that was only just financially stable. I was always acutely aware of not having money. Not only were we not comfortable - we were poorer than most other people. Even in the housing projects where I grew up, we were one of the poorest families. Only when I left school and found my first job did I understand that I could create financial stability for myself.

Financial Security

Positions 6, 7 and 8 refer to Financial Security. If the continuum were a bell curve, this is where the arch of the bell would be located. The majority of people, certainly in developed countries, live in a degree of financial security.

The term "financial security" is often used to refer to people who are wealthy, but that is not accurate. The word "security" also creates images and feelings of protection and safety, rather than abundance - and that's exactly what this stage represents.

When you have Financial Security you manage to take care of your everyday expenses, but it's a matter of control and management. At point 7 on the continuum, there may even be a little set aside for a rainy day, but any extra expenses - such as a broken washing machine or suprise bill - can really throw a monkey wrench in the works. However, people at this position don't worry too much about money - they have all they need to live a financially comfortable life.

Financial Significance

Positions 9 and 10 are where you own a strong enterprise - especially point 10. Financial Significance means that you have all the money you need and are constantly replenishing your supply of available money. This stage allows you to invest in wealth creating assets so that you can live very comfortably and enjoy the best of what the world has to offer. You are able to buy whatever you want whenever you want and enjoy your money to the fullest.

Most people I meet in the course of my seminars are currently somewhere between 2 and 7. Without exception, all want more and wish to head toward 10. The path and speed of that journey depend on where you are now and how you define the locations on the continuum.

This may all seem a little obvious, but it's very important to understand that wealth - in the final analysis - is something that you define. What each position on that continuum actually equates to in terms of cash and assets is as unique to you as your own DNA. Only you will know what "financial security" means to you. Does it mean that you have all the money you need to meet your everyday needs and a little laid aside for emergencies? Or does it mean much more than that?

I met one individual on the rich list who had just sold his company for $500 million - and felt that he had not yet experienced financial security!

Clearly, that's an extreme case, but part of the importance of Embracing the Future is *accepting the past* and quantifying exactly what you want to achieve in the future. Putting a figure on your 'endgame' - not just a label like "rich" or "richer" sharpens your focus and improves your chances of hitting that target. Plus, it's so much easier to know when you've arrived.

Establish a Clear Outcome

Once you've thought about your natural talents, where you are now, and what you enjoy doing, you will be in a far better position to establish your outcome. Law 2 is the key to becoming clear on what that target is, so that you can develop clear intentions, aims, and outcomes. Knowing your target has obvious advantages, but there are a few less obvious ones too.

For example, did you realize that part of the reason a clear target is so important is biological? In the brain, there is a mechanism called the Reticular Activating System (RAS). It has a number of complicated functions, but the important fact for this discussion is that the RAS is a filtration device. We are constantly bombarded with information that comes in through our five senses. If we were consciously aware of all that information, we'd never get anything done. The overload would drive us insane.

To help manage this process, the RAS limits what we become aware of by deleting what's not relevant to us based on our thoughts, beliefs, aspirations and goals.

The RAS "decides" what you become consciously aware of moment by moment. Dr. Daniel Simons of the University of Illinois and Christopher Chabris of Harvard University conducted some really powerful experiments that demonstrated just how impressive this process can be.

Students were asked to watch a video of two teams playing basketball, and their task was to count the number of passes made between one of the teams.

Halfway through the game, a person in a gorilla suit wandered through the players on the court for a full seven seconds! At one point the beast even turns its face to the camera and beats its chest. What makes these experiments so fascinating is that half the participants were so focused on the task of counting passes that they didn't even notice the gorilla.

Some were so incensed by the idea that they had missed the gorilla that they were convinced they had watched a different video. The two scientists were awarded the Ig-Nobel Prize for Psychology in 2004, which is awarded to sometimes bizarre experiments that prove nothing, something we already know... or, in this case, reveal something blindingly obvious but unnoticed... It made me laugh, then think.

If people who were given a task by way of others instructions could fail to see a gorilla, we have to ask ourselves: what else can we learn about this little known part of the brain?

At 7:51 a.m. on Friday, January 12th, 2007, a young man entered a Washington DC subway station and took a position against a wall near a trash can and started to play his violin. He played six Bach pieces for about 43 minutes. During that time 1,097 people passed him, most on their way to work. Only seven people stopped to listen - even for a minute or two. Without exception, children wanted to stop but were pulled forward by hurried parents anxious to reach their destination. Twenty-seven people gave money, mostly on the run, and the humble street musician collected the princely sum of $32.17. He finished, and no one noticed or applauded.

And yet perhaps they would have - if they had known that the man was Joshua Bell, one of the greatest musicians in the world. He played one of the most intricate pieces of music ever written on a violin handcrafted in 1713 by Antonio Stradivari and valued at $3.5 million.

Three days before, Bell had played to a sellout audience at Boston's stately Symphony Hall, where even pretty good tickets were selling for $100 and Bell's talents could command $1,000 a minute, instead of $32 an hour.

The experiment was organized by the *Washington Post* as part of a social experiment about context, perception, and priorities - it's another example of how powerful the mind can be in seeing a single outcome.

We are privy to a vast amount of information but delete most of it. Our target and focus will determine what we are aware of. If we can miss gorillas on basketball courts, or if we are able to ignore one of the best musicians in the world, playing some of the finest music ever written with one of the most beautiful instruments ever made because we are too busy or focused on other activities, then heaven knows what else we could be using this ability for that could transform our fortune.

That is why having a consciously chosen target is so vital for success. That target instructs your RAS as to what you are aiming toward and then filters data accordingly. It ensures that you become consciously aware of anything and everything that could help in the achievement of that single objective.

You will already have experienced the RAS in action. Perhaps you decided to buy a new car, and then suddenly you see that same car everywhere. You notice special offers and the colors it comes in. Nothing different has happened, those things were always there in your environment, but when you decided you wanted the new car, your RAS was activated so that your "observing" brain stopped deleting the information as unimportant and instead allowed it in so you could be consciously aware of it and move toward your target.

The challenge with working out where you are heading is that it requires thought and planning. And the trouble with that is that it's not always fun. The mere word makes some people burst out in hives! As it can feel restrictive, boring, dull and unimaginative.

Just think of someone you know that is really good at planning. If you had to describe them in five words, what would they be? be honest! For some strange reason those that fly by the seat of their pants are deemed interesting, spontaneous and exciting. Those that plan are not.

Yet nothing could be more inaccurate. Remember Chapter 2, we explored the idea of Mastering the Context, and I explained how we have choice, but sometimes we don't have choice as to how things will work out once we've made those choices. Planning is one of those things. You can choose to ignore or dismiss it as dull and not get what you want in life (or at least vastly reduce the possibility) - or you can embrace it and radically improve your results.

So forget some far-off, once-upon-a-time "I'm going to be rich" daydreams. Take a good hard look at yourself and what you have to offer, assess where you are, and use that information to establish a powerful and inspiring outcome.

Everything is Created Twice

Everything in life is created first in the mind and then brought to life and into reality through planning and execution. Everything, from the chair you may be sitting on right now to the TV you may watch later, was first created as a thought in the mind. That inspiration or creative idea would have been wasted if the person who'd identified it, failed to couple it with planning and execution so that it could be brought to reality.

That is why ideas alone are futile, and why action alone is equally impotent. You have to combine the two for maximum impact.

While thoughts themselves cannot affect the material world, they can certainly affect the way you behave in it. Most basically, if you believe you cannot improve your situation and become wealthy, then, short of the untimely death of a rich relative, you simply will not achieve the kind of success we are talking about.

Furthermore, positive expectations and optimism have an impact on the way you impress people. They make you alert to opportunities and personal connections that you might otherwise miss. They help ensure that you proactively move to take advantage of whatever opportunities that present themselves

Thoughts do have their own kind of power over the unfolding of your life - not so much the thoughts you have while you are waiting for the bus or the ones you have every now and again, but the habitual thoughts that are full of emotion - those make a real difference in your outcomes.

Everything is created twice - your happiness, fulfilment and enjoyment of life and most certainly your ability to create wealth.

Nothing great was ever achieved without enthusiasm.
Samuel Taylor Coleridge

You must have wealth-creating thoughts and back them with passion, energy and enthusiasm. You must turn those thoughts into action so that they are created for the second time - in reality.

Once you have mastered Law 1 and decided to take active and conscious control of yourself - your actions, behaviors and responses - you have to determine where you are going to focus that energy and power.

Charging off into the future without any clear idea of where you are heading is a waste of valuable time and energy. Instead, take a step back and engage in some honest self reflection in an effort to find your own path. Law 2 requires consciously deciding the future you want, applying the right thinking to that goal - and marrying it up to a method and process that will generate the results you seek.

The Wealth Quadrant

The Wealth Quadrant is a simple tool that explores how wealth is created by different types of people. There are infinite ways to wealth in terms of what you actually do to make money, but there is no point choosing a path that goes against your natural abilities. We are all unique, and there are innumerable ways to make money. Be smart from the outset and find a vehicle that is going to be a natural fit with your talents and personality. In the following pages the Wealth Quadrant will show you how.

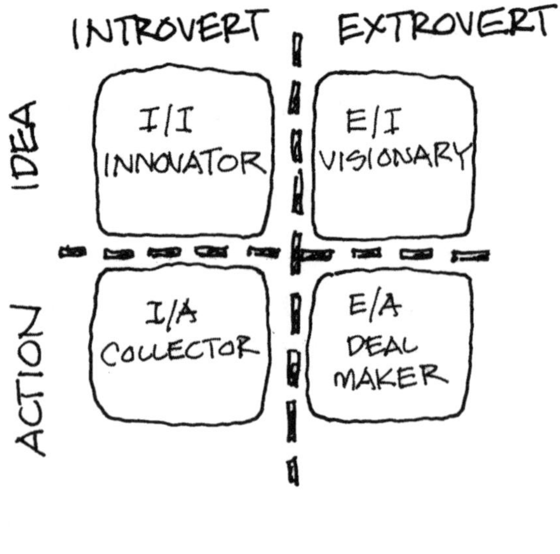

Horizontal Axis

The horizontal axis of the Wealth Quadrant relates to your natural inclination. Individuals are both introverted and extroverted, depending on a variety of circumstances and situations. We will naturally tend to lean more toward one than the other. Neither is better than the other and each has its own strengths and vulnerabilities; one is more suited to certain types of activities than the other.

Introverts are more inner-directed; they get their energy from being alone. They prefer to work on projects individually and are thus process orientated. Extroverts are outward focused and get their energy from other people. They prefer working with others and are people oriented.

In the old industrial economy, it would have been fair to say that wealth was created in the extrovert side of the quadrant. But the emergence of a new economy and the use and application of technology means that there are now just as many introverts making significant money too. Some without even getting out their pajamas...

Vertical Axis

The vertical axis of the Wealth Quadrant is about how to make money. Again, everyone has the capacity to make money from ideas and action. One of the greatest fallacies about how to create wealth is the notion that all you need is a good idea. Good ideas are everywhere. Ideas without action are futile. Action without ideas - going off half-cocked with no clue as to where you're heading - is just as ineffective.

We all have the capacity for both ideas and action, however we also have a natural propensity for one over the other. Some of us are naturally drawn to idea and innovation. We want to know how things work and how to make them better. For others it's all about the deal, the negotiation, the instinctive timing. One is not better than the other. They are just different approaches. And both should be understood and harnessed to make money.

Crucially, this axis identifies the fact that some people are happiest thinking and others are happiest doing. Knowing where your innate interest lies will save you a great deal of time, energy and stress.

The Four Wealth Quadrant Combinations

These four separate characteristics combine to create the four Wealth Quadrant profiles. These profiles will outline innate personality styles with potential money making approaches. Read each profile and see which one most clearly resonates with you. (If you would like a free Wealth Quadrant self assessment, sign up at www.7lawsofwealth.com).

1. Innovator (AKA Originator, Inventor, Designer)

Innovators are interested in new ideas. They love the fact that old information is constantly combining with new information to make new things possible. These people are natural philosophers and creators. Because of their introverted nature, their innovations tend to be related to processes and things rather than people. They are often appalled by the vulgarity of having to actually sell their philosophies and inventions to the world.

It's the Innovators, perhaps more than any other wealth profile, who are really coming into their own in the new economy. History is littered with famous inventors who died broke or who spent their lives fighting patent battles. Innovation is only part of the money making process; selling that innovation is vital to outright success. And yet many innovators hate selling. However in the new economy, technology is offering these individuals far greater opportunity to benefit from their unique skills.

Consider the 475,000+ applications, at the time of writing, that have been developed for the Apple iPhone. Apple made the application creation software available to everyone, so that anyone with a good idea could create an application and sell it through Apple's App Store. The developer got 70%, and Apple got 30%.

Suddenly, a certain kind of creativity became quite easy to implement. Kostas Eleftheriou from East London came up with the iSteam, which turns the touch screen into a steamed up window that you can write on. It may not change the world, but it made Kostas almost $125,000. Joel Comm, designer of the iFart (no need for explanations), has apparently raked in more than $1 million from his application brainwave! In a somewhat more practical vein, designer Jason Swain came up with SongBook, which turns the iPhone into a remote control for high-end stereos and at $75 a download, he made over $100,000 in nine months.

The Internet and advancement in technology has made life a great deal easier for Innovators. Not only by offering a sales channel *par excellence*, but by providing a playground for their talents. At last the Innovator is able to actually make money from all those good ideas.

The Innovators' Natural Weaknesses:

Innovators don't always see what others see. Because their attention and focus are directed inward, they can become myopic. Often it's sensible to gather external opinion and validation that an innovation is needed or wanted before going all out in the application.

The other challenge for Innovators is that they can be so busy innovating that they don't turn any of their ideas into a commercially viable product.

The Innovators' Natural Advantage:

Innovator see what others don't see. They see further ahead; they don't just Embrace the Future - they predict and create the future. They see problems as opportunities for inventing solutions, rather than obstacles to get upset about. Inventors are usually self contained, they can achieve a great deal without a great deal of external input.

Famous Innovator - Sir James Dyson

Sir James Dyson is perhaps best known for his bagless vacuum cleaner. Like a true Innovator, he saw what others either didn't see or saw and ignored - the annoying frequency with which a traditional vacuum cleaner will lose suction when the bag starts to fill up. The non-Innovator would simply get frustrated, curse a little, change the bag, and move on.

Not Dyson. He had seen cyclone technology working in a saw mill and wondered if the same technology could be adapted to the vacuum cleaner. Of course no one wanted to support him because the vacuum cleaner bag market was very lucrative, and there were powerful well established brands that were quite happy with the status quo. Dyson famously created over 5,100 prototypes of the Dual Cyclone bagless vacuum cleaner before it worked perfectly…which is, let's face it, about 5,100 more than most people would even consider.

Sir James is a classic Innovator: he saw what others didn't see; he cross-pollinated ideas from one industry to the next and was able to adapt ideas into new markets with new uses.

Failure is the key to success. Each mistake teaches us something.
Morihei Ueshiba

Dyson never gave up, it took five years of struggle to develop the successful prototype. Like most famous Innovators, he was caught between a rock and a hard place - needing to have people embrace his technology while also trying to protect it from being copied. But his perseverance has paid off, making him a billionaire and an extremely prolific and successful Innovator. His philosophy is "Always new and better."

Possible Wealth Creation Avenues for the Innovator:

- Invent something
- Be a product developer
- Be a writer / "info-preuner"

2. Visionary (AKA: Celebrity, Leader, Influencer)

Visionaries are also interested in new ideas, but their inspirations are much more connected to people. The Visionary is an influencer and leader they are able to persuade people of just about anything. The visionary has the unique ability of being able to bring the right team of people together to achieve a desired result.

The Visionary can see the future and develop the necessary relationships to make that future a reality. Where the Innovator can be a lone wolf, Visionaries acknowledge they are not good at everything and need to create a team rather than try to do everything themselves. This is where their genius lies.

The Visionary's Natural Weaknesses:

Human nature is complex, and most strengths can become weaknesses in certain situations. The Visionary's persuasiveness and influence can become manipulative. Visionaries are naturally people-orientated, but when the spotlight falls on them as individuals or on the business they create, they can become egotistical and may forget to acknowledge the efforts of the team that created the success.

The Visionary's Natural Advantage:

Whereas Innovators use processes and thinking to implement their ideas, the Visionaries leverage the gifts and talents of other people. Finding the right people for the right job and inspiring them to deliver their absolute best is where Visionaries excel. These people know how to get the best out of others and are thus seen as natural leaders.

Famous Visionary: Sir Richard Branson

Branson is perhaps the iconic Visionary. He started the Virgin brand as a mail order record business in 1970. Since then, the brand has grown to incorporate over 360 companies in areas as diverse as air travel, insurance, health care, and telecommunications.

The Virgin brand is probably the only brand in the world that includes such a variety of business types. What makes Virgin so special is that all the Virgin businesses have the same culture - one of expression, creativity, fun and adventure. Branson built his empire by empowering his staff and putting them before his customers, a philosophy which is still considered unorthodox.

He believed - and still does - that if you ensure that your people are happy, inspired and feel valued and cared for, there will be a positive impact on the customer experience. In other words, if your people are happy, your customers and shareholders will be happy. Even in Virgin, businesses that now have little connection to the man himself, the employees are of a certain caliber and type. They are creative, talented and enthusiastic individuals seeking to make a real difference. Virgin is the personification of the man who started it - flamboyant and competitive - and because of that, it's one of the most recognized forward looking brands in the world.

Possible Wealth Creation Avenues for the Visionary

- Build a company
- Develop a brand
- Excel in network marketing

3. Collector (AKA: Accumulator, Investor, Developer)

Collectors are naturally introverted and action-oriented. They are not much concerned with the outside world or with what other people are doing. They accumulate wealth through the application of process and systems.

The Collector is methodical and consistent and is thus able to bring a level of stability and perseverance to the wealth building process. Collectors are not inspired or swayed by the "big hit." They are more like the patient tortoise, compared to the Deal Maker's hare.

Collectors are usually calm, down-to-earth individuals who have no need or desire to flaunt their wealth. Consequently, there aren't very many well known examples of this type of wealth creator. And yet, as a type, there are probably more millionaires in this quadrant than any other.

When we think of millionaires, we immediately think of the Monte Carlo set, designer clothes, beautiful cars, magnificent homes, living the playboy lifestyle…and yet the truth is often far less glamorous. For many, millionaire status occurs after years of collecting and accumulating. These people are natural investors and often do so quietly and without fanfare.

The Collector's Natural Weaknesses:

Collectors are methodical and systematic. They know what they like and like what they know and don't often venture outside their comfort zone. This in itself is not a bad thing if their strategy works, but it does mean that they can miss opportunities because they are sometimes unwilling to be flexible in their approach.

The Collector's Natural Advantage:

Where Innovators use ideas and creativity to implement their wealth creation plans, the Collector uses time, timing, systems and common sense. There is often nothing creative about the Collector, but he or she has exceptionally keen judgment about when to take action and when to do nothing. Collectors don't have an impulsive bone in their body - and that can be incredibly helpful when your aim is to make money.

What people fail to appreciate about wealth creation is that often the key is consistency of action, and there is no one in the world better at consistent action than the Collector.

Famous Collector: Warren Buffet

Warren Buffet is a classic Collector. He's one of the richest men in the world - and living proof that this approach clearly works. There are a number of books written on Buffet and his investing strategy, but in a nutshell, he invests in businesses he understands, and he looks for bargains.

Buffet is a value investor. He's not interested in what the external world or other people think about a stock. He's become very wealthy by finding stocks that are out of favor with everyone else, buying them at bargain basement prices. and holding on as the market realizes its error. His indifference to external opinion is true introvert behavior. He couldn't care less about consensus or whether the media are talking about the stock or what the investment analysts think about it.

Can you imagine how much Buffet cleaned up in the wake of the financial crisis that began in 2007? Stock markets around the globe were crashing as the full extent of the mess became clearer. The crash affected not only weak companies but even healthy, well managed, financially sound businesses. When good businesses as well as bad took a hammering, value investors like Buffet realise that a lot is up for grabs.

That's not to say everyone enjoyed the financial carnage that followed the sub-prime collapse - but there were definitely winners as well as losers. There always are. In this case, the winners would have been the Collectors.

Possible Wealth Creation Avenues for the Collector

- Real Estate
- Stock market investment
- Creating a franchise

4. Deal Maker (AKA: Trader, Seller, Tycoon)

Because of their Extrovert/Action focus, Deal-Makers are always responding to the environment around them and jumping into action. They adapt to the environment perhaps better than people in any other quadrant. Consequently, they rarely have a plan and will fly by the seat of their pants. In conversation a Deal-Maker will be far more interested in what the other person has done as opposed to what he or she thinks.

It is this quadrant that has the most wanna-be's. You know the types - they look the part, with all the designer suits and fancy watches - even though they may be on the verge of bankruptcy. But they don't mind, because around every corner is their next "big hit".

Deal-Makers are determined and thick skinned. They tend to ignore the word "No." This is the quadrant where we find the classic, traditional entrepreneur - the never-say-die, quick-witted, look-out-for-#1 individual who can turn anything into gold.

Like Visionaries, Deal-Makers are exceptionally persuasive and charismatic individuals who can sell practically anything to anybody.

The Deal Makers' Natural Weaknesses:

With all their strengths, Deal-Makers are not always way ahead of everyone else and can be undisciplined and unprepared. They think "plan" is a four-letter word. They don't want to strategize; they just want to get on with the job. Their unwillingness to plan the approach means that they can just go off like a fire-cracker in ten different directions at once, and this can waste valuable time and energy.

They're also super enthusiastic, which can be a huge advantage - but it can also mean they get too caught up in the story of a business opportunity without looking at the facts behind the story. They want to believe that the next thing is the next big thing and their ticket to wealth, and this belief leads them to ignore signs to the contrary.

The Deal Makers' Natural Advantage:

They can sell anything. If you consider that no money is made until something is sold, then the Deal-Maker should be involved, at least potentially, at some stage of any business transaction. Such people are quick to move and are great at spotting gaps in markets and filling them. They can see what people want and will invariably find a way to give it to them.

Deal-Makers are natural negotiators and love the deal. They love the back and forth, the cut and thrust of business, the negotiation and bartering for the best price that are part of the process. They are good with people and can build up strong relationships - but they can sometimes run roughshod over those relationships in their desire to get into action.

Famous Deal Maker: Donald Trump

There is no accident that Donald Trump is the man who tells TV contestants, on the US version of *The Apprentice*, "You're fired!". Trump is a Deal-Maker in every sense of the word.

He is famous for his property development deals, starting with the renovation of the Commodore Hotel into the Grand Hyatt, followed by the famous Trump Towers, both in New York. Since then, Trump has expanded into the private charter airline business and casinos. His enthusiasm for expansion and making the deal has seen him in dire straits more than once, but he is a typical resilient Deal-Maker and always comes back even stronger than before.

Trump is known for his outspoken manner and ability to handle risk, often the type of risk that would make most feel nauseous.

Possible Wealth Creation Avenues for the Deal Maker:

- Buy and Sell Companies
- Real Estate

When it comes to wealth creation, you could look at the occupants of the various quadrants as athletes. The Innovator is the sprinter - usually great at getting out the blocks fast but in need of real discipline to see the race through. The Visionary is the relay runner - he or she is always passing the baton to others to fulfil the final dream. The Collector is the marathon runner who is not interested in sudden bursts of speed but has sights set on the target and moves relentlessly toward it. Deal-Makers are hurdlers - it doesn't matter what obstacle they encounter; they will overcome anything in their way.

Quadrant Movement

We all have elements of each quadrant within us and certainly there are plenty of very wealthy men and woman in the world who do not fall neatly into one box or another. Sam Walton or the Albrecht brothers who started the supermarket chain Aldi - their money was definitely made through timing and trading. They bought low and sold higher, albeit only a little higher.

They never created anything, so they are action oriented individuals, but they are also very reserved and down-to-earth. There is nothing flashy about either Walton or the Albrecht brothers, and in that regard they are more like Warren Buffet, who famously still lives in the same house he's always lived in, still drives an ordinary car (with the license plate "THRIFTY"), eats in the local diner, and still enjoys a Cherry Coke.

There are also people like Ray Kroc, who created the McDonald's franchise; he made money from accumulating real estate, as well as from his phenomenally successful dining concept (which he did not invent but acquired from the original McDonald brothers). Clearly there was an initial idea there and a degree of creativity, yet the on-going wealth of the business was largely created by other people.

Jeff Bezos, the man behind Amazon, is also more of a mixture of profiles. There is definitely an idea involved with Amazon, and yet once operational, it is the system that makes the money, the online buying and selling, first of books, then of a vast range of products.

This is the beauty of the new economy. In the past, the extroverted, go-getter personality was essential for success. But advances in technology, such as the Internet, have allowed both extroverts and their less dynamic cousins, the introverts, to access new sales channels that can massively leverage their effort.

So the traits and characteristics of each quadrant will be more or less pronounced for some people than others. In addition, you can move around the quadrants, depending on the situation or the life cycle of your business.

The purpose of the Wealth Quadrant is not to pigeon-hole you but to liberate you. Most of us have the capacity to adapt, but you will tend to "live" in the one quadrant where you are instinctively happiest. If you know which quadrant that is, then you are better equipped to create a future that works with your innate strengths - and deploy your vulnerabilities to the strengths of other team members.

This self-knowledge can also help you to turn your thinking later, to **Law 3 - Own a Strategy**. The Wealth Quadrant will help you to work out what sort of strategy might work best for you in creating wealth.

What You Can Expect If You Fail to Embrace The Future:

- Your aspirations will come to nothing
- You'll meander through life

Your Aspirations will come to Nothing

Embracing the Future requires looking at yourself and working out what you could do in order to make the money you seek. It's about seeing a future picture so you have a strong enough "why" to keep you going through the difficult moments.

Achieving anything worthwhile in life involves conquering difficult challenges. That is especially true if you aim to become a multi-millionaire. Unless you have taken the time to engage with your desires and paint a vivid picture of how your future looks, then you won't be personally committed enough to that future in order to do what it takes to bring it about.

You'll Meander Through Life

If you don't know where you are going, how will you know (a) how to get there and (b) when you've arrived? Without a clear aim, outcome and intention, you will drift through life.

One day you'll wake up, and you'll wonder where your life went. All the intentions you had will have fallen by the wayside because you kept jumping from one "great idea" to the next, never quite managing to stay focused on one thing long enough to translate it into significant wealth.

What You Can Confidently Expect If You Embrace The Future:

- Your future will be inspiring
- You will achieve your dreams faster

Your Future will be Inspiring

Fulfilment is often described as a journey toward a worthy goal. It is not always the attainment of that goal that really matters.

Just knowing you have a purpose is exciting and inspiring. Everything takes on new meaning. When we have a vision and are passionate about the attainment of that vision, it's as if we suddenly see color after years of black and white. We happily manage with a fraction of the sleep we used to "need"; we bounce out of bed full of excitement at the day ahead. Life is just more interesting and meaningful when we have a definite purpose.

People rarely succeed unless they have fun in what they are doing.
Dale Carnegie.

When you Embrace the Future, you will uncover hidden talents, and doors of opportunity appear before you - and that's when life gets exciting.

You Will Achieve Growth Faster

When you have a clear outcome, aim and intentions, you are far more likely to stay on track, which means you will reach your destination faster. Circumstances and events in life can only draw us off course when we don't have a target to keep us on course. Knowing the outcome also allows you to be adaptive and respond, with openness and flexibility, to circumstances as they arise.

In addition, if you have found something for which you have a natural affinity, then you are also much more likely to enjoy the process, and that enjoyment will almost certainly speed up your progress.

When I lost my first fortune, I ended up making even more money the second time around, in property development, but it wasn't a natural fit for me. I really struggled with the management side of things, organizing tenants and dealing with their various issues. Frankly, I didn't enjoy that side of the business one bit.

If I had known then what I know now, I could have shaved years and a great deal of heartache off that journey. If I had fully appreciated the importance of **Law 2** and understood my own strengths and vulnerabilities earlier, I would have taken the time to create systems and find ways to manage the areas I didn't like. We all have to do things we don't enjoy in order to create success, but it shouldn't be a lifestyle. Finding what you are best suited to is just common sense, but it's seldom common practice.

Mission Not Commission

Embracing the Future is about finding your mission, not just your commission. It's about chasing a passion, not just a pension. It's about finding out about yourself, understanding a little more about who you are and what you enjoy, so that you can find the right vehicle for your wealth creation goals. You can make money in any of a million different ways, but there will only be a handful that really suit your persona. By marrying your goals to your innate characteristics, you are in a far stronger position to create and maintain wealth.

After all, life is too short to do something you hate - regardless of the money that could be made from it.

Law 2 requires self leadership and taking charge of the "how," so that you can formulate plans and establish clear outcomes, aims and intentions. These plans will not be set in stone but will act instead as your guide posts, allowing you to see the end game. Where are you going to be in ten years, and how that is going to look?

Making money is a whole lot easier if you enjoy what you do. You can make money and be miserable, but it's not advisable. It's easier to persevere with something you enjoy; it's easier to get up in the morning and stay up late at night if you enjoy what you do. It's easier to forgo the parties and time with your friends when you believe in what you are trying to achieve and love the process rather than just the outcome.

Law 2 is also about setting your target. While this may sound like goal setting - it's not. Sir Richard Branson didn't have goals, Sir Philip Green didn't have goals, and neither did Sir Tom Hunter. What they created was a *standard*. They made a decision to stick to that standard, come what may. Law 2 demands that you find a *best way* and set a standard to do whatever it takes, to get that result.

You will have to adapt as the future unfolds, but if you know your end game, if you have the personal insight to find a suitable wealth vehicle, and the determination to see your plans through, then you will succeed.

Are You Aligned to Law 2 - Do You Embrace The Future?

Below there are seven sets of two statements - 1A/1B through 7A/7B. Read each pair of statements and check off which statement is mostly true for you. On balance, which more accurately reflects your opinions and view of life? It won't always be easy, but choose the one that best matches you. And check either A *or* B for each of the seven pairs.

Be honest - no one needs to see this. If you don't want to write in the book, if you want to keep your selections private, then make the selections in a separate notebook. Don't mark what you wish you were like or hope to be like in the future. Answer as you are right now. If you are unsure, then ask someone you know and trust to give you feedback.

	A	B
1	☐ I know what my natural strengths and weaknesses are.	I have no idea what my natural strengths and weaknesses are. ☐
2	☐ I believe that we all have particular talents and gifts that we can use to create wealth and fulfilment.	I don't believe we all have particular talents and gifts we can use to create wealth and fulfilment. Only the "chosen few" are so lucky. ☐
3	☐ I recognize myself in the Wealth Quadrant.	I don't recognize myself in the Wealth Quadrant. ☐
4	☐ I have taken time out of my busy life to think about what I want to achieve for my life.	I'm too busy dealing with today to waste time on tomorrow. ☐

5	☐ I know what my financial situation is right now, how much I have in savings, and how much debt I have.	I have no idea what my real financial situation is. I spend what I need to spend and hope it works out each month. ☐
6	☐ I know what I'm trying to achieve in life and I have clear defined goals.	I don't have goals. I don't have time for dreaming. Besides goal setting doesn't work. ☐
7	☐ I understand about the power of right thinking even though I may not always engage in right thinking.	I don't see how what we think about can make any difference in how things turn out.. It's just New Age nonsense. ☐

If you have checked five or more of the statements in the A Column, then you already have a good grasp of Law 2. If you have marked three or more statements in the B Column, then we suggest you read the supplementary guidebook; ***Law2 - Embrace the Future: Applications and Insights.*** This companion guide will give you further information about Law 2, together with practical techniques, ideas and insights into how you can successfully align yourself to this law and harness its power.

Law 3

Own a Strategy

Before all Else, Be Equipped Armed & Ready
Move Forward with Caution, Vigilance & Discretion

The man who enters prepared has his battle half won. He will be rated by his ability to anticipate his problems rather than to stumble upon then as they arise. Engineers can design bridges, calculate stresses and strains, and draw up detailed plans, but the great engineer is the man who can tell whether the bridge should be built at all. He who plans knows where he is going, how long the journey will take, and when he will arrive. All great accomplishment is won first, through strategy.

Chapter Five
Law 3 - Own a Strategy

EVERY MORNING IN Africa, when the sun rises over the plains, a gazelle wakes up and knows that it must start running and run faster than the fastest lion or it will be killed. Every morning, on the same plains, a lion wakes up and it knows that it must outrun the slowest gazelle; otherwise, it will starve. It doesn't matter whether you are a lion or a gazelle. When the sun comes up, you'd better be running, you'd better know where you're going - and, more importantly, know why.

For the gazelle and the lion, the strategy is simple - stay alive. The gazelle needs to be alert to danger at all times, and it needs to be nimble and swift to survive. The lion needs to be stealthy and clever to take advantage of opportunities as they arise in order to stay alive. Although the goals are often mutually exclusive, each knows what needs to be done in order to stay alive.

A simple strategy is always best. There can be few simpler strategies than "stay alive". And yet there are few more powerful. The more you complicate things, the easier it is to get into trouble. So take the first lesson from the lion and gazelle, and keep it simple.

Truth is ever to be found in the simplicity,
not in the multiplicity and confusion of things.
Isaac Newton

Strategy is the long term plan of action and is designed to achieve a particular goal or outcome. It is not to be confused with tactics - the details and individual actions that you need to take to meet that objective. Your strategy acts as a guiding light or road map on your journey from where you are now to where you want to be. So the simpler and clearer it is, the higher its likelihood of delivering your end-result. Unfortunately, it would seem that we are innately drawn toward complexity rather than simplicity. And that can cause us no end of problems.

In a famous cartoon, Pogo says, "We've met the enemy, and he is us." The enemy of good strategy is human nature, because we want to make it complicated, even when we know simple is stronger.

Social psychologist Professor Alex Bavelas designed a series of experiments that brilliantly illustrated our lust for complexity.

He had two subjects view slides of cells. They were told that the purpose of the experiment was to see if they could distinguish between a healthy and a sick cell. The two participants were shown the same slides at the same time, but they could not see each other or the responses they gave. Each had two buttons; one said "healthy" and the other, "sick." Subjects were simply to press the button they felt described the picture in front of them. Person A was given accurate feedback, so that when a slide of a healthy cell appeared and the subject pressed the "healthy" button, a light flashed "correct." Conversely, if the guess was wrong, the person would be told. Consequently, it wasn't long before person A was guessing with 80% accuracy through a simple process of deduction and comparison.

Person B, on the other hand, was not given accurate feedback, regardless of which button he or she pressed. Thus the selection of "healthy" or "sick" triggered a completely random response from the computer, and consequently person B was not able to deduce any patterns, and results were patchy. Neither participant knew that the other was getting different feedback.

At the end of the experiment, the facilitator asked the subjects to report their findings and discuss the rules they came up with to decide whether the cells were healthy or sick. Person A's rules were clear, straight forward and concrete. Person B's rules, on the other hand, were complex, subtle and vague, which wasn't surprising, given the circumstances of the experiment.

What was surprising, however, was that - far from thinking B's rules were stupid - A started to feel inferior, when it seemed their rules were too simple, and B seemed smarter. Person A was impressed by the brilliance of B! In fact, the more complicated and ornate the rules, the more convinced person A was of their inaccuracy, even though A scored significantly better in the experiment.

When asked to guess who would do best in the second round, almost everyone tested said that the person with the complex rules would score higher. They didn't, and yet the subject with the simple and clear rules started to fail because they gave up the clear, simple - and correct - rules in favor of the much more complex and (evidently much more appealing) complicated ones.

William of Ockham, a fourteenth century Franciscan monk from a village in Surrey, England, developed the "principle of parsimony," now called Occam's Razor. Essentially Occam's Razor advocates simplicity. If you can achieve an outcome in three steps, don't create ten. If you can get a result or arrive at an answer quickly, there is nothing to be gained by taking the long and more complex route. Money and finance are a hotbed of complexity, and yet when considering the best strategy for wealth creation, *simple is always more effective.*

In order to gain wealth, we have to make and keep commitments. And the best way to keep commitments is through developing an overall strategy. One must make the decision to act and move forward; only then will the specific components of the plan fall into place, including the tactical issues. Strategy is the big-picture vision of what you are trying to achieve, and the tactics are the nuts-and bolts-actions steps that you need to take in order to materialize that vision.

In many ways the first three laws of wealth are concerned with strategy and forming the big picture vision. Laws 4, 5 and 6 are the tactical considerations involved in bringing that vision to fruition.

Sacred Cows Can Create Herd Mentality

Choosing the right strategy can be tough. Deciding to change strategy after you've chosen it can be even harder. There is a real balance between giving something enough time to work and persevering long after there is commercial sense in doing so.

And therein lies the dilemma of strategy. How long is long enough? Corporate history is littered with examples of businesses that failed because they jumped around between strategies - and of those that failed because they hung onto a strategy long after they should have thrown in the towel or changed their approach.

The food company Quaker Oats tampered with a winning strategy by branching out into toys and restaurants. In doing so, they confused their customers and lost their dominance in the food business.

At the other extreme, where a business hangs on too long, you have companies like Motorola, which made a couple of classic strategy blunders, the most dramatic and costly being Iridium - a constellation of 66 low earth-orbiting satellites that would allow subscribers to make phone calls from any global location. Then-Chairman Robert Galvin and later his son Chris Galvin were convinced that Iridium was going to transform their fortunes.

Iridium was, as someone brilliantly described it, nothing more than a classic case of "techtosterone." It solved a problem very few people actually had, and subscribers would need to buy a cumbersome $3000 handset and pay up to $8 a minute. It was launched in 1998, with then-Vice President Al Gore making the first phone call. To reach that stage, Motorola had invested over $5 billion, $180 million of which was spent on an advertising campaign. It didn't go well.

Hindsight is a wonderful thing, but the problem should have been obvious even then. Motorola's perseverance in the face of a changing market was futile. In the 11 years it took from concept to development, cellular networks spread like wildfire to include most of the areas that Iridium previously considered hard to reach. The company thought its market was business travellers, however it needed 52,000 subscribers, just to cover the interest on its debt and they got only 10,000.

The cellular network ate into the market Motorola hoped to tap into and offered significantly better value and quality of connection. Motorola refused to see the writing on the wall and instead persevered with a product that had no future - wasting billions in the process. The company made the fatal mistake of falling in love with a product, and it hung on to a strategy that was fundamentally flawed.

Iridium was Motorola's sacred cow, and the company was seriously invested in it, financially and emotionally. But it created a herd mentality and blinded Motorola managers and executives to the real issues that kept them from acting on the evidence. And yet most of the damage could have been avoided.

Iridium was developed in two stages: 1987-96 (development of the technology) and 1996-99 (construction and launch of the satellites, by far the more costly stage of development). By the time stage two came around, Motorola knew much more. Its executives knew that the cellular network had grown dramatically and significantly and had eroded their market. They knew that they had still not solved design, cost and operational problems, and yet they continued anyway. You have to give your strategy a chance to succeed whilst putting everything you have behind it. But at what point do you say, "Enough is enough"?

Another example of strategy gone wrong is the world-famous Barney's department store. When Barney's tried to expand into new geographic areas, they assumed that a winning strategy in New York would work equally well in other areas such as Southern California and the Midwest. It never occurred to senior executives that what was viewed as the height of fashion in Manhattan would be seen as pretentious and borderline ridiculous in other geographic locations. Strategy requires thought and flexibility, where one size may not always fit all.

The evidence suggests that when it comes to our personal wealth-creating strategy, we often fail to develop one because we've never given it any serious thought in the rush to get moving; or we have one, but it's just the same as everyone else's because we like being in the herd. Or we stubbornly hang on to the wrong one without applying much-needed flexibility to changing locations, market conditions and demand.

Remember, most successful businesses today didn't start out with the strategy that they have today. There are numerous examples of radical shifts in strategy from Hewlett Packard to Google and PayPal.

It can also be helpful to appreciate that much of the time, you are battling human nature.

For example, social scientists have discovered that we are driven by basic principles of psychology that direct our behavior without our necessarily knowing about it. The two phenomena that are particularly relevant to this discussion are social proof and consistency.

Social proof illustrates how we "decide" what the right course of action will be. We instinctively look around to see what other people, like us, are doing to work out what we should do. This is especially true in unfamiliar situations or circumstances.

"Social proof" thinking is the reason why so many businesses "choose" a strategy based on what their competitors are doing. There is a perceived safety in that approach - the same feeling that comes from doing what you've always done in the past. If, however those results fail, then you need to have the courage to change course - as quickly as possible.

The second psychological principle that's relevant to strategy - and also explains why smart people do stupid things - is consistency.

Once we've decided on a course of action, there is a huge psychological pull to remain consistent with that choice. It would seem that once we make a decision or take a stand, especially if that position is public knowledge, we will experience a strong urge to remain consistent with that approach.

This consistency principle certainly helps explain Motorola's blindness about Iridium. The company put itself out there as the technology innovators and leaders in the field of communication. Motorola stuck its corporate neck and checkbook out for Iridium, so pulling back would be admitting they were wrong, and no one likes to be wrong - even when wrong is as obvious as a flashing neon sign.

It is this drive for consistency and commitment that makes people stay in jobs they hate or terrible relationships. It is clear - albeit subconsciously - that it's *"better the devil you know"*. Simply knowing this can help you not make those same mistakes. We will discuss these two psychological principles further in Law 6.

Strategy by Accident - Not Design

Most business strategy is not strategy at all, but a consequence of various actions and decisions taken over the course of the business's life. Strategy is therefore accidental and not created through conscious design. People go into business full of ideas and enthusiasm but rarely understand strategy. Yet a strategy is extremely important if you are to effectively minimize the journey time between where your business is now and where you want it to be.

If Law 2: Embrace the Future asks, "Where am I going" then Law 3: Own a Strategy asks, "How am I going to get there"? Without a strategy, you run the risk of falling into the trap that ensnares so many entrepreneurs and business people. They don't spend enough time working out how to actually make the journey efficiently. Instead, they jump into action, they re-invent the wheel, and they don't put any thought into process and systems. As a result, consistency of delivery and quality usually fail.

All too often, small businesses fail to make the transition to medium, and medium-to-large because they don't have a strategy to help guide that process. Problems arise because the infrastructure of the business is not in place. Quality issues arise because there is no agreed-upon "best practice." Growth is organic and by demand. This is a stressful and inefficient way to expand any business.

It is remarkable how easily and insensibly we fall into a particular route, and make a beaten track for ourselves
Henry David Thoreau

When business growth is so ad hoc - even if it is a successful ad hoc business - it won't be a saleable asset. If there is too much reliance on one individual or figurehead, for example, then the business is vulnerable. If there are no systems, then how do you effectively transfer the intellectual capital to a potential buyer?

If you want to make serious money, then you have to start with the target in mind. That means that you are creating a saleable asset right from the start, and the only way to do that effectively is to have a strategy and stick to it. If you consciously choose your strategy, then you are also less likely to be pulled off course by the latest fad or fashion. Instead, you maintain your position and give the strategy time to come to fruition.

How to Master Law 3 and Own a Strategy:

- Assess and accept risk
- Find a mentor
- Build a team
- Raise cash

Assess and Accept Risk

When you are taking the time out at the start of your wealth journey to discover what you want to achieve and how you plan to get there, you will also need to consider your attitude towards risk.

Whenever we go out to create anything - be it a business, a fortune, or a new mode of transport, there is a flip side to risk: opportunity. They're different sides of the same coin, and you can't have one without the other. What you try may not always work, but if you take the risk out of life, you remove the opportunity as well.

There are three ways to deal with risk

- Avoid it
- Reduce it
- Accept it

Avoid It

If you go through life avoiding risk, you will also go through life avoiding life, and that seems pretty futile. Those who avoid risk never try new things, so they're never stretched and tested to become better people. We don't learn from the safety and comfort of our living room. It's usually under extreme situations that we find out what we are really made of.

Science fiction writer Kim Stanley Robinson once said, "The distinguishing mark of true adventure is that it is often no fun at all while it is actually happening." I can relate to that. Some of the greatest adventures of my life were utterly terrifying at the time, and it was only time and distance that turned them from "nightmare" to "adventure."

He that leaves nothing to chance will do few things ill,
but he will do very few things.
George Saville, 1st Marquess of Halifax

Reduce It

This book is about helping you to reduce risk through understanding the laws that govern the process of making money. There are laws that govern everything, from how to have a wonderful relationship to how to become a multi-millionaire. Understanding what they are from the outset will put you in a far better position and avoid the need for at least some of the trial and error. Apart from being time consuming, trial and error is inefficient and damned stressful. Trust me, I know - I made the journey from poverty to wealth a round trip; I had to start again from scratch, because I didn't live the laws contained in this book. There are also techniques you can use to reduce the chances of failure. Getting educated is the first step that will immediately help to reduce your risk.

Accept It

In the end you have to accept that risk is a necessary part of creating wealth - especially the type of wealth I'm talking about. It is difficult to make millions without borrowing a great deal of money first, and that involves risk. All business ventures have an element of risk. No one really knows how a market is going to react or what people will like or what they will be willing to pay - until the market is actually tested.

Suffice it to say that if you are serious about creating wealth, then you have to accept risk and learn to reduce it wherever possible. You can't eliminate it, because if you did, you would also eliminate the upside.

Some people are naturally happier with risk than others. I have risked everything, and it wasn't easy, but it was a great deal easier than I imagined it would be. I've sold my own home, to get access to capital, but I was single at the time, and I had no dependants, so if the business failed, I was the only one in trouble. Your attitude and acceptance of risk - and therefore the strategy you choose to adopt - will be at least partly determined by your own personal circumstances.

If you are married with a small family, it would be unwise to bet the family silver or risk your own home to pursue a business venture. In fact I'd strongly discourage it. However, if you and your partner are committed and the business plan is sound, then the risk may be something you would both be happy to consider. Many have taken this route.

Only you can decide what level of risk you are comfortable with. Certainly your tolerance of risk will also expand as you progress. When I started, I felt deeply uncomfortable when I acquired a fair amount of debt. Now I can borrow significant amounts without a single sleepless night.

Why not go out on a limb? That's where the fruit is.
Will Rogers

Find a Mentor

Part of assessing risk is getting the right 'real world experience'. It is ignorance that makes things challenging - not the thing itself. Everything is a challenge when we don't understand it. So in order to Own a Strategy, you have to understand what strategy is about. You have to know your industry and understand what's possible, doing so will immediately reduce your risk. So getting up to speed in your area is imperative, and the best way to do that is to find someone who has already been successful in that industry.

Finding a mentor is one of those key steps that most people overlook. It may very well be that you've heard the advice before. My guess, however, is that you haven't done it. Put simply, finding a mentor is absolutely critical to your success - especially if you want to reach your target in the fastest possible time. Perhaps it's the terminology that puts people off. Or it's the idea that prospective mentors or advisors would be "too busy" that holds us back. But try thinking about it a little differently.

Human beings, who are almost unique in having the ability to learn from the experiences of others, are also remarkable for their apparent disinclination to do so.
Douglas Adams

Consider the Board of Directors in a company. Is it not a group of people who have particular strengths and knowledge that are especially useful in guiding a business? These individuals aren't always active in the business on a day-to-day basis. Instead, they have already done what your business needs to do and thus can bring experience and knowledge to bear on strategic and tactical choices.

When I recommend you find mentors, think of it as putting together your own Board of Directors. These people are essential in lighting your path, because they have already achieved what you wish to achieve, and that sort of knowledge and expertise is invaluable. A mentor will bring a new perspective and will short-cut the time in growing a viable enterprise. There is no rule that tells us that we have to learn all our own lessons. It's smart to learn as many lessons as you can from other people's experience - especially the really costly and painful ones.

7 Tips for Finding a Great Mentor

1. Find someone who is significantly more successful than you are
2. Find someone who has actually achieved what you want to achieve
3. Search both within and outside your geographic location

4. Make a compelling approach - ask intelligently
5. Don't pin your hopes on one mentor - find several
6. Family and friends do not count
7. A retired CEO is an excellent candidate

A Mentor is Significantly more Successful than You

Your mentor should be someone that you admire and respect. And they must be significantly more successful than you currently are.

So if you are making $50,000 a year and aspire to be making a few million, then you have to find a mentor who is making $1-3 million a year or has done so at some point in his or her past. There has to be this disparity; otherwise, the mentoring won't be a big enough stretch for you. The person's advice and recommendations will not compel you to grow fast enough, and you won't get the big wins.

When your mentor is really in another league, a few things happen. First, you step up, Even if you don't really want to, even if you're terrified or a little confused about what to do next, you will hold yourself to a higher standard. Even if you are scared to death, the prospect of letting that person down will always be infinitely more scary than the thing you need to do, and this thought will compel you to move forward and do things you currently think are impossible.

Anything that I have ever done that ultimately was
worthwhile initially scared me to death.
Betty Bender

A mentor who is significantly more successful than you is also inspiring; having that person hold you to account can cause quantum leaps in your progress. It is this accountability that is actually at the heart of the coaching boom. Over the last decade, there's been a huge rise in the number of people who are buying executive or personal coaching to help them meet their goals. It has always amused me that there are people who have set themselves up as professional coaches but have yet to achieve anything noteworthy in their own lives. Still, they happily dish out advice and recommendations about how others should run their business and life.

The simple fact is that much of this coaching is still successful. However, its success is not always due to the individual coach but to the automatic installation of an accountability system. It is accountability that gets things done. This is why slimming clubs work - it's not really the recipes or the T-shirt or the calorie counting charts on the website. It's because come next week, participants will have to be accountable for their actions and get on a scale in front of a room full of people and be weighed. That's what keeps them on track; that's what stops them from "getting fries with that" or reaching for the ice cream during a friday night film.

Now imagine that same accountability coming from someone who has already done what you want to do and achieved huge success from it. Not only will the person give you valuable information about how to achieve your outcome...but they will cause you to hold yourself to a higher standard than you ever thought possible. And that's incredibly powerful.

A Mentor has Achieved what you Want to Achieve

Think back to Law 2, and what you imagined for yourself in the future. You need to find someone who is already there. Your ideal mentor is someone who has done exactly what you are seeking to do.

Often people think of mentors as celebrities, but a great mentor doesn't have to be well known at all. There are millions of very successful and wealthy individuals all over the world who go about their business very quietly. Those people are every bit as valuable to you as someone who graces the covers of business magazines and are infinitely more accessible.

The key issue is that the person has done what you are trying to do. So if you want to build a construction company, you must find someone who has become wealthy building a construction company. If you want to become a stock market investor, then you find someone who has made money investing in the stock market. If you want to start a magazine, then find someone who has built a magazine empire from scratch and is now successful as a result of it.

This is the perfect situation because you benefit from the industry specific knowledge and expertise, as well as industry contacts that can fast-track your development. However, it's not always possible to find the exact person, so if you can't find someone who fits the bill exactly, then find someone who has created wealth in a similar or complementary field.

Being mentored by a self-made multi-millionaire in any field is still far superior to being mentored by someone less successful in your particular area. Ninety percent of business and business success is generic. Creating a successful fashion design house will require many of the same steps and approaches as building a successful publishing company or construction business, so there is still a great deal to be learned from a successful person outside your field. In fact, the knowledge you gain from learning about other industries may be the very thing that will give you an advantage over the competition.

Often it's just the encouragement you receive from your successful mentor that makes the difference. Knowing that you are on the right track and that someone with experience and genuine insight is supporting you and urging you on can be highly motivating.

> *The finest gift you can give anyone is encouragement. Yet, almost no one gets the encouragement they need to grow to their full potential. If everyone received the encouragement they need to grow, the genius in most everyone would blossom and the world would produce abundance beyond our wildest dreams.*
> Sidney Madwed

Seek a mentor both within and outside your geographic location, ideally at least one of your mentors should be accessible geographically, simply because all relationships prosper when there is opportunity for face-to-face contact. Just think about it for a moment - someone may have 121 "friends" on Facebook, but how many would they ever speak to in real life? How many would they meet for a drink? A handful at most - the rest are long forgotten school acquaintances, old colleagues or college friends you haven't seen for twenty years and don't really want to see in real life!

All the important relationships in your life require real communication and interaction, so if possible, source a mentor or two from your local area, because you'll have an opportunity to strengthen that professional bond - personally.

If that's not possible, then you'll need to widen your search outside your geographic location. You may live in a rural part of the country where there simply aren't people locally who fit your requirements.

If face-to-face contact isn't feasible, then there are still plenty of new methods of communication that can facilitate a great mentoring relationship. Today your mentor *can* be anywhere in the world.

My first formal business mentor was Denis Waitley, and the entire relationship was conducted via email, with each of us in a different country. I got in touch with him through his wife, who was a top distributor for a major network marketing company. I arranged to meet her while she and Denis were in London. I never did meet Denis face-to-face, but his wife gave me his email address and said she would talk to him about me. Twenty-four hours later, we had an agreement that he would mentor me for six months. I would email him once a week, and he would reply with a long email that answered all my questions every time. He was fantastic and really helped me in the early days of my training business.

Because of the nuances of business in particular areas, it is advisable to find a mentor in your cultural area, so that their information and insights are relevant to the market you are trying to conquer. But again, it's not 100% mandatory.

Even social networking sites such as LinkedIn can be really helpful in putting you in touch with people who could help you out with particular questions. On LinkedIn you can join specific interest groups and ask questions. You'd be amazed at what people are happy to share. Obviously, you need to be careful to listen to the right people, but so long as those providing the advice have the credentials to back it up, these business-focused networking sites can be a valuable resource.

Make a Compelling Approach - Ask Intelligently

First of all, don't overestimate how hard it is to speak to people and find a great mentor. Don't assume that the person you have in mind won't be interested or won't have the time. Most people fail to find a mentor because they fail to identify someone suitable and even if they do, they then fail to ask. You may need to tap into a little courage to ask, but if you don't ask, the answer will always be "No."

I remember when I first decided to interview the *Sunday Times* Rich List, there were plenty of people who told me it would be impossible and that "those sorts of people" would be totally off-limits to me. And yet, over the course of two years, I met and interviewed over 200 high-profile wealthy individuals. For me it came down to how badly I wanted to meet them - and it has to be the same for you.

The other part of asking intelligently is that you have to make the approach compelling for the other person. Try wherever possible to include some benefit for the prospective mentor. Remember that we are all trying to meet the same basic needs, even the extremely wealthy and powerful.

So how can helping you, help your mentor? How can helping you make them feel important and respected? Mentoring you may offer someone the opportunity to contribute and give back. Most people will not fall all over themselves and say, "Yes, yes, I'd love to help you," but if you appeal to something they want, need or enjoy, they are more likely to do so.

Find out about your prospective mentor and what he or she enjoys and likes to do; find some common ground outside the business arena. When I was just 16, I was mentored by a brilliant businessman who ran a successful company in Buckinghamshire in the UK. He enjoyed tennis, so we would meet and play tennis, during which time I would get all my questions answered.

If you find something that your prospective mentor enjoys then suggest combining a meeting with that activity, then the mentoring process becomes more enjoyable for both parties, and you will develop a better relationship. If you learn that your prospective mentor loves the theater, suggest a show and a meal. If the person loves Chinese food, find a great restaurant and book a table. And *always* be sure to pay the bill.

Developing your relationship in such a way is more natural and enjoyable. There is nothing worse than someone firing question after question. It can feel like you're trying to suck their brains out! Don't do that - step back, chill out, and relax. Your mentor will then enjoy seeing you, and once that happens, they will be more open to allowing you to draw on their experience and knowledge.

Don't succumb to conventional wisdom and dismiss your ideal mentor as being out of reach or inaccessible. Make as direct an approach as possible, take a deep breath, and ask intelligently. Be specific; actually ask, "Will you mentor me?" Make a formal arrangement, so that both parties know what to expect. It doesn't need to be legal; you're just clarifying the time commitment for the mentor.

Above all, don't give up at the first rejection.

Don't Pin Your Hopes on One - Find Several

Don't set your heart on one individual and give up if they decline. Finding a mentor can be a process of trial and error. Sometimes your choice may not work out; if it doesn't, find someone else and approach them.

If you get too hung up on having a certain person as your mentor and can't see past that one individual, then you limit your options and chances for success. In truth, there may be many different people just as qualified to help you.

The reason people get so bedazzled by one person is that they assume that they need just one mentor and that if they get that one particular person, everything else will fall into place. Certainly great mentors are worth their weight in gold, but you don't have to have one perfect person.

You can have different mentors for different parts of your business.

Often this is better than having just one person to call on anyway, because it broadens your perspective and increases your associations with successful people.

Who you spend your time with and associate with has a huge impact on where you end up. "The apple doesn't fall far from the tree" is a well-worn phrase, but it's true. Children don't end up very different from their parents because they spend so much time with them. The same is true when you get older. Who you spend your time with can determine your success trajectory as surely as your parents will determine certain personal characteristics.

If you can surround yourself with three or four extremely wealthy mentors who are coaching you on particular areas of your business, then you are getting a range and depth of experience that will be invaluable. You will also be getting used to how such people operate. You become more comfortable associating with them, and that helps you make the transition from where you are to being a well informed and knowledgeable individual yourself.

On my own journey, I have had to make very deliberate and conscious choices not to associate with certain people who were previously in my life, because whenever I shared my ideas and aspirations, they would try to knock them down or diminish them in some way. They were like a computer virus, whose sole purpose is to infect, infiltrate and halt progress. Be careful whom you interface with.

I never wasted my time arguing with these people. There's no point in trying to make a negative person a positive one - I just quietly stopped spending so much time with them.

Withdrawing from such people doesn't have to be noticeable or confrontational, but you have to protect your vision and stay focused on the goal. And that means surrounding yourself with positive people who have done what you want to achieve and can offer real insight without negativity and bitterness. We become like the people we hang around with. Underline it!

Family and Friends Do Not Count

When it comes to finding a great mentor, you can immediately discount all your friends and family. It's a sad fact of life that those that are often supposed to care about us can be the most critical of us or any changes we seek to make. The reasons for this could be the subject of a psychological tome, but they're really not important for now.

Forget about friends and family being your mentors - it doesn't work. Why on earth would you take property development advice from someone who has never even bought their own home? Why would you take wealth creation advice from someone who is constantly broke and worrying about his credit card debt?

It follows, therefore, that the only exception to this rule would be a friend or family member who is extremely successful and has done what you are seeking to achieve. But there's a very important caveat. Even if the friend or relative were super successful, you would still need to find at least one other mentor, because familiarity often breeds contempt.

If your uncle had built a huge business in your line of work and was a multi-millionaire, he is still your uncle. If you are going to use family as mentors, ensure that the arrangement is a formal one, because you've gotten used to them being part of your life. So used to it, in fact, that you didn't even realize how successful until your mother told you.

You may love your uncle, but the familiarity you feel toward him will affect the way you respond to his mentoring. It's possible that you won't have the same respect and reverence for him that you should have for your mentor. Remember: a great mentor will hold you to a standard far higher than you would even hold yourself, certainly at the beginning. If you don't have that reverence, then it's likely that you will not feel that same level of accountability that you would with someone you didn't know.

Seek out a Retired CEO

A brilliant way to find a mentor is to track down retired CEOs. To become a CEO of a medium to large business is a significant achievement. It indicates that one has been in business at a very high level of success for many years. However when they retire, no one calls them anymore!

These are people who have been deeply involved in business their entire working lives. All their expertise and insight then lies dormant in retirement - what a waste!

So find a retired CEO of a business that you aspire to. These individuals have done what you are seeking to do, they will have been more successful than you are at this stage, and they probably don't *need* the money. If you offer them an equity share, it may be nice, but the real reward and value for them will probably be getting involved again. They can choose to be involved as much or as little as they like, and being of service and offering their knowledge and insights can be just as rewarding for them as their input is for you. A true win/win.

Find a business in your industry that has done what you want to do or is doing what you want to do and look at their past leadership. See what happened to the previous CEO - where did he or she go? Track the person down.

I've done this myself on several occasions.

Finding a mentor in this way also raises some additional possibilities that can supercharge your business. Consider making that person CEO of your new business. You might be thinking, "Hold on, I'm just starting here." But I believe that you should set up your business properly from the start. Creating a public entity also creates seriousness about building the business and shifts it out of a "kitchen table enterprise" mode.

It might start off like that, and there is nothing wrong with acting small and thinking big. For example, there's no point in renting fancy premises or spending a fortune on signage, logo design, and the like, when you don't have the sales. That sort of facade is expensive and has been the demise of thousands of new start-ups. Setting up a public company can be done in about 24 hours, and it's not that expensive - yet it portrays a seriousness and commitment that are a powerful influence on the business. Making a retired CEO *your* CEO is also a shrewd move, as I'll explain in a moment.

All the people I know who have successfully grown a business have had a mentor in the early stages. All my mentors have had mentors when they started out - it's such a powerful strategy, and yet so few people look to find one. So be different - get a mentor.

Build a Team

It is impossible to create major wealth without involving others in the process. If you are serious about creating wealth, then you must accept that it is never done alone.

One of the biggest hurdles business people face in taking an idea to a multi-million enterprise is their reluctance to get other people involved. Instead, they refuse to delegate and get blinded by the details, because they mistakenly think that if something is to be done right, they have to do it themselves. They refuse to relinquish their tight grip on every facet of the business. And while it's true that no one cares about your business like you do, if you want it to reach its potential and fulfil your vision then, you must learn to let go.

Creating serious wealth demands it. Even if you were super-human, you could not do all that needs to be done, check all that needs to be checked, and see to all that needs to be seen to in order to create the success you seek. It's impossible.

John Knight, CEO of The Knight Group in London, knows a thing or two about getting the right people in place. Building a construction business from nothing to a multi-million-dollar empire requires courage, audacity, and a willingness to find the right people. When I interviewed John, he talked about the importance of hiring the best you can afford, paying them over market value, and always sending the right people to the right job.

Knight spoke about the importance of "buying the brains" that you may not have yourself. Bring in the best you can afford and let them educate you. Once you've found them, make it very hard for them to leave through "Golden Handcuffs."

So if the market rate for a position is $100,000 then you would pay the people in that position $120,000. Every time they are tempted to look around, they'll know they're being paid more than they could get anywhere else, and they will stay. Do that and treat them well, and they won't want to go anywhere else.

Knight spoke about getting the right people for the right job, "because of my upbringing and [strong cockney] accent, when we did certain deals I couldn't go and meet the top people. If it was an exclusive development, for example, that person would look down on me because of the way I spoke. So I sent one of my Managing Directors because he 'talked their talk'. If I'm buying a property off a scrap dealer, then I can do that deal because I talk his language." If you're selling pricey real estate in upper-class Manhattan, it's no good sending a salesgirl from Brooklyn.

This is the reality of business. There is no room for ego and sentimentality here - it's just simple business reality. People want to do business with people "like them;" they want to be assured that you understand them and that there is common ground. John Knight is a smart guy - because he knew this from the start, and he sent the right people to the right meetings to make the right deal. And if it wasn't him, then he wasn't going to get all prissy or offended. So send the right people in to do the right deal. Anything else is corporate suicide.

You must become the front man or woman and gather around you a team that will do all the things that will make the business successful. Every business of note, in fact every significant outcome of note, is the result of a team effort. The better the team, the better the results, so getting the right people in the right places is imperative. This is one of the other huge advantages of finding a great mentor and ideally making that person CEO. He or she has already walked your walk and will thus have a large network of contacts. The person will know the name of a great accountant, lawyer or designer - or will know whom to ask to find one. This can radically reduce the time it takes to build your team.

Tips for Creating Powerful Teams:

- Hire people better than you
- Pay them very well or give them equity (or both)
- Hire for attitude
- Seek cohesion
- Trust them to do their job

Hire People Better Than You

The key to building a great team is to ensure that you find people that are better than you. That means smarter, more creative, more imaginative and more ambitious than you are. Hiring someone with less imagination, less ambition and less intelligence doesn't propel you toward your vision; it hampers you. Instead of adding powerful jet engines, you are adding a ballast.

"The first method for estimating the intelligence of a ruler is to look at the men he has around him."
Niccolo Machiavelli

Everyone has strengths and weaknesses. Hiring more people like you simply exacerbates your weaknesses and over-supplies your strengths. You need to compensate for your weaknesses and find people who are even better at the things you are good at! That's how the business will grow. Think of it as a set of Russian dolls, one nesting inside another. If you hire people bigger than you, you'll have a big company. If you hire people smaller than you, then you'll always have a small company.

Find the best people you can, and don't settle for good. Good is the enemy, because great people will not join a team full of good people. Aim for the best.

And just as with finding a mentor, the best don't need to be on your doorstep - especially for tasks that are project based and don't require on-site participation. You may need a top-notch website designer to bring your business identity to life. That person doesn't need to be in your geographical location. In fact, there are many online marketplace websites where you can post your requirements and have professionals bid on your project.

For certain team members, it will not be necessary to be local, so you have the opportunity to find the best, not just those who might in your area. So forget about hiring *mini-me's* and find people who are different from *and* better than you. It takes courage - but it's worth it.

Pay them Well or Give them Equity (or both)

Building a team usually means mixing people you have identified by yourself with people your mentors have led you to. In any case, these people have to be willing to come on board and help you achieve your vision.

Depending on the person's role in the team, you need to ensure that you either pay them extremely well or offer equity in the business; many times, I have done both. If you want to attract and keep the best, then you will have to do the same. These people will be the best, and they will fast track-your growth and success - so reward them accordingly.

I said it earlier, but it bears repeating: if you pay them very well, they're more inclined to stay. Even if they do look around at other opportunities or find themselves headhunted by other organizations, they will know that they are already getting the highest salary they could in the marketplace.

Too often, business owners shoot themselves in the foot by trying to pay as little as they can get away with. One very effective technique is to ask your team member what they would like to be paid. Most people will suggest a lower amount than you had in mind anyway, because most people routinely underestimate their own worth.

And for those worried about financing this approach, consider giving away equity in your business to key team members. Or give them a share in the profits. Profit-sharing not only excites key team members and ensures that they will do everything in their power to make the business a success. It also makes the whole process more fun and exciting.

When you have confidence, you can have a lot of fun.
And when you have fun, you can do amazing things.
Joe Namath

Half the adventure of wealth creation is taking people with you: you're not just making money for yourself; you're helping others to make money too, so everyone wins in the end.

Hire For Attitude

A traditional business will have a vacant position and will create a job description so it can match a person to that position. The person is secondary to the position. Great entrepreneurs and businesses are more interested in the person and are more focused on the *need* than on a particular position. So entrepreneurs are always on the lookout for great people, whether there are vacant positions or not.

Attitude is more important than the past, than education, than money, than circumstances, than what others think or say or do. It is more important than appearance, giftedness, or skill. It will make or break a company, a church, a home. The remarkable thing is that we have a choice every day regarding the attitude we will embrace for that day. We cannot change the past. We cannot change the fact that people will act in a certain way. We cannot change the inevitable. The only thing we can do is play the one string we have, and that is our attitude.
Chuck Swindoll

When you are building your team, you are bringing together the people who will do much of the actual work of building your business. These are people who will become the face of your business, so hire for attitude as well as credentials. If someone is not enthusiastic by nature, it will be difficult to change him or her.

If we're talking about your accountant, attitude may not be that important, but if the person is going to be interacting with your customers or making sales, then it really does matter.

Find people who are not afraid of hard work. Building a business is not a 9-5 operation, and you need people to understand that right from the start. That may mean working on the weekends. You need to know that people are on board and up for the adventure; otherwise, they may hold the business back.

Seek Cohesion

A powerful team is not just a group of people doing their respective jobs. Real cohesion is necessary, because with cohesion, the activities of five people create the output of seven or eight. That's a real team.

You can see this in a sporting context. A soccer club buys million-dollar players, and yet the team doesn't gel. It doesn't matter how many superstar players a team has; it becomes a potent force only when the whole team plays as one unit intent on winning the game.

One of the best ways to create cohesion is by offering incentives so that everyone is committed to success. When everyone prospers with the company's success, not just those at the top, it's truly amazing what can be achieved. In my first business, my people knew that their paychecks were tied to company income, so they all continuously thought of ways to make more money. They all worked hard and the enthusiasm was incredibly compelling.

Like cohesion, saying thank you to your people is also highly underrated. Show them some respect - and be genuine about it.

It always amazes me how some companies will use money as a substitute for respect and how much nonsense people will take if the money is *good enough*. But you will never get the best from people and build powerful teams unless you appreciate your team and enjoy the rewards together.

Trust Them to Do Their Job

If you have hired the best you can and they are more experienced than you, if you have paid them well or given them equity in your business, then you have to let go and trust them to get on with their job. Otherwise, all of the preceding will be a complete waste of time.

People of the caliber you need don't expect to be second-guessed or have their work checked all the time. You have to allow them the freedom and creativity to experiment - and to make mistakes.

All too often, team members are not allowed to disagree with the boss. A business populated by yes-men (and women) is completely impotent. Even if the leader is right most of the time, the business will never really flourish, because no one is willing to stick their neck out and have a contrary opinion - even a good contrary opinion. Plenty of very smart businesspeople have made leadership errors because they didn't appreciate employees with an opinion.

I found in running businesses that the best results come from letting high-grade people work unencumbered.
Warren Buffet

In 1884, Thomas Edison hired a young Croatian engineer, Nikola Tesla, to work in his laboratory in Menlo Park, New Jersey. Edison was convinced that direct electric current was the way to light the world. Tesla believed that alternating current would be more practical. Already a world-famous inventor, the supremely self-confident Edison had little patience with employees who disagreed with him, and he fired Tesla. In 1889 Tesla patented an AC power system, and sold it to George Westinghouse, who built an empire generating AC electricity.

Few things help an individual more than to place responsibility upon him and to let him know that you trust him.
Booker T. Washington

This stage can be very difficult for business owners; you may feel as though you're losing control. Instead, you need to step back from the day-to-day activity and focus on providing strong leadership. You also need to recognize your own skills and strengths and adapt appropriately as the business grows. People who love to start businesses are rarely suited to actually running them. Running a successful business on a day-to-day basis requires very different skills from those needed to start it. You need to recognize that dynamic and build your team accordingly.

Creating a great team is a crucial part of the wealth creation equation because these are the people who will do the vast majority of the actual grunt work. You will very often find yourself taking credit for work someone else did. And that's just part and parcel of business. They are doing a job for which you are rewarding them with praise and encouragement, as well as money or equity. That's just the nature of business.

Raise Cash

Earlier in this chapter, I recommended that you set your business up properly from the start. Here's why: it fosters seriousness in the endeavor and lets everyone involved know you are there to make money.

If you have found a great mentor, especially a former CEO, and appointed that person as *your* CEO, and found other mentors that will form your Board of Directors - you have then created the potential to reap generous dividends. If you have a CEO with a great track record and a board of directors already in place, then raising capital becomes much easier, because you get to lean on their credibility.

No business will become successful without knowing how to raise money. So if you are held back by fear of asking for money, and the mere idea brings about a trembling lip, sweaty palms, and pounding heart - then get it in perspective. Every business will require a cash injection at some point, especially if you are seeking to grow rapidly.

Debt for many is a tricky issue. Many feel guilty about debt, but not all debt is equal. Credit-card debt or loans to buy things that don't add to your net worth is bad debt, and the only people getting rich from bad debt are the credit card and loan companies. Good debt, on the other hand, is money borrowed to buy an asset. Borrowing money to build or expand a business is good debt, and no one should ever feel guilty about debt of that kind. You need to get comfortable asking for money. This is easier in some cultures than others. Going into debt is no longer a crime as it once was. In 1833 the United States abolished Federal imprisonment for unpaid debts, and the UK Debtors Act abolished imprisonment for debt in 1869.

Good debt is an essential part of success. So getting used to asking for money is an essential prerequisite for success.

The standard advice is that you should clear your own bad debt first, before seeking business debt. If you use a credit card to finance a business or start a business when you already have bad debt that you need to service, then you put yourself under additional pressure. Starting a business, for example with a credit card, you will have to make, for example: 17% just to cover your debt charges from an average rate card, and no legal business in its early days can sustain that sort of return.

Ideally, therefore, you would not have any debt when you begin, because you will be making it harder for yourself. I didn't clear my debts before I built my first business or my second - I just went for it. But then, I didn't have any other choice at the time. However I knew I could generate enough equity within that time to pay it back. But it wasn't ideal, and I certainly don't recommend it.

Business Building Stages:

- Stage 1: Bootstrapping
- Stage 2: Loans from Banks or Financial Institutions
- Stage 3: Angels & Venture Capital

Stage 1: Bootstrapping

Bootstrapping is about being resourceful rather than just using resources. It covers all the creative ways that a business can start out and usually refers to growing a business the hard way through incremental growth.

Bootstrapping a business can be a slow process because you have to find the money to make a product or deliver a service, sell it, reinvest the profit, and repeat the process. At best, it usually promises slow growth.

There are many techniques for this stage of business development, such as customer or supplier funding. These involve selling your product before you've actually made it or going to the supplier and negotiating terms. Sppose you need 1000 widgets. You could negotiate with the widget manufacturer to give you 60 or 90 days' credit terms so that you have enough time to sell at least some of the widgets and pay the supplier. That way the manufacturer is funding the start of your business.

I've done this before with all sorts of professionals. Once I needed the services of a lawyer to oversee a big development I was doing. I suggested that he work out his breakeven on the deal so that worst-case scenario, I would cover his costs, but if the deal was successful, I'd pay significantly more than his hourly fee.

The lawyer was fairly compensated but was also super-committed to making the deal happen, because he'd get three times his normal rate. It's amazing what people will do when there is a success fee on the table. This has worked several times because the specialist has seen what I was trying to do and liked the business model. There was greater buy-in and attention to my work because it was in the other party's best interests to speed things through and to help me to be successful. It's a win for everyone, because everyone benefits when the deal comes off.

Although bootstrapping isn't that fast as a way to grow the business, it seems to be an essential incubator stage for every fledgling company. Personally, I don't think you should move on to the second and third level of financing until you've done this once or twice. This will help you to understand the true value of money.

There are many lessons to be learned by bootstrapping a business start up, lessons that will pay off throughout your entire business career. But if you are looking for faster growth, bootstrapping isn't always the best option.

Stage 2: Loans from Banks or Financial Institutions

There will come a time when you will need to borrow money. For many people, the first port of call will not be a bank or financial institution. Many times this involves seeking money from private individuals - usually friends and family. While it may be the easiest and cheapest place to secure money for growth, there can be serious downsides.

In the first place, if you borrow from friends and family, you are likely to get friends and family advice, which is usually the worst type of advice for a business. And perhaps most damaging of all is the potential for dispute. Often in the initial enthusiasm of a business venture, friends and family are only told of the anticipated returns, with no mention of the potential downside. If things go wrong, nothing can sour a relationship faster and more permanently than losing money.

If you do insist on borrowing from friends and family, then you need to make sure that everyone understands the worst case scenario, not just 'hoped for' projections. You need to have a watertight agreement so that everyone is aware of the risks as well as the rewards. The agreement should also clearly set out an acceptable exit strategy for the lender who wants their money back for any reason. Managing expectations on both sides will go a long way to helping avoid disputes. This type of lending is nevertheless fraught with challenges.

There is nothing wrong with gifting money to friends and family for a business venture. This doesn't carry the same risks, because there is no expectation of return, however, the safer option is to borrow from a bank or financial institution. There are literally thousands of options available to you, and they're not limited to prestigious banks or traditional lending institutions.

Some argue that the financial landscape has changed dramatically since the global financial crisis that began in 2007. And certainly fear gripped the lending markets as banks and investment houses struggled to come to terms with the US sub-prime fallout. But to think that the lending business will somehow grind to a halt is crazy. Banks and financial institutions make their money from lending money, so they are still eager to lend to suitable businesses that can demonstrate a sound model and make a profit.

When you are seeking a loan, however, there are certain things your bank or institution will want. They will want to see past accounts, and they will want to know if the business has assets that can secure the loan. Obviously, with a new venture, this question can sometimes prove difficult. So if you are new to business or have only been trading for a short time, then you will be asked for a personal guarantee, a guarantor, or an asset as security.

A guarantor is someone else who does have assets and guarantees your loan on your behalf. If things go wrong, then that person will be liable for the debt. If you have equity in your family home, i.e., the value of the house far exceeds the outstanding mortgage on it, then you could put that asset up as security for the loan. There are obvious dangers in this approach - if things don't go according to plan, you could lose your home.

I've done this before, I've been on a razor's edge, but I knew that if it went wrong, I was the only one who would have suffered. I wouldn't do it again, and I certainly wouldn't recommend it to any new start-up.

The question the bank or financial institution is always thinking is, *"How do we get our money back if this person dies or becomes incapacitated?"* In order to get access to capital, you will need to think like the lending institution and anticipate those questions.

Stage 3: Angels & Venture Capital

Angels typically invest their own funds and in my experience, this is usually limited to under a million dollars. Unlike Venture investors who typically invest from a pooled fund, Angels are wealthy individuals who will seed a business in return for an equity stake in that business. They are not always active in the business on a day to day basis but often will have been successful before and can offer advice and contacts to further the enterprise. Again, retired CEO's can be a possible source of angel investment.

Venture capital has its place in business growth, but there are significant upsides and downsides for business owners. On the upside, the investment is not just about money; a venture capital firm will bring expertise, credibility and experience, as well as a vast network of contacts that can literally transform a business and put it on a fast track to success.

But the cost of that is usually a controlling interest in the business. You may have to give up the leadership of the business - for some entrepreneur's, a bitter pill to swallow. This route is not suited to someone who is too emotionally attached to the business. However, if your intention is to sell the business or take it public in a relatively short space of time, a venture capital partner may be the smartest option.

A venture capital firm will raise a fund that borrows or invests from usually large financial institutions for a promised return over a period of time. If the fund raises $100 million from private investors and institutions, the venture fund managers will invest in, say, 20 companies. Usually they will have a 3-5 year time-frame, during which they hope to find one or two winners. They will take those one or two to flotation and make maybe $600 million or a billion dollars each.

If your business happens to be one of the winners, then great - but if not, you are just a small percentage of their overall portfolio.

So it's important to understand that a Venture Capital strategy may not be the same as your overall strategy. You are just one horse in the stable, so the Venture Capital firm may not always have your best interests at heart. If they find their winners, they will collect the prize money and cash in the entire fund within that 3-5 year window.

Venture capital also invests on a preferred basis. So suppose they liked your business plan and decided to invest $5 million in your business. They may take 35% of the business for that investment. If you do reasonably well and the business is then sold in four years for $200 million, the venture capital company would usually take the first $5 million as payback for the initial investment *and* 35% of what's left.

So if you sold for $200 million, they would get $70 million plus the $5 million initial investment, and you would get $125 million. Hardly a disaster - but most people think that they would get 65% of the $200 million, not realizing that most Venture Capital firms will take the initial investment first and calculate the split from what's left.

Whether venture capital is the right route for you will depend on your personality and what you want to achieve. If you just want to make money in the shortest time possible, then Venture Capital can be a really great solution. You may have to give a whole lot away, but who cares if you are left with more than enough to do what you want with the rest of your life?

Starting a business is like flying a plane - most of the money is burnt at take-off, where the plane must gather enough speed to get off the ground.

The same is true of business, and often business owners ask for too little. Soon they realize they're running out of runway and don't have the speed to take off...which forces them to go back and raise more money.

Once in bed with a Venture Capital firm, it's very hard to get out, and if you have to go back for more money, then you will have to relinquish more equity, meaning when the business does finally lift off, you're left with a smaller share. At that point, you've sold part of your business, and you may have lost right to control.

Always overestimate what you need when raising cash. It is far easier to get the money the first time than it will be if you have to go back for more. This is true of both banks and Venture Capital firms. If in a bank ask the person you are meeting with what their lending limit is. If you are looking for $10 million, and the person in the meeting is authorized to lend up to $1 million, then you're not going to get the money you want - you need to be speaking to someone else. Don't waste time selling yourself to the wrong person. Unless you are direct with banks, they won't tell you this. If their lending limit is sufficient for your needs, then always ask for the upper end of that limit.

Remember: your goal is to create a successful business, with the aim of selling it for a great deal of money. That has to be your ultimate strategy, and so everything you do in your journey toward wealth must keep that clearly in focus.

What To Expect If You Fail To Own A Strategy:

- You'll be forced to re-invent the wheel
- Your growth with remain slow and incremental

You'll Be Forced to Re-invent the Wheel

If you don't Own a Strategy, then, although you may have a vision for the future, you haven't put the people and plans in place to make that happen. So you're left to rely on trial and error, which is inefficient and slow. Why waste time trying to work out the best way to re-invent the wheel, when you could find someone who has already done what you're seeking to do and ask that person for the best way? That sort of insight can shave years off the time and costs required to build a successful business.

Your Growth will Remain Slow and Incremental

Not all businesses are on a growth trajectory, and some business owners are happy just to do business - they like the process and the actual game of business. There is nothing wrong with that. I can relate to it myself, as I love making deals and pulling things together. I love the pace of business; I love to discover what's possible when good people come together to create something. The traditional way of building a business can be needlessly slow. If you want to make it easier and faster - and, quite frankly, more enjoyable - then *follow Law 3 and own all the aspects of your strategy*. Put the right people in the right places. Find great mentors and raise a enough cash to see you through - if you don't, you will be doomed to slow and incremental growth.

What You Can Confidently Expect If You Own A Strategy:

- You'll get where you want to go faster
- The journey will be less stressful
- You'll set the business up correctly from the start

You'll Get Where You Want to go Faster

If you have a clear strategy, if you've found some great mentors and, set them up in key positions in your company, if you have built a great team and used the credibility of that team to your advantage, then you will be able to raise cash with surprising ease. Do all that, and you'll get where you're heading faster than you dreamed possible. Having the right people in the right places doing the right thing at the right time can create amazing results. And if you take your time to get this law right, it will generate its own rewards.

The Journey will be Less Stressful

If you have a strategy and the team has a shared vision and a personal stake in that vision, then you create momentum toward success. The decisions that you and everyone else will face along the way are easier when everyone knows what they are trying to achieve, because you don't have to sit and deliberate over every opportunity or possibility from a standing start. All you have to do is check the opportunity or decision against your strategy and end-game, and if it takes you closer to that target, you pursue it. If it takes you further away from your target, you ignore it and move on. This focus will massively accelerate the journey from where you are now to where you want to be. And, additionally, it will remove the inertia of inaction.

You'll Set the Business up Correctly from the Start

Most businesses muddle along. They start after years of deliberation or perhaps as a result of redundancy. Whatever the reason, most businesses evolve over time - but evolution is really slow! Somewhere in that evolution, a business owner may decide to try and sell. However, unless you have the structure and systems in place, there really isn't anything to sell.

94% of failure is a function of poor systems
and strategy rather than people.
W. Edwards Deming

You have to set a business up properly, with board members, key roles, policies and procedures for consistent delivery. If you don't do that from the start, your aspirations of selling the business will be adversely affected. At best, it will take you a year or so to go back over old ground and transform the business into something that can be sold. But if you follow Law 3, you will have set it up properly, right from the start.

Producers vs. Consumers

When formulating your strategy, keep in mind that it is producers, not consumers, that create wealth. You can't make money by being a consumer. Sure, wealthy people spend their money on nice homes, cars, and all the finer things in life - but only after they have first produced something, be it products, services, or jobs, through innovation, ideas or creativity.

A consumer, on the other hand, is always buying things, never creating them. Consumers take value; they use other people's products or services, ideas and creativity. They are the end-users who add no value. They make other people wealthy, not themselves.

Owning a Strategy requires you to take the right steps to become a successful producer. Whether you are creating ideas, products or services, you need to own your strategy so that you can fast-track your success. It means putting the right people and systems in place to make that journey and finding the money to make it happen.

Are You Aligned to Law 3 - Do You Own A Strategy?

Below are seven sets of two statements - 1A/1B through 7A/7B. Read each pair of statements and mark the one that's mostly true for you. On balance, which more accurately reflects your view on life and opinions? The choice won't always be easy, but pick the one that best matches you.

Be honest. No one need see this. If you don't want to write in the book or want to keep your selections private, make the selections in a separate notebook. Don't mark what you wish you were like or hope to be like in the future; answer as you are right now. If you are unsure, ask someone you know and trust to give you feedback.

	A	B
1	☐ I know what I'm good at, and I am able to convert my talents into a plan of action to achieve my objectives.	I may or may not know what I'm good at, but it doesn't matter either way, as I can't translate that information into concrete results. ☐
2	☐ I accept that risk is involved in all great endeavors, and I am relatively comfortable with at least the idea.	I'm not comfortable with risk and would rather play it safe than find myself in hot water. ☐
3	☐ Once I've decided on the right course of action, I will rarely change my mind.	I tend to change my mind a lot. This indecision can be tiring. I'm just never that sure if I'm doing the right thing. ☐
4	☐ I can see how important planning is in the achievement of goals. All the goals I have ever met have been a result of good planning.	I prefer just to get on with the tasks at hand and work out the issues as they arise. I don't have time for planning. Besides, it's dull. ☐
5	☐ I have had mentoring relationships in the past even though they may not have been called that.	I have never considered asking someone to be a mentor. It feels silly for an adult to ask for help in that way. ☐
6	☐ I believe that success is a team effort - you can't really achieve anything major on your own.	I prefer to keep things to myself and work alone; I don't want others to let me down. ☐
7	☐ I have experience in raising money - either personally or professionally.	I don't like asking for money and would prefer to grow organically. ☐

If you have checked five or more of the statements in the A Column, you already have a good grasp of Law 3. If you have marked three or more statements in the B Column, then we suggest you read the supplementary guidebook; ***Law3 - Own a Strategy: Applications and Insights.*** This companion guide will give you further information about Law 3, together with practical techniques, ideas and insights into how you can successfully align yourself to this law and harness its power.

Law 4

Always Execute

Boldness & Audacity Yield Results, But be Observant & Adaptive in Attack

For successful action, nothing is more useful than narrowness of thought combined with energy of will. Intention means nothing, results are everything. Unless a capacity for thinking be accompanied by an equal if not greater capacity for action, we are doomed to fail. The inspired ideas of even a superior mind will perish on the rocks of endless contemplation. The thought is the seed, but only action can propagate it. The end of all knowledge should be valiant and bold execution.

Chapter Six
Law 4 - Always Execute

King Philip II of Macedon (382-336 BC) was an ambitious ruler of a land in the northern part of Greece. He set out to unite the various city-states of Greece under one ruler - himself. He raised a great army and systematically waged war on various parts of Greece, bringing them under his control. One of the few remaining states was an area in the southern part of Greece known as Laconia - home to the Spartans.

According to legend male Spartans were removed from their mothers when they were just seven years old, when they would enter the Agoge system. The boys lived in communal messes and were deliberately underfed to encourage them to master the skill of stealing food. Discipline, physical toughness and military skill were instilled in these boys, along with an emphasis on the importance of the Spartan culture. The Spartans were noted for their bravery, ingenuity, and skill in expressing themselves in a few carefully-chosen words. Even today, short, terse speech is often described, "laconic" after the Spartans' homeland. Indeed, during their military schooling, which also included reading, writing, music, and dance, any boy who could not answer questions in a sufficiently "laconic" manner received special punishments. The Spartans' custom of using few words to express themselves conveyed an image of strength and austerity.

Philip knew that he had to subdue the Spartans if his expansionary vision of a united Greece were to succeed. So he sent them a message: "You are advised to submit without further delay, for if I bring my army into your land, I will destroy your farms, slay your people, and raze your city." After a few days, Philip received an answer by letter. He opened the letter and found only one word. That word was... "if."

The implication was clear: *if* he chose to invade, those things might occur - or they might not. Would he have the courage to actually follow through? In similar way, you and I could achieve incredible things - but only *if* we follow through. If you look at where you are right now, you can usually determine whether or not you live by this law. If you are broke but want to be wealthy, then chances are you will not be consistantly doing what is required to create wealth. If you are single but wish to be in a relationship, then chances are you are not doing what needs to be done to meet a suitable person. If you are unfit and want to run a marathon, then you will need to do what needs to be done to run a marathon. Whether or not you are able to transform your life in any direction rests on your willingness to adhere to **Law 4 - Always Execute**. All of the 7 Laws of Wealth are important, but it is Law 4 which is the foundational key to mastering the others.

If you think of the 7 Laws of Wealth as forming an arrow, then the first three laws form a platform for the apex or tip of the arrow. "Always Execute" is the tip that slices through obstacles and soars to the bull's-eye. You have to Gain Control and take responsibility for where you are now, work out how you are going to create a compelling future, and plan a strategy - but unless you execute and take action, your dreams will bounce off target, just like an arrow without its tip. Without action it doesn't matter whether you Gain Control, Embrace the Future, or Own a Strategy - nothing will actually change.

The first three laws are ineffectual without the fourth. If you haven't taken action, there is nothing to Create Value with. If you haven't taken action, there is nothing to grow, and without action, you have nothing to Give Back. Thus the 4th Law of Wealth is the linchpin that holds the others in place. Without execution, nothing happens.

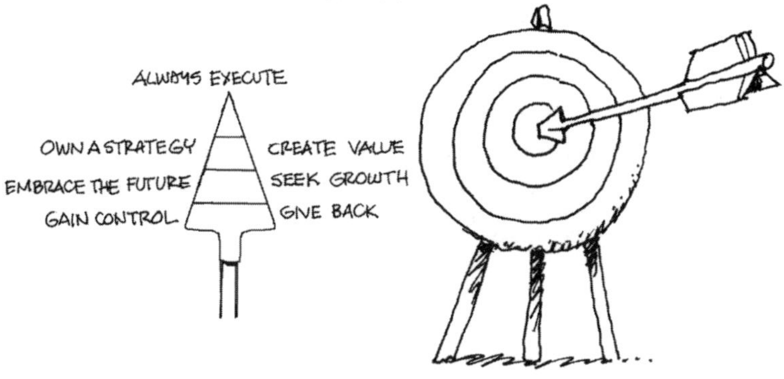

In this respect the 4th Law of Wealth is perhaps the most important. It is the message of the biblical passage (James 2:14-26) "Even so, if it hath not words, is dead, being alone."

Thought + Action = Power

You will remember from Law 2 that intention is a powerful thing and that everything in life is first created in the mind and then in it's physical form. Everything that exists in the world today first sprang to life in someone's mind as an idea or inspiration. But it was action that made it a physical reality.

Human beings can make detailed, long-range plans and act upon them, that is what makes us different from all other species. And yet far too many people allow life, other people, and circumstance to act upon them. They wait for others to make their life better instead of finding out what skills they have to offer whilst seeking to make a positive contribution.

You must have a target and a plan to achieve it, but once you do, then the *only* thing that will bring that ideal to life is *action.* Lofty thoughts without action are useless. It's nothing more than pleasant daydreaming.

It seems to me that man is made to act rather than to know.
Frederick the Great

Thought and action belong together - they are two sides of the same creation coin. Most personal development literature over the last fifty years has successfully emphasized the vital importance our thoughts have on our reality. However, they have played down the need to unite right thinking with right action. So we have thousands, possibly millions of disillusioned seminar attendees the world over who are improving their thinking and faithfully visualizing their goals - but who continue to fall short of their intentions. Why? Because they were led to believe that the right thinking alone would mysteriously manifest their hopes and dreams like a rabbit from a magician's hat.

Not All Action Is 'Right' Action

There are plenty of people who are busy from the minute they wake up to the minute they finally fall asleep. Every moment of their day is accounted for, but being busy does not necessarily mean you're being productive. It is productive action that we are seeking, not just activity.

Far too many people, especially in the western world, go through life being busy. They are always in motion and pride themselves on their activity. They love being busy and having things to do but pay little or no attention to the outcome. There is no assessment as to whether their busyness is productive or just a way to fill in their day and make them feel useful. We're all trying to meet needs, and being busy is a great way to feel important and loved. It is also a great way to add variety to a life - jumping from one meaningless task to the next at least offers variety from the monotony of boredom. If you look more closely at a busy person, very often you will see that they are moving things around rather than making things happen. Nothing is being produced, finished or progressed.

Beware the barrenness of a busy life.
Socrates

The great French naturalist and entomologist Jean-Henri Fabre conducted a now-famous experiment that brilliantly demonstrates the difference between activity and progress. He filled a large plant pot with soil to create a flat surface and placed a sequence of processionary caterpillars around the edge of the pot. The lead caterpillar was positioned at the tail of the last caterpillar to form a complete circle. Processionary caterpillars are so named because they will blindly follow the caterpillar in front in a neat little procession.

Fabre wanted to know if he could change their conditioning without physically moving or obstructing the caterpillars. The obvious first choice was food - so he put the caterpillars' known food; pine needles, in the middle of the pot to see if this reward would entice the caterpillars to break their procession and seek food.

I often ask audience members in seminars what they think happened. Invariably, logic kicks in, people say that eventually they would break the procession and ensure survival. But they don't. Fabre's busy caterpillars didn't flinch. Instead, they marched for seven straight days until they died of starvation, even though their means of survival was inches away the whole time.

Too many of us behave like processionary caterpillars: we confuse activity with accomplishment. Sure, those caterpillars were busy - but they were not productive. Being busy without regard for your achievements is futile and every bit as futile as thought without action.

It is not enough to stay busy. So, too, are the ants.
The question is what you are busy about.
Henry David Thoreau

In today's technology driven world, it's so easy to get sucked into "busy." Apart from any of the needs we may be seeking, we have also become addicted to technology. We confuse the immediacy of communication with it's importance. When we get a phone call, check our emails, or receive a text message, there's an almost immediate compulsion to open, read, and answer. So even if we do manage to get down to useful action, we will be routinely interrupted by technology that for the most part delivers nothing but drivel. Social networking facilities such as Twitter and Facebook must be responsible for a dramatic drop in productive action. Is it really wise to be interrupted by a tweet from your friend to tell you "gone for milk" or "waiting for a bus"? Was that piece of information really worth the distraction? In cases like these, seriously - where is the value?

The new information and networking technologies provide us with untold opportunity. They also pose a huge threat to financial success, because whatever is demanding our attention right now…distracts us from what we need to attend to in order to meet our objectives. You can either use technology to your benefit so that it serves you effectively…or you can become a slave to it and waste huge amounts of your most precious resource.

Wasting time and productivity have always been an issue for business. Even before the distractions of mobile phones and social networking sites, business mangers and executives have wrestled with *activity* instead of *productivity*.

In the 1920s, a man named Ivy Lee, considered by some to be the founder of modern public relations was called in to help Charles Schwab with a productivity challenge. Schwab, the head of Bethlehem Steel, wanted to know how to make his managers more effective. The story is told that Lee offered to give Schwab the secret to productivity and allow Schwab to decide how much that secret was worth. He was simply to implement the idea for a minimum of one week and send Lee a cheque.

Schwab agreed and implemented the simple system. At the end of each day, his managers had to list their top six priorities for the following day and rank them in order of importance. At the start of each new day, the managers were to take action on the #1 priority until it was complete (or no further action could be taken) and then move to priority #2 and repeat the process. Schwab sent Lee a check for $25,000, which today would be equivalent to $250,000!

The basic problem in business and life is that we think too much and act too little. And if we do act, we act on the wrong things. That's why the previous three laws of wealth are so important to get right *before* you take action. Laws 1-3 allow you to assess where you are heading and what your priorities are, so that you can take meaningful action instead of following blindly like the caterpillars.

The Spartans were such a fearsome force because they let their actions do the talking. They didn't sit around discussing what they were to do; they had a definite aim and they did what needed to be done.

If we did all the things we are capable
of doing we would literally astonish ourselves.
Thomas Edison

And by the way…if you're wondering what Philip II of Macedon did when he received his one-word response - neither he nor his son Alexander the Great ever marched on Sparta.

Motivation

So what is it that separates those who achieve stellar wealth from those who do not? Do they want it more? Do they have inside knowledge? Are they naturally motivated? Or is it something else?

Some people think that if they just work everything out and make a logical case for action, then action will occur. But it's not what we know - it's what we feel about what we know that really makes the difference. We think that we need to understand logically before things will work out. The fact is that we don't act on logic but on emotion. The English word *emotion* derives from Latin *emovere*, where *e-* means 'out' and *movere* means 'move.' Thus emotion and feelings, not logic, are what make us move out and take action. In fact the word *emotion* derives from the verb '*move*' which means 'agitate, stir up'. If lower animals were capable of logic, then the processionary caterpillars would have broken rank for a moment to eat the pine needles and save themselves from starvation. Similarly, logic told Philip of Macedon that his army was far larger than Sparta's (and his vision too ambitious) to turn back, regardless of the Spartan's laconic repost. But he still didn't attack.

Logic will not change an emotion as an internal motivator but action will. The same is true of external motivation. People sit around waiting to be motivated to action. They think that if only they could get motivated by something or someone, they would spring into action and everything would fall into place. Waiting for external motivation is as hit-and-miss as waiting to feel "in the mood." Sure, taking action is easy when you feel like it. But what happens when you don't feel like it? Do it anyway.

In my experience of wealth creation and my research on the super-rich, the one characteristic that stands out is the willingness to adhere to the 4th Law of Wealth, come what may. Successful people will execute *whether they feel like it or not.* They will execute whether it's *logical* or *rational* or not. They will execute whether they are motivated to do so or not. They are subserviante to how they feel. If they need to, they will force themselves to do what needs to be done. They have gained such personal control that mood, feelings, logic, or motivation are irrelevant to action. They simply adhere to a higher personal standard of operation than the average person, and act based on decision.

Sir Alex Ferguson once said, "David Beckham is Britain's finest striker of a football not because of a God-given talent but because he practices with a relentless application that the vast majority of less gifted players wouldn't contemplate." Daley Thompson, Olympic Gold Medal Winner in Decathlon once said, "I trained every single day, including Christmas Day, in order to achieve what I wanted. I never wanted to leave any stone unturned."

Do you think he wanted to train on Christmas Day in the freezing cold, while everyone else was busy unwrapping presents and eating turkey? Probably not, but he wanted Olympic Gold more, and he took the action necessary to ensure that he did everything in his power to secure it.

You can't sit back and wait for the feeling to arrive. You can't wait for the external motivation to present itself. What if it doesn't show up? You must act. Define your target and take action.

An acre of performance is worth a whole world of promise.
William Dean Howells

Did you know that emotion is a two-way system? Science has discovered that we feel emotion as a result of events, but we can also create events or take action that will generate the emotion. Every emotion has a chemical and physical signature in the body. For example, everyone knows what depressed looks like. There are neurological attributes of depression that trigger the physical signals and tell the body to be depressed. If you hunch your shoulders, look down, breathe shallowly and frown, it's actually very hard to feel happy.

But if you change your physiology and look up, smile, and breathe deeply, it's very hard to feel depressed. In fact do we smile because we're happy, or are we happy because we smile?

Your emotion is affected by your physiology. Even if you don't feel like going to the gym but you force yourself to go, your body will soon create the chemical signals required to do your workout. In other words if you "just do it," you will start to feel like doing it. And the internal motivation you crave will arrive in spades.

Knowledge is Overrated

Most people have heard Francis Bacon's immortal words "knowledge is power," but it's at best an unfinished sentence. Perhaps Bacon was interrupted before he finished - because knowledge by itself is only *potential* power. The only way to realize that power is to use action. A more accurate statement would therefore be "*applied* knowledge is power."

The great end of life is not knowledge but action.
T H Huxley

Knowledge on its own is not what we thought it would be. If it were, then university professors would be making the seven-figure salaries that many deserve. Those with the most education would be the wealthiest, and yet if you look at the Rich Lists of the world, much of the world's wealth is held by people who didn't even finish school or who dropped out of college to pursue a business career. Knowledge alone is never the key to wealth.

The new economy and technological advancement has allowed the dissemination of knowledge and information in a way never before possible. The opportunities thus created, however, are as dependent as ever on the implementation of this law, this truth will not change or alter.

Regardless of the available knowledge or your ability to access it, knowledge only offers potential power, and its promises are realized only when you *do* something with it.

We have all met people with three academic degrees and entire alphabets after their name - and that are dead broke. You know the kind of people I'm referring to. Don't get me wrong: getting informed is absolutely crucial. When I first ventured into property development, I had to learn what to do and how to make it work. Gathering information and knowledge was a crucial part of that process, but none of it would have been worth a anything if I hadn't bought my first property.

Intelligence and logic are no match for courage, boldness and persistence. Gathering excessive information is usually a defense mechanism, a way to remove uncertainty. But in the end, nothing removes uncertainty better than experience. And experience is not the result of adequate knowledge; it is the result of adequate action. You don't have to know everything. Just get *enough* knowledge - and get into action.

What we think, or what we know,
or what we believe is, in the end, of little consequences
The only consequence is what we do.
John Ruskin

How to Master Law 4 - and Always Execute:

- Develop courage, boldness, audacity and persistence
- Just do it!
- Ask and ye shall receive
- Continuous action
- Monitor results

Develop Courage, Boldness, Audacity and Persistence

When it comes to courage, boldness and audacity, I think of Christopher Columbus. The son of a middle-class wool weaver, Columbus went down in history as the first European explorer to finally bring the Old and New Worlds together.

But it wasn't all smooth sailing for Columbus. He first proposed his plans to John II, King of Portugal, in 1485. He suggested the king equip him with three sturdy ships and give him a year to explore. He also wanted to be made "Great Admiral of the Ocean" be appointed governor of any lands he discovered and be given one-tenth of all the revenue derived from those lands. This was a bold and audacious request, by anyone's standards.

The king took the matter under advisement, but his experts rejected it because they felt Columbus's estimates were wrong. But he didn't give up.

Three years later, he approached the court of Portugal and was rejected again. He went to Genoa and Venice but got no support. He even had his brother sound out Henry VII of England. He was looking to raise cash.

However, on the first of May, 1486, Columbus was granted an audience with monarchs Ferdinand II of Aragon and Isabella I of Castile. Advisors again stated that Columbus's estimations of travel were inaccurate and the proposal was rejected. Again Columbus did not give up; he continually lobbied at the Spanish court until finally Ferdinand intervened and his plan was accepted.

If we did all the things we are capable
of doing we would literally astonish ourselves.
Thomas Edison

Columbus was made "Admiral of the Seas" and would receive a portion of all profits. He'd shown courage, boldness, audacity and persistence - and he got what he wanted. The terms of his agreement were unusually generous because the king and queen did not expect him to return. It took seven long years for Columbus to bring his dream to fruition, and he went on to be one of the first great European explorers of the Americas.

In a similar vein, the most successful people I've met and observed have been those who have gone against the grain with a certain amount of audacity.

The qualities of courage, boldness, audacity and persistence don't arrive at birth; they arrive with practice. No one is born bold. We are made bold by taking bold action and making brave choices. No one is born timid. We are made timid by not taking bold action and by making timid choices.

Columbus was the son of a wool weaver and part time cheese seller and yet his modest origins didn't keep him from having grand plans and wanting to be Admiral of the Seas. He demanded to be treated with respect, and so he was.

You have to believe in yourself before anyone else ever will believe in you. This is especially true in business. Managing perceptions and presenting the right image are essential to success. You need to look the part and display courage, regardless of whether you feel courageous or not. Courage and boldness are like a muscle - you just need to use them, and they will grow. Start small, make little changes, act a little more bold, and you'll soon develop boldness as a natural trait.

Boldness in business is the first, second and third thing.
H G Bohn British Publisher

When Sir Tom Hunter, founder of Sports Division and later Private Equity firm West Coast Capital, was a boy, he worked in his father's shop. Later, when Sir Tom was at college, sort of "bumbling along," he would come home occasionally and help his Father sell shoes from a market stall. He noticed from the sales figures that trainers were the big seller. Meanwhile, he'd graduated from college, and no one would give him a job. But these trainers kept nagging at him. So he had some letterhead made up with "Super Shoe" emblazoned at the top. He wrote to existing retailers to tell them that he was a fast expanding footwear company and asked if the retailers had any space in their stores for his shoes. One retailer replied, and after a meeting in North of England, they agreed.

Sir Tom told me when we met, "I remember going back home and telling my Father, "There's good news and bad news. Good news, they said yes. Bad news - I have no idea what I'm doing." At the time, he was 23 years old, had no money, and was living at home with his parents in a small village in Scotland. What he did have was courage, boldness, audacity and persistence in spades.

Fourteen years later, Sir Tom Hunter sold the business he started on that day, to JJB Sports for $467 million. At the time, the business was bringing in almost $570 million. He employed 7,500 people and was making over $56 million in annual profits. Sir Tom Hunter was only 37 years old.

Nothing great is ever achieved without courage, boldness, audacity and persistence.

When David Haye was scheduled to fight Russian Nikolai Valuev in Nuremberg, Germany, it was dubbed the "David vs. Goliath" fight. David was 6'5", weighed 215, and had an 81-inch reach. His Goliath, Valuev, was a towering 7'2" tall, weighed 322, and had an 88-inch reach. Each had lost only one fight, but Valuev had won 50 to Haye's 22. Four times as much money was bet on Valuev than Haye. The odds and the statistics were heavily stacked against him. November 7, 2009, David Haye beat "The Beast from The East" to become the first British heavyweight champion since Lennox Lewis.

Courage is the first of human quaities because it is the quality which guarantees all the others.
Winston Churchill

One of the most famous boxing victories of all time was the "Rumble in the Jungle," when, on Oct. 30, 1974, Muhammad Ali regained the world heavyweight crown from George Foreman in Zaire. In another demonstration of boldness and audacity, Don King convinced both boxers to fight for $5 million each - but he didn't have the money. He sought an outside country to sponsor the event. Zaire's flamboyant president Mobuto Sese Seko put Zaire forward, and the rest is history. Ali, a man known for his bold super-self-confidence, regained his title against the odds - and against a younger, stronger Foreman.

Courage and boldness are not just reserved for the boxing ring. When Gillian Ramsay, a confectionary maker on the tiny island of Lerwick off the coast of Scotland, was contacted by Asda to tell her she couldn't call her chocolate nuggets "Puffin Poo" anymore, most people would have thought the war was over. Asda, after all, is a part of Wal-Mart - a multi-billion- dollar global company.

Life shrinks or expands in proportion to one's courage.
Anais Nin

Asda claimed it owned the name "Puffin" because it held a trademark for its Puffin brand of biscuits. In another example of a David and Goliath battle, Gillian went to court and represented herself against Asda's expensive legal team...and won! She acted with courage, boldness and audacity. She stood up for what she believed in, and after the case, she said, "I'm delighted - they listened to me and saw through Asda's legal jargon."

Just Do It!

The law of diminishing intent says that if you decide to take action or you know that there is something that you have to do, the longer you put it off, the less chance there is of achieving it. The hesitation weakens your resolve and makes it far less likely that you will follow through. It is the law of diminishing intent that leaves houses half renovated all across the country. If you move into a new home, statistics show that unless you make the renovations you envisage within six months, it's very likely you'll never make them. It's the same law that results in exercise equipment gathering dust in the top of the closet. Unless you use it immediately, as soon as it arrives, the chances of your ever using it diminish with every passing moment.

In the dim background of our mind,
we know what we ought to be doing but somehow we cannot start.
William James

As soon as you know what you have to do - take immediate action. If you don't, then your mind gets used to thinking it's going to be like all the other times you had a good idea and nothing happened. Whatever it is you need to do - don't put it off; follow Nike's immortal advice and "Just do it!"

Even when things look too big and too daunting, more information is not going to help. Action is the only cure. Instead of sitting back and saying "I'll never start" or "I don't know where to begin"...just begin. Sometimes it's best not to know what's ahead. Sometimes it's best just to start and resolve to continue. It's like the question "how do you eat an elephant?" Start at the bottom, take little bites - and don't look up.

There comes a point in all great adventures where you just have to start, and after you start, you have to keep going. A friend of mine climbed Kilimanjaro for charity. It is 19,340 ft high - the largest freestanding mountain in the world. The group needed four days just to get to base camp. They set off for the summit at midnight - illuminated only by moonlight (and a head-torch.). There are several reasons for this, the main one being that the climbers reach the summit at sunrise, which adds to the majesty of the experience. The other reason, according to my friend, is that you can't see what's ahead. If you could, you would simply turn back. Instead because she couldn't really see that far in front, she simply kept putting one foot in front of the other. She followed her guide's advice and kept moving, thinking "pole, pole" or "slowly, slowly". She kept walking beyond the point when her water froze, her breathing hurt, and her mouth was bleeding. Seven hours later, she, along with a few others, arrived at the summit.

Whatever you dream of, you must first start. Goethe said it best when he wrote, "Whatever you can do, or dream you can, begin it. Boldness has genius, power, and magic in it!"

You've probably heard of Goethe's famous quote above, but this is only a piece of the wisdom he imparted. Here's the rest: *"Until one is committed, there is hesitancy, the chance to draw back, always ineffectiveness. Concerning all acts of initiative and creation, there is one elementary truth, the ignorance of which kills countless ideas and splendid plans: that the moment one definitely commits oneself, then Providence moves too. All sorts of things occur to help one that would never otherwise have occurred. A whole stream of events issue from the decision, raising in one's favor all manner of unforeseen incidents and meetings and material assistance which no man could have dreamed would have come his way. Whatever you can do, or dream you can, begin it. Boldness has genius, power, and magic in it."*

There are those that say that the "magic" Goethe refers to is some sort of mysterious serendipity that conspires to help you reach your goal. It's as though the world is waiting for you to show up and take a stand and when you do, it joins with you to ease your route. But only once you have taken action.

Perhaps it's not serendipity at all, perhaps it's just the law of averages taking effect, and you simply notice the results because they meet your needs so perfectly. Whatever it is, there is no doubt that when we take action in the direction of a major purpose, things happen to help that process.

Napoleon Hill coined the term "definite major purpose" when he wrote "truly thoughts are things, and powerful things at that, when they are mixed with definiteness of purpose, persistence, and a burning desire for their translation into riches, or other material objects."

Knowing what you want and focusing all your available energy on that target is essential for success. The alternatives are either a vague notion of what you want or too many targets - neither of which works. If you can't see what you are trying to hit, the attainment of that goal comes down to luck and chance. If you want too many disparate things, then you split your focus and dilute your energy pursuing too many goals.

Purposeful action is key. Sometimes action requires a leap of faith; we're not fully sure of the outcome, but we accept that the status quo is untenable, so we jump anyway. In *Raiders of the Lost Ark*, Indiana Jones' father has been shot, and the only way to save him is to recover the Holy Grail and give him some water from the fountain of eternal life.

Navigating the various perils in his way, he comes to a ravine with no bridge or visible path. He is in that moment called to take a leap of faith and step out into nothing. Of course, the nothingness is an optical illusion, and once he steps out, the bridge beneath him becomes visible. Achieving anything worthwhile in life usually requires us to take that leap of faith, muster all our courage, and take action with boldness, audacity and persistence.

Ask and Ye Shall Receive

The Bible says, "Ask and ye shall receive" - and yet so few people are actually prepared to ask for what they want. Everyone knows the sentiment and can paraphrase the saying, but few people do it. It's also worth noting for the record that the statement is not "Complain and ye shall receive". You have to ask tactfully and intelligently.

There are five things you have to bear in mind if your asking is to be successful.

1. **Be precise.** You have to be clear about what it is you are asking for. Don't allow other people to fill in the gaps. Be clear, concise and precise in your requests. That way people are not left confused by your request and are far more likely to grant your wish or reject it quickly, so that you can re-negotiate. Being vague delivers vague results.

2. **Ask the right people.** Always ask people who have the ability to help you. There is no point asking someone for something they can't give you. Far too many would-be entrepreneurs, for example, ask their family and friends for money rather than asking a financier.

3. **Reciprocate**. If you are asking someone for something or for some help, then work out how you can make it worthwhile for that person. Find something that you can give in return that is of value to that person, and you stand a far higher chance of success. Make it as easy as possible for the person to give you what you want.

4. **Ask with conviction.** You have to believe that you will get what you are asking for; otherwise, there is no point asking for it. If you don't believe that you will be successful and that you deserve what you are asking for, then how can you ever convince someone else of that fact? Your lack of faith will alter your attitude, preparation, and the request itself, making success virtually impossible. So ask with boldness, confidence and conviction - even if you have to fake it for a while.

5. **Ask continually.** Asking for something is not a one-off event. If you listen to kids asking for something, you notice that they don't ask once and then stop. They are incessant. This approach can be extremely tedious for a tired parent, but kids use it because it works. It's only after we've been told it's rude or that "'I want' gets nothing" so many times we stop asking. You have to keep asking. Not in the same way and perhaps not for the same things - but keep asking. And don't take "No" as the end of the conversation. See it as nothing more than an opportunity to renegotiate.

It's difficult to say why we are so poor at asking for what we want. There are certainly countries and cultures that are better at it than others. In the UK and China, we are not that great. In China the issue is probably the culture, which sees the group as more important than the individual. Individual wants and needs are in many ways secondary to the health of the society, the economy or the company. In the UK, asking for what we want and being forthright about it is often seen as rude.

In the US things are very different. The entrepreneurial spirit is practically written into the Constitution. It is much more acceptable to take a shot and see what happens, to fly by the seat of your pants and ask for whatever you need.

There is undoubtedly a conditioning element at work when it comes to asking for what you want. It has been estimated that the average one-year-old child hears the word "no" or "don't" two hundred times a day. Even if we assume that this is the height of negativity, over the course of an entire childhood, the average boy or girl must hear these phrases hundreds or thousands of times. In effect, we get so used to being told "no" that we stop asking.

In parts of the world where they are used for transport and construction, elephant's are trained from a very young age. While still a baby, the elephant has a rope tied to his back leg with the other end secured to a stake in the ground or large tree. The baby will tug and pull and struggle to escape for weeks, maybe even months, until finally it gives up and stays put. What the baby doesn't realize, however, is that as it grows up, its strength multiplies exponentially, until as an adult it could pull the tree completely out of the ground. By then, the elephant doesn't believe escape is possible, and so it never struggles again. As an adult, the elephant could have a noodle tied to its back leg and it wouldn't go anywhere, such is the power of its early conditioning.

The same is true of people. We get knocked back once or twice; we take it personally, and soon we stop asking for what we want.

Most people have heard of OPM (Other People's Money) in the context of wealth creation, but there is a similar, although less known acronym that is every bit as essential for success and getting what you want in life - OYM. If you are serious about making more money and achieving that desired outcome, then you'd better learn how to Open Your Mouth.

It doesn't mean you have to become a gifted speaker or great communicator (or a pest); it just means you have to be clear, succinct and persistent in asking for what you want. Don't sell yourself short. Be brave and remember no one ever died from rejection. If someone says "no," then ask someone else or re-think your request until you get the "yes" you need.

Nothing can be achieved without asking others for various things along the way - so don't forget to Open Your Mouth.

Continuous Action

Once you make the decision to take action, you have to do it continually. Taking action and going hell-for-leather for a month or two and then stopping…is as pointless as never starting. If you begin and pull back, you will create a pattern in your mind of inconsistency and weakness. You wouldn't go to the gym twice a day for a month, get all buffed up and toned and then stop and expect the results to last. Janet Jackson may indeed be able to re-discover her washboard abs after some heavy duty effort in the gym, but a quick flick through the celeb magazines in a dentist's waiting room or at the checkout of the supermarket will demonstrate only too graphically that extreme action followed by inertia delivers poor results. The results you get in any area of your life will always faithfully reflect what consistent action or inaction you have taken over time.

In the final analysis, sporadic action is as useless as no action at all. At least if you never even try you can comfort yourself with the delusion that you "coulda been a contender." If you are serious about making major amounts of money, then you have to embark on a whole new way of life. The 4th Law of Wealth is not something you can tap into when you fancy it, or when the mood takes you or you have nothing better to do. It has to become a constant companion.

Once you start, you don't stop, and never take your foot off the accelerator either. I've seen this happen time and again. Colleagues have set lofty goals and financial aspirations, formed a plan, and taken action toward the goal. Many of them succeed beyond their wildest expectations. All too often, this first flush of success is accompanied by an expanded ego. They start to believe that their success is due to some personal genius, rather than the predictable result of the consistent action they took. Invariably, they begin to take their foot off the gas, move to the back seat, and effectively stop doing the very thing that made them successful in the first place. Law 4 is never a destination; it's an on-going process.

Monitor Results

Success is usually the result of good judgement and process of trial and error. In my own life the result I achieved was often not what I expected. At no point have I ever considered myself "successful" because the process has often felt more like "failing forward." If you imagine a set of stairs toward your goal - you will often "fall up the stairs."

Even when the results have not worked out as I hoped, I have never failed to produce something. Granted, sometimes what I produced was not what I hoped to produce, but the process always taught me something and took me forward. You have to accept failure as part of the learning process - and fail forward as quickly as possible. Fast failures always lead to fast learning and fast learning means more distinctions that will help you judge the next move.

One of the reasons people resist this law so strongly is because they are afraid of failure. But the best and only remedy for fear is direct action. Failure occurs only when you stop taking the initiative. Everything else is just feedback that enables you to alter your approach.

You don't drown by falling in the water.
You drown by staying in there.
Edwin Louis Cole

If you have taken the first three laws to heart, then you will have Gained Control and taken responsibility for where you are, you will have Embraced the Future and come up with a Strategy to take you to that outcome. By following Law 4, you will work that strategy and Always Execute. However, that doesn't mean blindly taking action without feedback. It means that you take conscious, deliberate action while being observant and adaptive in your approach. You monitor the results you achieve, fine-tune your action, and persevere until you hit your target.

What To Expect If You Fail To Always Execute:

- Nothing will change
- Your confidence will spiral downward

Nothing Will Change

I can't really say it any clearer than that - if you do nothing, then nothing will change. And for the record, nothing much will change when you stop executing either. Action has momentum in it; that's why this law is "*always execute*." Occasional execution will be about as useful as no execution at all. Unless you are committed to Law 4 and moving forward, then your efforts willcome to nothing.

Your Confidence Will Spiral Downwards

If you are a dreamer - always coming up with exciting plans for how you will make your fortune but never actually implementing anything - then eventually you will create a pattern where ideas are followed by inaction.

It's as if you had a friend who's always telling you about what they are going to do but they never get off the couch. Eventually all your confidence in that person would evaporate. It wouldn't matter what they said - you wouldn't believe it. If that person made plans with you to go somewhere, you wouldn't get ready because you'd have learned from experience that they won't show up. The same will happen to you if you continually make plans and promises to yourself without following through. In this case it's your confidence in yourself that will spiral downwards.

You can see this happen with attendees at personal development programs. Some of these courses have really great information. But...the problem is that people leave all hyped up about how they are going to change their life. They rush back to family and friends to tell them of their new found enthusiasm for life and the adventures ahead. But family and friends are notorious party-poopers. They know that after the attendee blabs about their new plans...nothing happens. No new action is actually taken because in the razzmatazz of the seminar, the individual didn't really take that much notice of the "how to" information (if there was any).

Days and weeks pass, and nothing changes at all. Once-cynical family and friends are now laughing. Before long, the enthusiastic seminar attendee is dejected and despondent about the future, having lost confidence in their ability to execute. Taking action builds confidence - even if it doesn't always work out the first time, the act of doing is always good for the individual.

What You Can Confidently Expect If You Always Execute:

- Progress
- Increased confidence
- Expanded perspective
- People will seek you out

Progress

You will never know if you have Gained Control, Embraced the Future and Owned a Strategy - unless you get into action. Action is the measuring stick of how successfully you've been able to adhere to Laws 1, 2 and 3, because action makes things happen. Things change when you take action. Sure, they may not always change in the way you wanted, and the outcomes may not be quite as you had envisaged or expected, but progress and movement are inevitable.

It isn't possible to Always Execute and have nothing happen. Progress is a natural consequence of action.

Once you are in action, you can monitor what's happening; you thus have the power and control to alter the process and fine-tune your behavior.

Without feedback from action, you can re-think your plans till you get a headache, but you won't know the consequence of those musings until you actually do something about them. Execution can be terrifying - especially at the start, when you just don't know what will happen. But it's also exciting, because you begin to see your ideas and plans come alive before your eyes.

Increased Confidence

Once you have moved into action and taken a few chances, your confidence will soar. If your action works out well, and you begin to see the fruits of your labor, then you'll feel more motivated and inspired to continue. You'll come to realize the irony of thought versus action. We can so easily build things up in our mind to the point where we're terrified of what we must do - and yet if we just find the courage to do that thing, we invariably realize that it is far easier and less intimidating than we ever imagined.

This was my exact experience when I was first asked to sell. Our neighbor had a market stall and asked if I wanted to work for him on weekends. I was 14 years old. I started at 4:00 a.m. and didn't finish until 7:00 p.m., but I loved it. I would help set up the stall sell household goods and then pack things away at the end of the day.

One weekend my boss told me that the following weekend I was going to have to go to the middle of the market and sell. I was petrified. I'd seen the sellers at work, standing in a crowd of strangers hawking their wares. I felt physically sick. I don't think I thought of anything else that week, and by the time Saturday rolled around, you may as well have asked me to slay a dragon with a butter knife. I was scared. But I needed the job, so I just did it. I didn't love it, and it wasn't easy to start with, but it was nowhere near as terrible as I'd imagined it would be. I survived, and by the end of the day I was exhilarated. Just doing something I thought impossible filled me with confidence, and I got better and better at it. I never loved it, but I improved and always sold more than the other employees.

Even if you get into action and it doesn't work out right away, or the wheels fall off in a major way and you're thrown into panic. In the heat of battle, you will find a solution and begin to make progress again. In fact, experiencing difficult situations and finding a way through will dramatically increase your confidence. Once you've had a few disasters, you realize that life always goes on, and you will be able to access inner resources that you didn't even know you had.

"The truth is that our finest moments are likely to occur when we are
feeling deeply uncomfortable, unhappy or unfulfilled.
For it is only in such moments, propelled by our own discomfort,
that we are likely to step out of our ruts and start
searching for different ways or truer answers."
M. Scott Peck

The outcome of the action is therefore almost irrelevant. The mere fact that you did it, survived it and took another important step toward your target will inspire you with confidence and pride - and that is always a great outcome.

Expanded Perspective

One of the standard, although controversial techniques in therapy is to force someone to do something they never thought possible. A therapist who has a seriously shy client may engineer a situation where that person's shyness is tested to the absolute limits - singing in front of an audience, for instance. You can sometimes see this approach on TV shows like *Spendaholics*, which tries to help those who are drowning in personal debt. Finance specialists and psychologists enable people get to the bottom of their spending and take control of their lives again. In one episode, a man was taken to a comedy club and asked to do a set.

The man was distraught. He was extremely upset and stormed off. Eventually he did calm down and returned to the club, where he was coached through his feelings, and he did the set. The sheer elation and shock that he experienced afterwards was mesmerizing. He was literally a changed person because his understanding of what he was capable of was irrevocably altered, and in that moment he had a greatly expanded perspective on who he was and what he could achieve in his life.

The same is true for any of us when we face our fears and take action. I experienced it first when I was asked to sell from the market stall and many times after. It's an incredibly liberating thing to do.

People Will Seek You Out

The world is full of talkers, but those who can actually translate that talk into quantifiable action are surprisingly rare - perhaps that's another reason why super rich people are few and far between.

If you are going to make significant money, you have to take radical action. If you do, you will get results. Those results will stand out like neon signs, and people will seek you out. It may not be that they will seek you out for reasons of mutual benefit that will fit into your plans and help you toward your goals. But you will stand out and be noticed because you take action.

Action is inspiring and impressive just because it is so rare. Too many people think that the world owes them a living and they should be paid for showing up. Action breeds confidence. Inaction breeds timidity, fear and despondency. Which would you prefer?

Never retreat. Never explain. Get it done and let them howl.
Benjamin Jowett

William Boetcker once said, "The individual activity of one man with backbone will do more than a 1,000 men with a mere wishbone." This is what "Always Execute" requires - developing a backbone and getting into action toward your outcome. There is always a price to pay for any reward in life. If you are unwilling to pay that price, then don't complain about it and enjoy the life you have. But if you're willing to pay that price and create the life you want, then always let your actions speak louder than your words.

Mastering this law can be a real challenge. Perhaps it's because we live in an instant world - everything from instant noodles to instant communication to instant success. We have been taught by the media and credit card companies that we can have whatever we want, whenever we want it. But it's simply not true. Expecting success without any effort is a violation of the 7Laws and will deliver nothing lasting or worthwile.

As I said earlier, we overestimate what we can achieve in a year and grossly underestimate what we can achieve in a decade. If you internalise Law 4, there is no end to what you can accomplish. You won't always achieve what you set out to, but if you Always Execute, you can't help but create. When I try to achieve something, I manage to hit the target only about 60% of the time - the rest of the time, the actions I take often move me in new directions I hadn't even considered. Sometimes they don't pan out, and sometimes they end up being better than I could have ever imagined.

The world is moving so fast that the man who says it can't be done is usually interrupted by the man who is already doing it. Peter Ustinov once said, "If the world should blow itself up, the last audible voice would be that of an expert saying it can't be done!" Forget the past. Seize the future and make it yours. Act, never be acted upon.

Are You Aligned to Law 4 - Do You Always Execute?

Below there are 7 sets of two statements - 1A/1B-7A/7B. As before, read each pair of statements and check the one that's mostly true for you. On balance, which one more accurately reflects your opinions and your view of life? The choice won't always be easy, but pick the one that best matches you.

Be honest. No one need see this. If you don't want to write in the book or want to keep your selections private, then make the selections in a separate notebook. Don't mark what you wish you were like or hope to be like in the future. Answer as you are right now. If you are unsure, then ask someone you know and trust to give you feedback.

	A	B
1	☐ I'm pretty good at making plans, and I usually follow through on those plans.	I have plans coming out my ears - I just don't follow through on many. ☐
2	☐ If I start a project, I finish it.	I'm definitely a better starter than I am a finisher. ☐
3	☐ I play a sport or go to the gym regularly and have done so for years.	I have joined the gym about three times in my life and usually go a few times and cancel. ☐
4	☐ I believe that you should do what you say you are going to do, and do it when you say you're going to do it - regardless of what pops up in the interim.	I believe that you can't commit too much to anything these days because there is so much choice and things change too often. ☐
5	☐ I strongly believe that fortune favors the bold.	I think it's smarter to be safe than sorry. ☐
6	☐ I have no problem asking for what I need. It's an important skill to be able to articulate what you need and ask for it.	I hate asking anyone for anything. I feel awkward. I feel that I'll owe the person something, and I don't like owing anyone anything. ☐
7	☐ Planning and action are equally important - you need to assess results and fine-tune your approach for the best outcome.	I prefer the planning stage to the doing stage. ☐

If you have checked five or more of the statements in the A Column, then you already have a good grasp of Law 4. If you have checked three or more statements in the B Column, then we suggest you read the supplementary guidebook; ***Law4 - Always Execute: Applications and Insights.*** This companion guide will give you further information about Law 4, together with practical techniques, ideas and insights into how you can successfully align yourself to this law and harness its power.

Law 5

Create Value

Service to the Many is the Key to Riches; Profit to the Giver is the Consequential Effect

If you feel that your rewards are unjust, begin your efforts to rectifying the situation by examining the service you are rendering and especially the spirit in which you are rendering it. Great enterprise is built not on deception and manipulation, but on providing goods and services that create more value for customers than what they pay in return. The true measure of a business is not the number of customers it has, but the number of people it serves.

Chapter Seven
Law 5 - Create Value

In Greek mythology, Daedalus was a skilful architect and innovator. He created the labyrinth, where the Minotaur was kept. To prevent the secrets of the labyrinth from spreading to the public, King Minos had Daedalus and his son Icarus imprisoned in a tower. Even if he managed to escape, Daedalus couldn't leave Crete by sea because the king kept strict watch on all ships, insisting they were thoroughly searched before departure. The land was watched by countless spies, so Daedalus deduced that the only possible way to escape was by air. He constructed a set of wings to mimic the wings of a bird. The largest feathers were secured by thread and the smaller ones by wax. When he was finished, he was able to flap his new wings and found that he lifted off the ground.

Excited, he made a duplicate set for his son Icarus. Before they set off to freedom, Daedalus warned his son not to fly too high because the heat from the sun would melt the wax, and he would fall into the sea and drown. He was also warned not to fly too close to the sea because the spray and foam would make the wings wet and they would no longer work.

They successfully flew past Samos, Delos and Lebynthos, but then Icarus became over-confident and began to fly upwards, as if to reach heaven. As predicted, the blazing heat melted the wax in the wings, and he fell into the sea and drowned.

Apart from demonstrating how children rarely listen to their parents - sometimes with disastrous consequences - the story also demonstrates the idea we explored in "Mastering the Context." The world is governed by natural laws that simply can not be violated. These are cause and effect relationships that do not vary. Icarus wasn't unlucky to fall to his death - his fate was the inevitable consequence of his actions.

You must Give before you can Receive

In the same way, your wealth is the inevitable consequence of your actions. You *can't* make money without adhering to the Fifth Law of Wealth. Business sustainability requires that you create value and be of service.

Your rewards in life will always match your effforts. If you have a religious background, you may have heard this idea expressed as "As ye sow, so shall ye reap." Most people have come across this notion before in some form or another. They'll even agree with it and tell you how it makes sense - and yet very few people actually take it to heart and grasp the enormity of its application and implication. Law 5 is not something you can pick up and put down when you feel like it. It doesn't apply occasionally. It is an all-encompassing law of the world we live in.

Everything you think, do, or fail to do either adds value or diminishes value. As with the scales of justice, there is a balance between two factors.

On one side is all that you are, think and do - the value you add. On the other side is the reward you receive for that value. The more value you add to the scales of wealth creation, the more reward you or your business will receive.

If you do not feel that life is rewarding you well enough - then you are likely not creating enough value. Your rewards are in direct correlation to the amount of value you create and the service you deliver to others.

Somewhere along the line, too many of us have stopped appreciating the truth of this law and decided instead that we should *get* before we *give*. That we want to reap a bountiful harvest without sowing a single seed. We have all met people like these - they want the promotion before they make any effort. They don't see the point of working hard unless they get a raise. They want the rewards before they add value. But natural laws do not operate this way. You wouldn't sit in front of a fireplace and expect it to keep you warm without adding wood and setting it alight.

Yet all too often people expect to make money without adding value and being of service to others. They don't realize that by working and Creating Value first, they reach a stage where they qualify for the desired result or outcome. Why would someone give you a promotion for being lazy? Why would you get a raise if all you did was the bare minimum? Why would your customers buy from you instead of your competition if you were always late or rude? Why would they come back to your business if their experience was not positive and you didn't make their life easier or better in some way?

They wouldn't.

Amazingly, there are now families in the UK and US who haven't worked for two or three generations! That means that not a single member of the household has held down a job or created any value to the marketplace. Instead they live on state handouts. They complain that they don't get enough, and yet they offer no service and add no value to society or the community they live in.

Adding value and being of service are not just about making money; they're about developing healthy self-esteem. There is something innately satisfying about doing a hard day's work, of knowing that you've done the best you can and that your contribution has made a difference.

Whether you are an employee or a business owner - or whether you're just starting out to make your fortune - you have to find ways to Create Value. You have to consistantly give before you get. Becoming a millionaire is not an overnight event. If you are serious about it, I can tell you that there will be times you wonder why you bother - when all you seem to meet is brick wall after brick wall. There will be times when you think you are no further forward than you were the year before, and yet you just have to keep on giving and adding value. Your reward will come, enhanced by goodwill and service.

Too many people are caught up in what they can get out of something or someone without giving any thought as to how they can serve others and Create Value. You just have to get used to looking at life from a different perspective. Instead of lamenting that your boss won't promote you, or your customers won't buy from you, change your attitude and actively seek ways to be better at what you do. What could you do *right now* that would make you more valuable in that role? Accept that you may not ever get paid for it; you may never even get thanked for it - just do it anyway. Make it your mission to find ways of making and saving your business more money.

That sort of approach is aligned to the 5th Law, and the outcome will always be inevitable. It may take a few months, it may take longer than you expect, but you will be rewarded for it - even if that reward is that you gain more self-respect and a sense of personal satisfaction. You will be a different person because of the experience, and that can lead to all sorts of new and exciting opportunities.

To paraphrase John F. Kennedy, "Ask not what others can do for you; ask what you can do for others." Whatever you seek in terms of rewards you must first earn in the form of service to others. All efforts to reverse this law will meet with absolute failure. Icarus found out the hard way that you can't violate a natural law, and he paid the ultimate price. If you truly want to create serious money in your business, then you must Create Value and be of service to others; *otherwise, you too may find yourself dead in the water.*

All your effort to circumvent this law will be useless. You would be far better embracing Law 5 and re-directing that effort toward making it work for you.

We Are All Born Equal

Consider that we are all born with an imaginary plot of land. There is nothing on it, it's completely barren. You have several options. First, you can ignore it and let it run wild with weeds. It will end up being a completely useless piece of land. You can sit on the sidelines and complain about the fact that there is nothing to eat and that other people's plots are bursting with vegetables and a few have even struck gold. Or you can get up and start sowing.

You will only be able to reap what you first sow. This requires effort and activity. So ask yourself: what do people need? What could you grow on your plot that other people are prepared to pay for? Have you taken a shovel and dug a little deeper to see what value may be hidden from view?

There is a great story of a minister driving by a beautiful farm. He decides to compliment the farmer, who's busy tending his crops. As he approaches the immaculate driveway, he stops at the yard; the buildings are clean and freshly painted. The farmer sees him approach and stops his work. The minister gets out of his car and walks over to the farmer, "God has blessed you with a beautiful farm." To which the farmer replies, "Yes, He has, and I'm grateful, but you should have seen it when He had it all to Himself."

The farmer knew that his farm was beautiful and bountiful because he worked hard all year round to make it that way. It didn't just fall out the sky like that!

The same is true for all. We each own a potentially beautiful farm more than capable of providing wealth and prosperity, but not by wishing for it or hoping that your lottery numbers will come up each week. You have to make it happen. You have to apply some thought, energy and action to the question of how you can Create Value. Before you can ever expect to receive a reward, you have to take what you have and make it better, then find ways to offer it to others. You can't just pick and choose when you want to do it. It's a lifelong pursuit. Not something you can try out for a week or two. The farmer doesn't stop when the weather is bad. He can't just decide to have a "mental health day" and not feed his livestock. The 5th Law of Wealth never sleeps.

Adding value and providing service is the mindset of all wealthy people; either it's instinctive or they have learned to adopt it. The fastest way to make money is to find out what people want and help them get it. Find out how you can benefit others and how you can deliver value to them, consistently.

because service to the many is the key to riches. Profit to the giver is the natural consequence.

How to Master Law 5 and Create Value:

- Understand what value is
- Understand how value is created
- Find opportunities to Create Value

Understand What Value Is

What you value is without question different from what I value. That makes the 5th Law so powerful. Value is not concrete and definite. It is both tangible and intangible and thus offers infinite opportunities to those wishing to create it.

In essence, value is how much a desired object or condition is worth relative to other objects or conditions. In other words, a product or service is only worth what an individual or company is prepared to pay for it.

Real Estate, for example. A professional appraiser could say the home is worth $500,000, but it's a meaningless number until the exchange is made. That home is actually worth $500,000 only if the owner is willing to sell for that price and a buyer is willing to pay the same to secure it. That's the really exciting thing about value.

What people pay money for is an eternal mystery. The idea and perception of value is as varied from one person to the next. I don't have any interest in stamps or old coins, and yet there are people who would happily chew off their right arm for a truly rare specimen. That's what makes business so exciting. That's what gives life variety.

The development of eBay is a wonderful example of how value can be created. In 1995 an Internet enthusiast Pierre Omidyar thought he'd create an auction site to help his then girlfriend (now wife) find Pez™ dispensers to add to her collection. The first item he put up for sale to test the site was a broken laser pointer, which sold for $14.83. Astonished, Omidyar contacted the winning bidder to make sure he realized that the laser pointer was actually broken. The buyer answered, "I'm a collector of broken laser pointers." In that moment, Omidyar knew he was on to something. Omidyar and his co-founder Jeff Skoll are now billionaires.

eBay is so powerful and successful because you can sell what you own but no longer value for a profit to someone who does value that item. This is an important distinction, because often when we are viewing our own skill-set or figuring out what we can offer the world and where we can Create Value, we ignore things that we take for granted or wrongly assume others wouldn't value.

So whatever you decided in Law 2 that you could use your talents for to make more money, then that is the beginning of creating real value. You'd be truly staggered at what people will happily spend money on.

Perceived value is every bit as important as real or tangible value. In the end, value is only produced when a customer will willingly pay the price you ask. In most cases you add or Create Value in the following ways:

- More - the pursuit of quantity
- Better - the pursuit of quality
- Faster - the pursuit of speed
- Different - the pursuit of innovation
- Cheaper - the pursuit of price

Business at its core offers a way for people to meet their needs in the fastest, shortest time possible. We are always looking for shortcuts. We buy a loaf of bread because for most of us it's faster, cheaper and easier than making it. We hire a lawyer because we don't have the time and money to learn the principles of law ourselves. This drive for speed and advancement means that opportunity is everywhere. You just have to open your eyes to it.

Understand How Value is Created

The purpose of a business is to provide value to customers. If a business can do that, it will make money and be successful, and if it can't, it will not survive. If what you do is not improving someone's life in some way, then you won't make money. Remember, everyone is seeking to meet their six basic human needs, and all buying decisions can be traced back to those needs.

Here are the six:

- to live
- to love and be loved
- to experience variety
- to make a contribution
- to grow
- to feel important

People buy products and services because they hope they will:

- make their life easier
- make their life more fun
- make them healthier
- make them feel loved
- make them feel better about themselves
- make their life happier
- save them time
- save them money

We all want to feel safe, loved, interested and valuable. We want to feel that we are growing and making progress. We want to feel important, so we'll buy all sorts of products and services that promise to deliver those experiences. People listen to the promises and usually buy with their heart - then rationalize the purchase with their head, even when there is no rational explanation!

Botox, is a good example. It contains a natural neurotoxin and is injected into various parts of the face to remove frown lines by paralyzing the facial muscles. Before Botox, Botulism was a form of food poisoning caused by eating something containing a neurotoxin produced by the bacterium *Clostridium botulinum*. Botulism causes paralysis and in some cases can be fatal, however in small doses it relaxes facial muscles. So in effect people knowingly and happily have a deadly substance injected into their face! It's crazy, and yet it's a billion dollar industry because men and woman want to look younger (and thus be loved).

Is that logical, rational, or even very sensible? No, but it doesn't keep people from doing it. The idea at first may have seemed crazy, but surely whoever came up with this ingenious use of a nerve poison was really thinking outside the box when it comes to adding value.

Charles Revson, the founder of Revlon Cosmetics, said, "In our factory we make lipstick; in our advertising, we sell hope." Revson added value by selling hope and created a global brand and a billion dollar company.

So what creates value? Value is created at the intersection of these three circles:

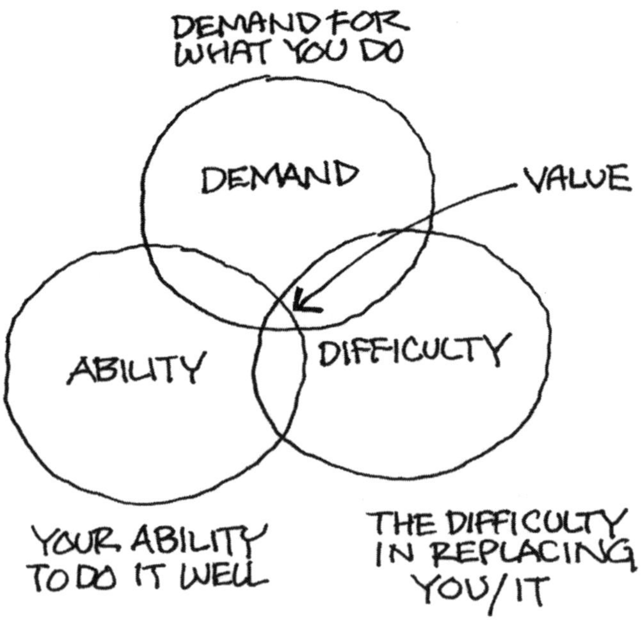

Demand

Value is created when there is demand for what you do. This is distinctly different from *need*, and the two should not be confused. Do we need an iPod to survive? No, but there is a huge demand for them - so huge, in fact, that the humble iPod saved Apple from obscurity. Do we need to inject Botulism into our faces to feel young? No, but there is clearly a huge demand for it. Do we need 500 channels of TV to survive? No, but there is a huge demand for it.

Value can be found wherever there is demand for a product or service, and people are willing to pay much more money for what they want than for what they need. For example, the demand for diamonds is higher than for a glass of water, most people would choose the diamonds (unless they were crawling out the desert on their hands and knees). Yet we don't need diamonds, but we absolutely need water to survive. If you never owned a diamond your entire life, you would survive quite happily, yet you would die within a matter of days if you didn't have access to water. Clearly it is desire and demand, not necessity, that drive value.

So if you want to Create Value and make money, you need to identify your "starving crowd." If I asked you what you needed to make a successful hot dog stand, you might tell me "delicious buns, tasty fresh meat, good quality mustard and tomato ketchup, a good location, nice uniform, and clean stand." All of those things may be relevant if you are to be successful in the hot dog industry. However more than anything else, you need a starving crowd. You need demand.

Ability

The second component of value is your ability to deliver the product or service. Recognizing that the demand for Irish dancing was reaching fever pitch in the 1990s. That demand was only an opportunity if you were a proficient Irish dancer or knew people who were. You couldn't reach that level of proficiency quickly enough to be able to *tap* into the demand.

This is why a realistic self-assessment is such a crucial part of wealth creation. Your first port of call in the quest for the right wealth creation vehicle has to be the knowledge resources and skills you and your team already have. Only when you have exhausted them would you consider starting from scratch, because the learning that would be required to demonstrate sufficiently high ability takes time to attain.

It has been estimated that to be an expert at anything takes about ten thousand hours of practice. If you practice relentlessly at your chosen skill for eight hours a day, seven days a week, it would still take you almost 3½ years to become proficient in that skill. Talent alone is worthless, without the application of that talent and the willingness to put in the time to become an expert. In every field, notably arts and sports, we find that the greatest achievers never rely on skill alone. They practice relentlessly; they put in their ten thousand hours and then some.

In the same way, you have to find your natural abilities and work on them to make them into viable commercial skills.

The other issue to be mindful of when it comes to ability is that often when we are good at something, we assume that everyone is good at it. So if you are struggling to highlight your own talents and abilities, you should ask your colleagues what they think you are especially good at. You may get a powerful insight into what your innate abilities may be.

Difficulty to Replace

The more unique you are or the more unique your product or service is, the more value you can create. This is why people with specialist skills make big money. Soccer stars Wayne Rooney and David Beckham are paid huge amounts of money every week because they are very unique and difficult to replace. Oprah Winfrey makes a great deal of money as a talk show host because she is very difficult to replace. Janitors are not paid very much because the skills they use to do their job are extremely easy to replace. They simply don't add the same perceived value. Once again, emotions rule: in real life, we need janitors much more than we need Oprah.

This can be hard for some people to hear because they assume that it's a value judgement on a person as opposed to an activity. As human beings, there is no value difference between a famous soccer player and a janitor. Each life is as important and valued as the other. Each is loved and cherished by friends and family, and each has the same human rights as the other. However, when it comes to making money, the famous soccer player adds more perceived value, because they can do something that few others can do. That uniqueness of skill is a valuable commodity in the commercial world.

The more unique your product or service, the more value it has. There are plenty of people sitting at home watching their favorite soap opera, lamenting their lack of money. They want more. Yet they are not providing the exchange in value and therefore they are not making more money. It's just a simple equation of cause and effect.

Find Opportunities to Create Value

One of the biggest mistakes businesses make is to benchmark the best companies in their industry and set goals to emulate that performance, only to arrive at that target and find that (a) the best are still way out in front or even farther ahead; or (b) the market no longer wants what they are creating. Sometimes business can be so focused on the competition that they forget to notice what the customer is asking for and how they can add genuine value.

I remember when the CEOs of the Big Three US car manufacturing giants - GM, Ford and Chrysler - flew to Washington D.C. in November 2008 to request a government bailout. They didn't get it. Their cause was not helped by the fact that they travelled to the meeting in a private luxury jet.

The country and much of the world was in recession, but the Big Three's problems were largely self-made and not entirely a product of the economic downturn. They were very late in meeting the quality benchmarks set by the Japanese (who added tremendous value by providing fuel-efficient quality products that didn't break down); by the time GM and the others learned quality, the industry had moved on.

It was the oil crisis that began in 2003 that caused the most damage. Oil prices were escalating which caused customers to turn away from large gas guzzling SUVs and pickup trucks. Demand for their product had changed, the big three had not responded accordingly and got sloppy.

You have to find new ways to Create Value and elevate your product or service above the competition, and often you can't do that effectively if you are too focused on what everyone else has already done in your industry. That can be a great starting point, but it will not deliver the big returns.

Any income you derive is due to the service and value you provide. More service = more money. But before you realize that wealth - and activate the money-making power of creating value - you have to decide how you are going to compete in the marketplace. Money is made when something is sold. That's not rocket science, so whatever you've decided as your wealth creation vehicle from Law 2, you now have to work out how you will compete and make money from that venture. In business, trying to be all things to all people is a recipe for disaster.

There are three ways for any business to sustain a competitive advantage:

- Cost leadership
- Differentiation
- Focus

Cost Leadership

You succeed because of how well you compete on price. You stand out because you are the cheapest or most expensive provider of a product or service.

This is a very risky strategy and one that has only worked for a handful of people. Sam Walton of Wal-Mart became rich using the cost leadership strategy. Tesco is another example of how size can inhibit competition through economies of scale. The reason Wal-Mart and Tesco can sell many of their items at such low prices is that they buy in such huge volumes, and push hard on price. These economies of scale mean that small and medium operators simply can't complete. They don't have the negotiating muscle to drive down the price with the suppliers. Retailers such as Primark have also made a name for themselves for selling clothes and accessories at rock bottom prices. But you have to ask yourself, "How is that possible?"

Business doesn't have to have winners and losers. But when you compete on price and price alone, someone in the supply chain is going to lose out. When suppliers are ground down by powerful bargaining muscle or products are shipped in from factories overseas with questionable work practices, then people do lose out. Remember all the trouble Nike and Gap got into for their sweatshop operations overseas? That sort of exposure can really damage a business, brand or industry.

The other reason cost leadership is a risky strategy is that once you've brought the price down to the lowest point, you not only bring the entire industry down - you now have nowhere to go. Your margins have been crippled, and you soon run out of strategic options.

For example, imagine you were going to have a swimming pool installed in your back yard, and you decided to ask three local contractors to give you a quote. The first contractor came in at $80,000, the second one quoted $75,000, and the third, $35,000. Immediately you'd question why the third contractor could offer such a low price when the first two were pretty similar. You may be tempted to choose on price, especially if the contractors offered a no-questions-asked, money-back guarantee on the quality of their workmanship. But let's say the one contractor that doesn't offer such a guarantee is #3. When faced with this situation, very few people would choose based on price alone, because the risk is simply too high.

Remember that sustainable businesses are usually not so price driven, but value conscious. They understand what customers really want and execute against that standard.
Ben Benson

Although people say they buy based on price, only a certain section of the population actually does. People may tell you that they are not going to buy your product or service because of the price, but their objections usually lie elsewhere. The other reality about the demographic group that does decide purely based on price is that they are usually the hardest people to make happy. It's not always about price. In fact, I'd go so far as to say it's never about price; it's about value, price is what you pay and value is what you receive. So competing on price alone is almost always a mistake.

Differentiation

Work dilligently to stand out from the competition. But remember that the difference is useful only if the customer appreciates and values the difference.

A restaurant may differentiate itself by the quality of its food, exceptional service or by serving ethnic cuisines. A bank may differentiate by opening all day on a Saturday, and a corner shop may differentiate by offering a home delivery service.

Differentiation is a more productive strategy than cost leadership, because you can always make yourself better and different - and charge appropriately. You can always find new ways to stand out and deliver added value.

One of the best ways to differentiate is to find out what customers hate about your industry and promise to solve that problem. For example, contractors are notorious for never turning up when they are supposed to and always taking twice as long to finish a job than promised. If a new competitor in your area wanted to differentiate himself from the competition, he could offer an extraordinary guarantee: he would finish when promised or the job was free. That would get people's attention.

Whatever you decide to do to stand out from your competitors, you have to ensure that it is something that your customers want or value. You might be excited by the quality of the shampoo you use in your hair salon or the quality of the pipes you use as a plumber, but unless the customer *appreciates* the benefits of those aspects of your service, your efforts to differentiate will go unnoticed.

Differentiating doesn't have to be complicated. Often stating the obvious can be extremely powerful. When Domino's Pizza advertised that their pizzas would be "delivered to your door within 30 minutes or the pizza was free," they were not the only pizza place making that claim. But they were the only one that made it an obvious selling point. They articulated their unique selling proposition to their customer and turned a local pizza shop into a global brand.

Another example: Schlitz beer. A smart marketer named Claude Hopkins visited the plant and was taken through the beer making process. What he learned was that despite being located on the banks of Lake Michigan, Schlitz ignored that water source and dug five 4,000 feet artesian wells to source even purer water. Hopkins learned about the 2,500 different experiments to find the yeast which would produce the best taste. They showed him their research facility, which included five different three-foot thick plate glass rooms where beer was condensed, distilled and re-condensed for purity. Hopkins met the five tasters who each sampled the beer at five different intervals in the brewing process. Finally he saw the bottling plant where the bottles were cleaned and re-cleaned 12 separate times before the beer was bottled.

Sounds impressive, doesn't it? And yet even back in 1919, when this took place, it was standard beer making practice. All Hopkins did was tell consumers about the process. He made the invisible visible and transformed the fortunes of Schlitz beer; within six months it was the number one selling beer in America.

So what is your value proposition? What will make you stand out from the other businesses in your industry? What value do you add that your customers don't know about?

Look Beyond Your Industry

To differentiate successfully, you should consider getting out of your own industry and looking at things from a new perspective. If you are working in a service industry, then look at what manufacturers are doing, and vice versa.

Remember James Dyson from Law 2? He saw cyclone technology, which would be the center of his bag-less vacuum cleaner, first demonstrated in a sawmill. He was able to transfer that insight into a completely unrelated field and become a billionaire in the process.

The story of the Sony Walkman is now the stuff of corporate legend. Sony had a product called the Pressman, which they marketed to professional journalists as a way to record interviews. Masaru Ibuka did a lot of corporate travelling as head of Sony and wanted to break up the monotony, so he instructed his tape recording division to see if they could modify a Pressman for his own personal use. The result was the Walkman, which would eventually change the way we listen to music.

Value is added when you create something new and useful, when you take something old and create a new purpose for it. Or when you create a new market for what you have to offer.

Focus

Focus is slightly different from the other two ways to gain competitive advantage because cost leadership and differentiation apply to the whole market. Businesses that operate successfully through cost leadership do so because their market is broad. They make their money by selling large volumes - low margins multiplied by high volume still makes a lot of money. Differentiation is also a whole-market approach - it's a way to stand out within that broad market.

Focus, on the other hand, is about finding your market niche(s); you can go after market segments based on price or differentiation. A differentiation focus offers more opportunity - especially in the early days of a business venture.

For example, suppose you have a carpentry business, that you really enjoy. You are a very good cabinetmaker and are keen to exploit your gift, but you're not sure how. You could compete as the cheapest carpenter in the area, but that's not going to make you rich. You could differentiate and say that you will do the work and clean up afterward, so that you leave the premises cleaner than when you found them - guaranteed. That would get you noticed. Or you could differentiate focus and target affluent neighborhoods. You could call yourself a craftsman rather than a carpenter and build up a reputation for outstanding custom-made furniture, perhaps with unusual woods or materials. Designers such as Prada and Gucci have become very wealthy through differentiation focus.

By narrowing your focus from broad market to niche market, you stop being all things to all people and become a specialist. Big fish in small ponds are always fatter than little fish in big ponds.

Profit and Pricing

Once you know what vehicle you are going to use to make money and you've worked out what sort of competitive strategy you should be following, then you need to price your product or service for success. After all, there isn't much point going into business or creating a product or service if you can't make a profit from it.

Profit in business is nothing more than a function of what's going on in the hearts and minds of your customers. In other words, profit is a direct result of your doing something right. The more profit you create, the more value you are delivering to people. If you deliver value, you will make money - it's a principle that never fails.

How much money you will make depends on how you price. Most people engage in "cost plus" pricing. This is what accountants would recommend: work out your costs and then add some extra for the profit. So the selling price is arrived at by calculating the production and distribution costs and adding an arbitrary profit margin. But this is costing in the wrong direction!

Start instead with the selling price for the customer in terms of value. What is this product or service worth to your customer? How willing are your customers to pay for it? Figure out what the market will bear, and price accordingly. In the case of a designer suit, cost-plus pricing would never result in the prices that are charged for designer garments. And yet the market wants them and values them sufficiently enough to pay 500%-1000% mark-ups for the prestige of owning a certain name or brand.

You don't want to offer a product or service to happy clients who, unbeknownst to you, would have gladly paid double what you are charging. To maximize your profit, you have to test your offering to see what the market will bear. This is especially true if you're selling yourself as a specialist. There are only so many hours in the day, so better to have fewer clients paying more for your skill than pulling your hair out trying to supply at a lower price point. If there is a huge demand for your product or service, you have the option of either increasing production to capitalize on the demand or simply increasing the price to reduce the demand to a manageable level. Both strategies will make you more money.

This process of getting the supply and demand right has been greatly assisted by the Internet. Before e-commerce, a product or service would be priced, and the brochures and marketing collaterals would go to press. Now businesses can use automated metrics like online pay-per-click advertising to gauge whether their product or service is price sensitive before printing the marketing collaterals. If you discover that the response rates to your marketing hover around 15%, whether or not you charge $50 or $95 or even more per unit (or hour of service), then that knowledge can make a massive and immediate difference in your profitability and ongoing success.

There are countless examples of products and service categories where the more expensive offering out-performs the cheaper one. This often happens because people equate price to quality, but the two don't necessary belong together. Just as buying the most expensive version does not guarantee you quality, buying the cheapest does not guarantee you value for money.

It's not really about price. It's about delivering value and matching that value to what the customer will pay. When working out what to charge, *always work backwards from your market rather than forwards from your cost.* Your price should reflect the value and perceived value your customer receives from your product or service. Don't worry about what's "fair." The market isn't driven by fairness - it's driven by demand.

Remember: customers are not so much *price sensitive* as they are *value conscious.*

The Psychology of Pricing

The need to better manage how much money was taken in each day was a big factor in the introduction of cash registers, which led to all the "99"'s that are almost ubiquitous in pricing. The idea was that if the price was $7.99 or $59.99, cashiers would have to ring the sale up on the till so they could open the register and give the one cent change.

Also, whether by design or coincidence, odd numbers are more attractive to shoppers. That's why marketers still use apparently random odd numbers when pricing a product.

Spending Money - and How We Value It

- You spend your own money on yourself
- You can spend your own money on someone else
- You can spend someone else's money on yourself
- Spend someone else's money on someone else

Value Ladder

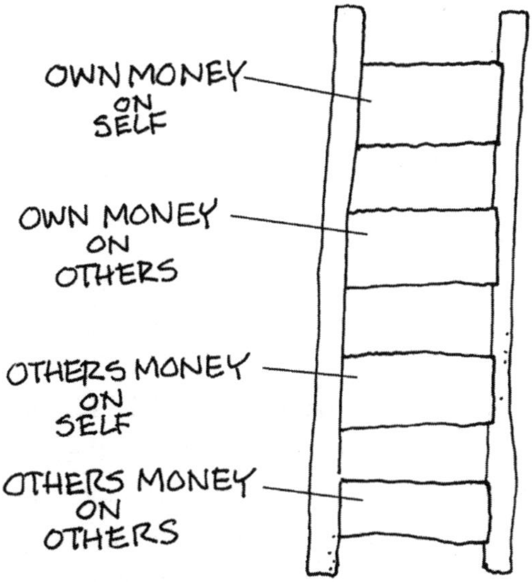

We value our own money the most and are most invested in purchases that involve our own money being spent on ourselves. We will take the most interest and spend more time deciding on purchases that involve our money, because we value our own money far more than we will ever value anyone else's. That might sound inherently selfish, but it's just the nature of human beings.

Next, we value spending our own money on someone else, especially friends and loved ones, almost as much as we value spending money on ourselves. We still think quite deeply about how we spend our own money on other people.

Third is spending someone else's money on ourselves. It's much easier to spend other people's money because we are not so invested in the outcome, although we will consider the purchase more carefully because we will be the beneficiary. Finally, we place the lowest value on spending other people's money on other people. We are not so connected to the outcome, and consequently care far less. This causes carelessness: perhaps this is why so many government programs fail, and government in general wastes such a huge amount of money - our politicians are spending other people's money on other people. Zero personal investment.

This value ladder is important to consider when you're working out what you are going to offer to the world. Be aware that people will require more selling and more persuasion when they are spending their own money. You will need to make sure you add enough value to make the proposition appealing enough to move your customers to action.

Become Your Own CVO

We've all heard of a Chief Executive Officer (CEO) or a Chief Financial Officer (CFO), but how many of us have heard of a Chief Value Officer (CVO)?

In every company someone must be focused on the big picture and on navigating the road ahead. Someone must be focused on the financials, managing the cash flow and revenue projections. The CEO and CFO are crucial roles in every successful business. But creating value and focusing on how and where it can be created is also crucial to a successful business - and yet there is never a CVO. No one is focusing on that aspect of the business, even though adding value is required if the company wants to make money.

You will have to become your own CVO, along with all the other functions you'll have to fulfil in order to make the money you're commited to.

As CVO, you must also protect the value that you add. If you bring innovation and ideas to market, you must protect them with the appropriate patents and trademarks. Although such protections may not stop everyone from trying to muscle in, they do deter a great many opportunists and copycats.

The 5th Law is about what you can bring to the commercial transaction. More broadly, it's about how you can serve others and make your contribution to society, so that you can benefit from the rewards that value delivers. Wealth may be held in tangible assets and money in the bank, but it is created from value. Thus, it starts in the hearts and minds of people who want to make their customers lives and their businesses better and more prosperous.

What To Expect If You Fail To Create Value:

- You won't make money
- People will ignore your product or service

You Won't Make Money

You only get one chance to make a first impression. If you have been so focused on getting started and making money that you have not stepped into the shoes of your clients and customers to understand what they want, then your efforts will be short lived.

You have to find out what they want - not what you want to deliver. You have to listen to them and make their experience extraordinary. Customers are not stupid. They may buy once based on a promise, but if that promise is not kept, then you will seldom get a second chance.

People Will Ignore Your Product or Service

You've probably heard that "any publicity is good publicity." Oscar Wilde once said "The only thing worse than being talked about is not being talked about." That may be true if you are aspiring to be a pop star or B-list celebrity, but it's not useful if you're attempting to create significant wealth.

If you fail to deliver, then the only publicity you'll get will be negative. The best-case scenario is that you will be ignored. If you fail to deliver real value, then you may create very vocal critics. People who are unhappy about product quality and service are likely to tell far more people about their experience than customers who are happy with their experience.

What You Can Confidently Expect If You Create Value:

- You'll make money
- You'll make an impact
- People will talk positively about your product or service

You'll Make Money

Businesses that Create Value make money. If you Create Value and therefore make your customers lives happier, better, easier or more successful in some way, then the natural consequence of that action is revenue. Tapping into unfulfilled needs and meeting those needs will result in a very predictable outcome - profitability, sustainability and success.

Adding value doesn't always have to cost that much. Sometimes it's as simple as taking the time to understand the real needs of the customer, or a better service than the competition. Sometimes it's information, which is often very easy to provide and may have a high perceived value. Finding out what your customer wants and finding cost effective ways to offer it to them are the foundational keys to Law 5.

You'll Make an Impact

Far too many businesses are cookie-cutter replicas of their competition. They find a common standard, where no one is willing to push the boat out and say, "That's not great. We can do better."

History proves that those that serve better are the winners. The history of business is full of examples of companies that have chosen to do things differently, to hold themselves to a higher standard - and have profited as a result.

Ricardo Semler is the "sometimes CEO" of the Brazilian firm Semco, a thoroughly unique company. Since taking over the family business from his father, Semler has systematically broken just about every management and business rule in the book. There is no organizational chart or mission statement, no policies and procedures, no planning, no managers, no HR department, no head office, no secretaries, and if you want a cafe latte, you get it yourself. Employees decide their own pay and who they want to work with. But this doesn't mean there is nowhere to hide. Far from it. If an employee doesn't do a great job, they simply won't be included in the team requirements for the next six months, and that's the end of the road.

Semler believes that employees should be encouraged to meet their personal goals before corporate ones, because he recognizes that happy, inspired employees are better employees. Being the father of young children himself, he encourages his employees to "retire-a-little." This is a program that allows employees to buy days back from the company so they can enjoy a little more time with a young family - or pursue a dream. Then, when the employee does reach retirement age, they can "sell" those days back to the company. The retiree still feels that they are a valued, important member of the team, while the company retains valuable expertise. People and businesses that find ways to add real value make an impact.

People Will Talk about Your Product or Service

One of the easiest, cheapest, and most reliable ways to generate sales is to ensure that you get talked about for all the right reasons. Word-of-mouth advertising still beats all other forms of marketing, hands down.

There simply is no substitute for an individual telling friends or colleagues about a great experience with your product or service. Adding value and doing so consistently will get you talked about in a positive way. People will tell others about your product or service, and ultimately, it is this conversation that will make your efforts remarkable.

The 5th Law of Wealth may require you to shift your thinking. Being able to create value successfully means that you have to view your product or service from many different angles. You have to step into the shoes of your customers to see what they want and value most highly. If you don't know, then ask them. You have to see your product or service with the eyes of your customers and other business partners, to discover how it could be revised, improved or created more efficiently.

You have to view your business the way your employees see it. What could you do to create value for them, so that they feel appreciated and enthusiastic about promoting your product or service?

And what about your competitors? What are they doing that could offer clues for you to increase the value you create?

In short, leave no stone unturned. You need to view what you do from all angles, up and down the value chain, so that you can identify opportunities and impress customers by delivering stellar products and services that continually appeal to them.

Are You Aligned to Law 5? Do You Create Value?

Below are seven sets of two statements - 1A/1B-7A/7B. As before, read each pair of statements, and mark the one that's mostly true for you. On balance, which more accurately reflects your opinions and your view of life? They won't always be easy, but choose the one that best matches you.

Once again, no one need see your answers. If you don't want to write in the book or you want to keep your selections private, then make the selections in a separate notebook. Don't mark what you wish you were like or hope to be like in the future; answer as you are right now. If you are unsure, then ask someone you know and trust to give you feedback.

	A	B
1	☐ I rarely play the lottery or gamble my money because pinning your hopes on random chance is just futile. I'd much rather make my fortune than win it.	I buy my ticket religiously. You have to be 'in it to win it'. I'd much rather win my fortune than have to make it. ☐
2	☐ I often do more than I'm expected to do. I'm not even sure anyone notices, but I notice and I prefer to do a good job.	I rarely do more than I'm expected to. I do the hours I'm paid for, and that's it. Why should I do more? I'll get no thanks for it. ☐
3	☐ I would consider taking a pay cut to change my career, and/or I'm always interested in learning new skills.	I would never consider taking a step backwards to change my career. I hated school, and my education finished there. I don't need anything else. ☐
4	☐ I have been promoted several times, or I get a lot of business through word of mouth.	I have rarely been promoted, if ever. Or I have to advertise for every bit of new business I get. ☐
5	☐ I've never been made redundant (or it's only happened once).	I have been made redundant two or more times. ☐
6	☐ I appreciate that so much of business is relationships, so I always try to under- promise and over-deliver.	I often get myself in hot water because I tell clients things and don't deliver on the promise. It's not my fault - I'm always let down by others, and it makes me look bad. ☐
7	☐ What I do is quite difficult to replace.	People like me are a dime a dozen. I believe that it's impossible for me to stand out. ☐

If you have checked five or more of the statements in the A Column, then you already have a good grasp of Law 5. If you have marked three or more statements in the B Column, then we suggest you read the supplementary guidebook; ***Law5 - Create Value: Applications and Insights.*** This companion guide will give you further information about Law 5, together with practical techniques, ideas and insights that will enable you to successfully align yourself with this law and harness its power.

Law 6

Seek Growth

Change is One Thing - Inevitable & Assured
Progress is Another, Cultivated & Created

To grow and know what one is growing towards - that is the source of all strength and self-confidence. Character is forged by surmounting difficulty while proceeding toward a worthwhile outcome. We must seek to surpass that which we have already mastered if we are ever to progress and prosper. There is no royal road to riches. One thing at a time, and all things in succession. That which grows consistently, endures. All life is growth.

Chapter Eight
Law 6 - Seek Growth

If a tree is given limited nourishment, it will live, but it will never thrive and grow to its full potential. If it has access to plenty of clean water, sunlight, and nutrients from the soil *beyond* what it needs for survival alone, it will naturally Seek Growth. It will be healthy, with lush green leaves. Its roots will reach down into the ground for added strength and security, so that no matter what the weather above the surface, the tree will bend with the conditions and remain strong.

The tree never asks when it should stop - it will always Seek Growth, using all the resources it has available. If the tree is further nurtured over and above what it needs to merely support life, it will produce fruit. The fruit is the reward for growth and reaching its highest potential.

Your business is like a tree. If you follow the preceding five laws, you will nourish your business and create a healthy vibrant enterprise. But it will bear fruit only if you continue that nourishment over and above what it needs to survive. You must Seek Growth at all times.

To understand how growth can be achieved, we first need to explore the growth process. At the beginning of the value chain, there are commodities - basic raw materials that are traded around the world. These commodities are then converted into products and services, adding value in the progression and therefore selling for a higher price. As the numbers of products and services grow, so does the need to stand out in order to survive - and so the brand is born.

Brands offer businesses an opportunity to compete on something other than price; to gather a following, to charge a premium, and to grow exponentially. Today a brand must stand for more than a list of superior product or service attributes. People are demanding more - they are now looking for an experience. If you are seriously committed to growth, then you have to offer something different from the norm. You have to give your customers an experience that will bring then back to you time and again and convert them into loyal advocates.

For example, consider the coffee bean. Coffee is a commodity traded on global markets. The beans result in hundreds of different coffee products and related services, from supermarket products to filter coffee served at roadside diners. There are countless coffee brands - Nescafe, Douwe Egberts, Maxwell House, Green Mountain, Folger's, and many others. But there are very few companies who have taken their brand one step further to make coffee an experience. Starbucks is one of those success stories.

Starbucks was originally a popular little coffee bean store in Seattle. Howard Shultz, who at the time worked for a coffee machine company, was visiting them because Starbucks had been buying a lot of his machines, and he wanted to take a look at their store.

Starbucks was inspired by Peat's Coffee & Tea, the company widely credited with starting the specialty coffee revolution in the US. Starbucks had mastered the product and service part of the equation and was dedicated to high quality coffee and equipment. Shultz was so impressed he decided he was going to work for them, although it took him a year to persuade them that it was a good idea.

While on a trip to Italy in 1982, Shultz noticed that there was a coffee bar on every corner of every block. They formed part of the social glue and were central to the Italian way of life. It was this insight that led to the Starbucks we know today. He spotted a way to transform a commodity into an experience, and the rest is history.

In order to Seek Growth successfully, you have to aim to provide an experience, whether you are delivering a product or a service. Stand out, be different and create new markets. Shultz was convinced that people would flock to high-end coffee bars even though nothing like that existed at the time. There may have been the odd specialty coffee shops dotted around large cities, but there was no chain.

At one point, Shultz paid over $500,000 for a feasibility study into launching in a new international territory. Expert opinion indicated it was not a prudent move - after all, nothing like this had been done successfully before. But Shultz was sure the report was wrong and pursued his dream anyway. Today Starbucks operates over 15,000 locations, with a mix of company-owned and licensed stores across 43 countries serving an estimated 30 million customers a week.

Starbucks experienced phenomenal growth over a relatively short period of time because Howard Shultz wasn't interested in what everyone else was doing.

If you're doing what everyone else is doing in your industry, then you might as well reconsider, because you *will* become invisible to customers, and you won't make the quantum leaps in growth that will bear fruit. The only way to grow in a major way is to become visible by becoming extraordinary or remarkable in some way.

That means going to the periphery of your industry and looking at other industries for inspiration and ideas. Good ideas stand out in all industries. Often the best businesses have taken something that worked in one industry or region, adapted it, and made it even better in another. That's exactly what Starbucks did - Shultz saw the possibility for Italian-style coffee bars as a global idea. A place where people would meet and hang out, work, play and enjoy good coffee. It worked - despite all the naysayers.

Additionally, you must have a competitive advantage; otherwise, *don't compete*. You have to have something highly appealing to the customer, and its execution has to be flawless. There's no point getting them through the door if you can't fulfil your promise.

Law 6 - Seek Growth is about capitalizing on early success and really making a business fly. In really simple terms, growth happens when you generate more revenue. And despite the thousands of books on the subject, there really are only three ways to generate more revenue in business:

- Sell to more people - increase the customer base
- Sell more often - increase the frequency of sale
- Increase your prices - increase the unit of sale

That's it. Sure you can reduce expenses, but no one ever got rich from cutting back on their stationery. Sustainable growth is where the money is, and Law 6 is all about the various ways you can achieve that end.

How to master Law 6 and Seek Growth

- Internal growth
- Market penetration
- Diversification
- External growth

Supercharge Your Internal Growth: Market Penetration

Although I'm not a huge fan of business theory, there are a few business models that are really helpful to keep in mind when growing your business and seeking opportunities. One such model is the Ansoff Product-Market Growth Matrix. This marketing tool was created by Igor Ansoff and was first published in his article "Strategies for Diversification" in a 1957 edition of the *Harvard Business Review*, yet it remains as useful and relevant today.

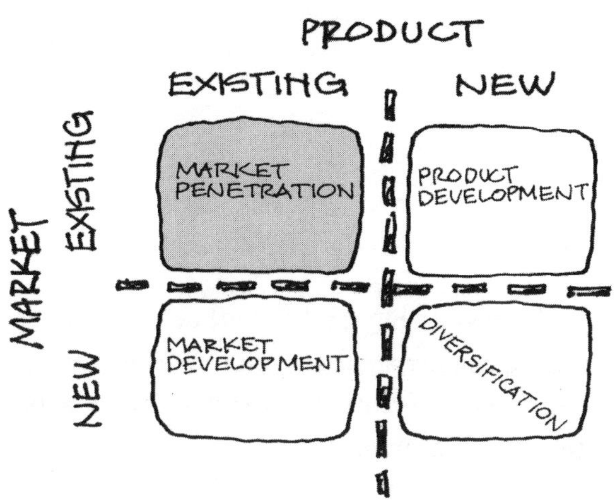

When people talk of internal growth, they are usually referring to the least risky but slowest form of growth - market penetration. You focus your energy on promoting your existing products to existing markets, hoping to increase your exposure and market.

The best way to achieve this is through effective marketing and promotion to convert customers away from your competition, thereby increasing your market share. Penetration also means attracting new users to your product or service...or convincing current users to use your product more often.

This type of internal growth is one of the main ways that businesses grow, but it's rarely a fast track. It involves all the usual techniques that you would learn about in a standard business course. However, instead of getting bogged down in techniques, it would be more beneficial if I help you understand why people do what they do. This knowledge will help you to innovate and create new ways to grow your business and increase your customer base.

Psychology of Effective Market Penetration

Social scientist Robert B. Cialdini has simplified the task of understanding consumers by identifying six unconscious psychological principles that constantly influence our behavior. These principles are often referred to as:

- Social Proof
- Consistency
- Liking
- Reciprocity
- Authority
- Scarcity

If you understand why people buy and how they are influenced, then you can use those insights to shape the tactics you use to grow your business. We've mentioned two of these principles in **Law 3 - Own a Strategy,** but they are also relevant to internal growth.

Social Proof

Research has conclusively proven that, whether we are conscious of it or not, we are deeply influenced by people like us. We will look around to find someone or a group of people we consider similar to us, see what they are doing, and use that information as guidance on how to precede.

Social psychologist and researcher Stanley Milgram is famous for a number of ground-breaking experiments and discoveries in human behavior. He discovered that we are all connected by just six degrees of separation. In an experiment on group behavior, he had one of his research assistants stop and look to the sky in the middle of a busy New York street. Most people kept walking, but when he asked four more people to join his assistant, and all five stared skyward, the number of passers-by that stopped and looked up quadrupled. We are instinctively drawn to do and behave in a way that is consistent with others around us. We find comfort in that decision.

This is especially true when we find ourselves in unfamiliar territory or situations. If for example, you are driving in a city you've never visited before, you are more likely to match the driving behavior of other people, than you are to adhere to road signs or instruction from other less "personal" sources.

So why is this important to you as you Seek Growth? Simple: Social proof is imperative for influencing more people to buy more often. This is why testimonials and endorsements have such a powerful influence on our buying decisions.

If you are a busy mother who's in the market for a new washing machine, and a particular brand has a testimonial from another busy mother on how quick the wash is and how efficient the machine is, then that endorsement will influence your decision to buy. If I asked you if it had any bearing, you would probably deny it vehemently, but research suggests that we are indeed strongly influenced by what others choose. This is true even if we don't personally know the other individual; just knowing that another individual has similar challenges and is in a similar situation is enough.

A great example of social proof in action came from Colleen Szot, who is one of the most successful writers in the paid programming industry. She is famous for changing a few words in an ad and smashing a twenty-year sales record for a home shopping channel. Instead of the usual call to action, *"Operators are waiting for your call, please call now,"* she changed it to, *"If operators are busy, please call again."*

The inference and imagery created by this small change in wording made a huge difference. Instead of imagining countless bored operators waiting patiently for the phone to ring while painting their nails, the caller imagines a busy switchboard buzzing with orders from "other people just like me" who were making the purchase.

This result is especially interesting because the wording change actually implies that the caller may be inconvenienced by having to try several times in order to get through. But far from putting people off, this subtle change also tapped into another one of Cialdini's principles - scarcity, which I'll explain in a moment.

When we are unsure about whether something is right or not or whether we should buy or not, we will see if other people "like us" have made that choice. If they have, we are much more inclined to buy. By inferring that the lines were busy, callers were reassured that they were not alone in their purchase decision - and so they called!

But beware - social proof is a double-edged sword and can cause great damage if you are not aware of it. If you visit Arizona's Petrified Forest National Park, you will realize that the park is in danger because so many people take pieces of the petrified wood as souvenirs. All over the park there are signs that say, "Your heritage is being vandalized every day by theft losses of petrified wood of 14 tons a year, mostly a small piece at a time."

Bearing in mind what you now know about social proof…is that sign going to help the situation or make it worse? It's making it worse because people read it and say, "Wow, 14 tons a year. Everyone is doing it - I better get my bit before there is none left!"

To test the theory researchers placed alternative signs at various places in the forest and planted small pieces of wood as bait. What they found was that the "14 tons" sign tripled the instances of theft compared to a neutral sign that did not tell the tourists how much was stolen but instead simply asked them not to remove the wood. Moral: *If you don't want people to do something, don't reassure them that the wrong action is popular!*

However, if you do want someone to do something - like buy your product or service - then be sure to reassure them that other people like them have already bought and are happy with the purchase. One of the most powerful and simple ways to tap into this principle is to gather testimonials and endorsements from happy clients. Oh, and please don't make them up! Deliver stellar service and get legitimate testimonials.

Consistency

Consistency and commitment are about our desire to remain congruent with our stated ideas, values, opinions or choices. Once we commit to something and invest in that approach, we are very reluctant to change our mind, especially if that change will imply that our original judgement was flawed in some way. As I said in **Law 3**, everyone avoids being wrong. It is this psychological principle that would explain why smart people do dumb things. Once a business has committed to a strategy and has publicly declared its intentions, it can be hard for senior management to accept that the strategy is clearly failing.

So why is this necessary for you as you Seek Growth? If you have brought a customer through the door and delivered a product or service, then the hard part is done. You have got them to part with their cash, and so long as you continue to add value, there is no reason why they wouldn't buy from you again and keep buying from you into the future. And yet so many companies turn their back on existing customers and instead focus almost all their efforts on trying to get new ones. Attracting new customers is considerably more expensive and difficult than keeping their current customers happy.

Once you've made that initial connection and people have bought from you, then you can introduce more buying opportunities. Track what they buy, and suggest other products or services that may be helpful to them. They are thus more likely to buy again, and so long as you tailor your approach with relevant offers, then you can increase buying frequency and grow your business dramatically.

Liking

Liking is pretty obvious - we like to work with people we like. If you think back on your own career and the people you've worked with or met, isn't it true that you would rather have good service from a nice person than perfect service from someone who is uninterested. We will forgive more with someone we like and we are more influenced by someone we trust.

Although this is obvious, it's still remarkable how many companies get this wrong. The liking must be sincere. Traditional sales training might suggest that sales reps smile when they answer the phone or smile at the customers. And yet we can usually tell when someone is not being genuine. We know when someone is being sincere or not.

Social scientist Alicia Grandey and her colleagues tested this idea; they wanted to find out if perception of effectiveness and satisfaction were influenced by a smile. Based on previous findings that demonstrated that people are able to distinguish between an authentic and inauthentic smile, they wanted to see if smiling affected customer satisfaction.

Participants were asked to watch several video clips of conversations between a hotel employee and a guest. The employee was to perform a task. The situation was always the same, but the employee behaved slightly differently. In the first video the employee was to be authentic. Obviously, you can't instruct someone to be authentic, so the employee was asked to generate positive feelings toward the guest and think about how she could make the guest feel good. In the second example she was told to smile - inauthentic.

The employee was then asked to perform a task well and then poorly. Unsurprisingly, the guest was happier when the task was done well. When it was done poorly, the type of smile was irrelevant. However, if it was done well with an authentic smile, observers registered a far higher customer satisfaction.

So what does this mean for you as you grow your business? You can't instil a customer service mentality into someone - they either have it or they don't. Forget trying to fit round pegs into square holes. Hire front-line personnel who genuinely enjoy working with customers.

It's also worth noting that no one likes a *'know it all'*. People are much more likely to like someone who can admit their flaws and seem human. Some of the greatest advertising campaigns in history have been created by taking a negative aspect of a product and making it positive and almost loveable.

The Volkswagen Beetle's introduction to the US is a classic example. At the time, Americans were buying large American cars, and the domestic market was strong. So when VW decided to introduce the small and quirky German Beetle, it was considered by many as an insurmountable task. Advertising firm Doyle, Dane & Bernbach thought otherwise and created ads with taglines like *"Ugly is only skin deep"* and *"It will stay uglier longer."* The Beetle wasn't attractive and streamlined - and yet drawing attention to that quite obvious fact made VW seem honest and trustworthy; therefore, people were more inclined to believe the other benefits of price and fuel efficiency. VW sales went through the roof.

How can you convert perceived negatives into growth? If you have a negative in your product or service, then sometimes it's better to take the bull by the horns and identify it. Be direct and obvious - people respond to that. Look at Stella Artois lager - their major problem was that they were more expensive than many other beers. So what did they do? They created an advertising campaign that told customers that Stella Artois was *"reassuringly expensive."* They took a negative and put a positive spin on it and it worked.

Another example: Avis, the second largest car hire company in the world. Instead of trying to avoid that issue, they drew customers' attention to it and used it. Their famous tagline was *"Avis. We're #2, but we try harder. (When you're not #1, you have to)."* The inference was clear - when a company is #1, it gets lazy and complacent, and those attributes rarely work in the customer's favor.

We only confess our little faults to persuade people that we have no big ones.
Francois Duc de La Rochefoucauld

Clearly, if your product or service has major flaws, then this approach will not work. But admitting to small faults can boost sales.

Reciprocity

Reciprocity is about returning favors or balancing the books in some way. If I give you something - even if it's not something you particularly want - then you will feel an innate drive to reciprocate that action in some way, so that we are even again and you don't feel a sense of indebtedness.

It would be fair to say that the Hare Krishna Society struggled in their fundraising activities until they discovered the transformational qualities of reciprocity. Orange robes and shaven heads didn't endear them to the general public, but once they started handing out gifts before asking for a donation, things took off. The most cost effective of these gifts was a small flower. What's especially fascinating about reciprocity is that it appears to beat liking as a powerful influencing motive. So even when would-be donors didn't want the flower, tried to return it, or felt offended by the approach, they still gave a donation.

Researcher Dennis Regan conducted a study that demonstrated the power of reciprocation. In the experiment those people who had been given a can of Coca-Cola from 'Joe' a stranger, purchased twice as many raffle tickets from him as those who were not given the can of Coke. This happened even when there was a time delay between the unsolicited gift and the request to purchase raffle tickets and when there was no reference to the original gift or encounter when Joe made the request.

The easiest way to get what you want is to
find out what other people want and help them get it.
Frank Bettger

Liking Joe had no bearing on how many raffle tickets the individual bought. Those who were given the soft drink, regardless of when or whether they even liked Joe, were driven to reciprocate in some way and bought twice as many tickets.

So why is this principle important in growing your business? Because you can tap into its power through a number of tried and tested techniques.

When companies offer free samples or free gifts, they are activating reciprocity.

I would suggest, that instead of trying to trick people into helping you, think about how you can help others get what they want, because those actions will eventually come back to benefit you.

Authority

Whether we like to think so or not, social scientists have demonstrated time and again that we are incredibly susceptible to requests made by people in positions of authority. One of the most disturbing demonstrations of just how far we will go to adhere to requests made by authority figures was given by Stanley Milgram in what are now famously referred to as "the Milgram experiments."

In one experiment, participant A had to administer electric shocks to participant B on the instruction of a researcher in a white coat who was the authority figure for the experiment. What person A did not know was that both the researcher and person B were just role playing and there was actually no electric shock being administered. However, person A was asked to systematically increase the shock voltage until person B was screaming and begging to stop. In many of the cases, the people administering the "shock" were also deeply upset by what they were being asked to do and pleaded with the researcher to allow them to stop - and yet when pressed to continue, most of them did. Such is the power of an authority figure.

We instinctively trust amongst others, scientists in their white lab coats, people with letters after their name, and police officers in their uniform.

This is important to remember when growing your business, because we can use that trust of authority in our favor. Testimonials and endorsements from authority figures can also positively influence buying behavior. If you were a tire manufacturer, you would want your tires endorsed by a Formula one driver who's an authority figure - and who knows all about good tires. This sort of official seal of approval from a trusted figure can make a big difference to sales.

Authority in this instance means anyone who is either a recognized name or celebrity… *or* someone who is recognized as an expert. A doctor in their crisp white coat exerts a great deal of authority. In fact, it is this innate trust of authority that is suspected to be at least partially behind the amazing results of placebo medicine. When a patient is given a saline injection or a sugar pill and told of the pharmaceutical properties of those treatments by a trusted doctor, then truly amazing things have happened.

One of the most famous examples of placebo medicine is Mr. Wright, a patient in the 1950s suffering from far advanced cancer of the lymph nodes. He was given an experimental drug called Krebiozen - hailed in the national press at the time as the "cure for cancer." It had miraculous effects. Later, however, press stories appeared that raised questions about the effectiveness of the new drug, and Mr. Wright suffered a relapse. His doctor, Dr. Bruno Klopfer, was desperate so he told his patient that he had secured the new double-strength version of Krebiozen, which was actually a placebo. Klopfer reported that his patient's tumors *"melted like snowballs on a hot stove."*

More recently, in 2002, Baylor School of Medicine published a study in the *New England Journal of Medicine*, which demonstrated the power of the placebo effect - this time in surgery. Dr. Bruce Moseley wanted to establish what part of knee surgery was causing the most improvement, so he split his patients into three groups. In the first, Mosley shaved the damaged cartilage in the knee. In the second he flushed out the material thought to cause inflammation. And in the third, he made three standard incisions, and then talked and acted as though he was doing the operation - even splashing salt water to mimic the sound of the knee-washing procedure. After 40 minutes, Moseley sewed up the incisions. All three groups were given the same aftercare and physiotherapy program.

Those who received the traditional surgery improved as expected. However, what shocked Dr. Moseley was that the placebo group improved as much as the other two groups! So much so that he suggested, *"My skill as a surgeon had no benefit on these patients. The entire benefit of the surgery for osteoarthritis of the knee was the placebo effect."*

There is surely more going on with placebo medicine than we currently understand, but one thing is for sure: we put a great deal of faith and trust in an authority figure - so make sure you trust the right ones, and make sure you do what you can to legitimately tap into that potent force in your marketing and growth efforts.

Scarcity

Things appear more valuable to us when they are less available. Recall the home shopping channel advertisement - the reason scarcity worked was that the message "If operators are busy, please call again" implied that the phones were red hot, and if you didn't call right away, you may miss out. We hate missing out - even when what we are missing out on is something that we didn't actually want that much.

When Pope John Paul II died on the evening of April 2, 2005, his funeral was scheduled for April 8 - the same day that Prince Charles was due to marry Camilla Parker Bowles. The Royal Family quickly rescheduled the wedding, so that Prince Charles could attend the funeral. What's interesting, is that this event saw a stampede of souvenir buyers - everything with the wrong royal wedding date was snapped up by people who thought they could cash in.

People who normally wouldn't have cared about either event bought up the souvenirs because they thought they would be scarce and valuable. The idea of missing out on a potential opportunity meant they were buying up tea towels, mouse pads, coffee cups and key rings by the truckload.

The assumption was that shop owners would have thrown the wrong dated items out and so those that could secure these items and didn't miss out on the opportunity would benefit. Ironically, however, more people own a souvenir with the wrong date than the right one. It turns out that the error did not make the items rare at all.

We can also see the power of scarcity at Christmas. Each year there is a "must have" toy or game that keeps millions of parents up at night for months as they struggle to secure that product for their child. Time and again, game console manufacturers will deliberately depress volume to create a sense of scarcity, which drives up desire and demand.

Another example is the Hermes "Birkin bag." The price of a Birkin starts at about $5,000, not including sales taxes. Prices can reach five and six figure sums, especially when the bag is constructed from exotic animal skins. Allegedly, the waiting list for a Birkin is over two years. So not only is the bag expensive, it's incredibly difficult to get, and that scarcity makes it even more appealing. Hermes successfully tapped into the power of scarcity. The lack of product created a buzz about the product and increased demand.

This is important to remember when you are marketing products or services, because customers will be more inclined to buy what you are selling if they believe that by not buying they will miss out. Make sure your call to action tells people that they have only a limited time to take advantage of the opportunity. Marketers tap into this principle by telling customers that there are only a limited number for sale or that buyers must act before a certain date; otherwise, they will miss out on a particular early-bird rate or discount.

So, not only are we motivated by rare and unique opportunities, but if we think we may miss out on those opportunities, we are even more influenced to act. This phenomenon is known as "loss aversion," and it can be a useful tool in generating more sales, more often.

The other interesting psychological aspect to scarcity is that more choice does not mean more sales. Behavioral scientist Sheena Iyengar analyzed company-sponsored retirement programs for nearly 800,000 workers to see how the participation rates correlated to the number of programs offered. What the research found was that when *more* choice was offered, the *less* likely the employees were to participate. When only two funds were offered, the participation was about 75%, but when 59 funds were offered, participation dropped to about 60%.

This idea was further tested in other areas, and it held true. A little choice is compelling, but too much choice was detrimental to sales. Logic would tell us that too much choice can be confusing, and the decision is relegated to the "too hard basket." It also indicates that when there isn't enough scarcity, the value of the choice is diminished.

The focus in market penetration is to access more of your market with your existing product range. If you understand what moves people to action, you can ensure that all your communication, especially your marketing initiatives, tap into as many of the six principles as possible. All the best marketing minds and advertising people know this. Most of the really good ones know it instinctively and probably wouldn't be able to tell you the specific factors at work - they just know it works. *So remember; those who fail to master these principles will always be mastered by them.*

Supercharge Your Internal Growth: Diversification

Once you have created a business that is working and is making consistent returns through market penetration, then - and only then - can you think about diversification. Law 6 is about how to turbo-charge growth once you successfully get off the ground. Trying to start as a diversified company is risky. Start with one business and learn to master it. Then you diversify. That's not to say you can't get moving on diversification quickly; it's just easier to diversify if your main business is working well and you have time and energy to develop new income streams.

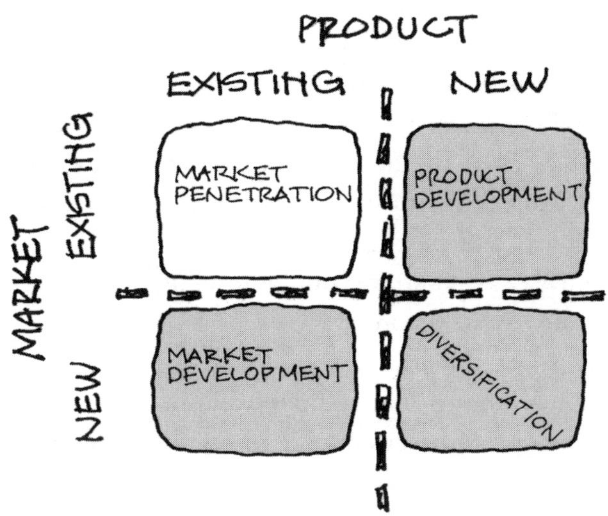

According to Ansoff's Product-Growth Matrix you can diversify in three ways:

- Product - product development
- Market - market development
- Both - *[multi-dimensional?]* diversification

Product Development

Here you try to diversify your product range and create new products or services that you can then sell to your existing market.

Cosmetics companies do this brilliantly, because they know that many women prefer a particular brand. So all they need to do is come out with a new product, and many of their faithful customers will buy it - especially if prompted to do so with a good offer, free samples, a discount, or an advertising campaign.

If you bend over backwards to make sure your customer experience is second to none, then those customers will become loyal, not only to the product or service, but to your company. If you successfully diversify your product line, that loyalty will be translated into additional cash flow and profit.

Product development has to be smart. It needs to be congruent with the rest of the business and make sense to the customer. Remember the Quaker Oats example from Law 3? If the new product or service does not make sense to customers, it will confuse them, and confused customers don't buy. Quaker Oats making toys and moving into restaurants didn't make sense. This type of wrong move can even make your long-standing customers question their original loyalty to the brand.

A better example is Caterpillar's move into CAT-branded clothing and footwear products. According to its corporate website, Caterpillar is "the world's largest manufacturer of construction and mining equipment, diesel and natural gas engines, and industrial gas turbines." On that basis, a move into clothing and consumer products may have seemed odd. However, it was inspired. Caterpillar is a strong masculine "man's-man" brand. By licensing the manufacturing of consumer goods, the company successfully transferred those brand values to a clothing line. The CAT brand was Initially targeted at construction workers who would use the Caterpillar equipment but has since successfully moved into new, mainstream markets.

Product development and diversification are like spreading your eggs in different baskets. All too often, business owners become emotionally attached to the initial product or service and refuse to acknowledge a shift in demand.

The most spectacular example of this behavior in recent times is the music industry. For decades, record companies made a great deal of money charging a very healthy margin for vinyl records, tape cassettes, and then CDs. They notoriously paid the artists poorly and created vast wealth for themselves. But the Internet changed the way people bought and listened to music. Napster was the first to offer a vast range of music illegally, and people were all too happy to download it for free. CD sales went into freefall, and the record companies lost billions.

Instead of seeing this sea-change in consumer demand and looking for ways to harness it, the industry put its considerable muscle and money behind shutting down music sites such as Napster. They were so distraught at the loss of their sacred cash cow that they failed to appreciate that everyone had become vegans overnight.

The fact of the matter was that they were never going to stop this type of music transfer, so fighting it was a pointless waste of time and money. Instead, they should have got on board, slaughtered the sacred cow (or at least put it out to pasture to live out the remainder of its days in peace) and focused their energy on working out a way to give the music lovers what they wanted in the format they wanted, while also making some money for themselves and their artists.

This idea is often referred to metaphorically as the "Barbarians at the Gate": when your market is screaming for something more or different and banging down your door for that new thing, then you'd better figure out how to give it to them rather than wasting time trying to convince them that what you sell is still really what they want.

If what you offer is no longer wanted, then let it go and get busy on working out how to deliver what they do want. Create new baskets into which you can distribute some new eggs. It was completely pointless for the record companies to try to stop music downloads - instead, they dragged their heels long enough to allow Apple to dominate the new market space. Apple was originally known for computers, not innovative music and communication devices. As they dropped the word "computer" from their name, they acknowledged that their sacred cow was no longer sacred - and they moved on to related fields.

Hindsight, of course, is a wonderful thing. It's incredibly hard to accept that the thing that made you money, the product or service you've poured your heart and soul into, is no longer what the market wants - but you have to be prepared to walk away if the market demand changes. You have to constantly monitor what your customers want and adapt accordingly.

Product diversification allows you to sell more things to more people. It allows you to spread the risk of your business across many baskets so that if one basket of eggs suddenly gets squashed by a new business or market demand, then you can simply shut it down and move on without being financially or emotionally crippled.

Nothing stays the same for long. What you are doing successfully today may not be successful for you tomorrow. If you can accept that at the start, you'll save yourself a lot of heartaches later.

Often business owners worry about product diversification because they think that the new products may cannibalize their original market share. Often it will - but you have to remember that customers want what they want. If you don't offer it, they'll go somewhere else.

As long as they buy something from you, it's a win. If they now buy product A instead of product B, who cares? They have still bought from you. However, if you don't appreciate what they want and offer it, then you run the risk of losing that customer to a competitor who does offer product B, C and D as well.

Consistently ask yourself: what else would my customer buy? If you don't know, then ask around, do your research. Call up some of your best customers and ask them what they would change about your offering if they could.

Market Development

Here you Seek Growth through market diversification. You take an established product, tweak it slightly, and direct it toward a whole new untapped market.

That's what the vitamin and nutritional supplement industry did. Instead of focusing on the product, e.g. Vitamin C or iron, the companies got smart and targeted the end-user's needs. And in doing so they opened up vast new markets. Today you can buy vitamins that have been formulated for pregnant woman, over 40s, teenagers, and other groups. They have also associated their products with various health issues; joint, eye, skin health etc (without claiming to cure any disease), enabling consumers to self-medicate.

The product is essentially the same as ever. The marketers have just targeted their message toward niche groups in the market, who perhaps didn't previously know they needed dietary supplements. The companies may argue that the products are tailored to particular groups, but if you take a look at the ingredients, you'll see that there's very little actual difference. All that has changed is the pitch.

Another great example of this is Lucozade, which was initially marketed in the UK as a health tonic to help sick people recover faster. But that's a pretty small market, so the marketers took the exact same product and directed it toward a new market - athletes and those aspiring to be an athlete. It became an established energy drink and massively expanded its reach and profit. Now energy supplements constitute a huge - and hugely profitable - category.

The company that makes the home lubricant WD-40 transformed their sales from $2 million a year to $34 million a year, just by getting creative about how customers could use their product. They didn't change the product in any way. All they changed was the customer perception about what sorts of problems WD-40 could solve.

The product was originally developed in 1953 by Norm Larson to repel water and prevent corrosion, "WD-40" is an abbreviation of "Water Displacement 40th Attempt." because Larson had failed 39 times to find a formula for water displacement to prevent corrosion. He finally succeeded on his 40th attempt.

WD-40 was later found to have a multitude of household uses. The WD-40 slogan is now *"Dirty, jammed, rusty, squeaky or damp - just WD-40 it!"* By advertising the alternative uses for WD-40, the company massively expanded its market and increased sales. Food companies have been following this strategy for decades, bombarding consumers with new recipes and other uses for their products.

Remember: we each like to think we're a little bit different from everyone else, and we like the opportunity to buy products and services that are tailored directly to our individual and "unique" requirements. So when a company homes in on our exact needs through astute product development and marketing, then we are much more likely to buy that product.

This is the principle of social proof in action. When faced with a dizzying array of vitamins on a pharmacy shelf or your local supermarket - what do you buy? You naturally narrow your search to the product that matches your situation. So if a pregnant woman is looking at that selection of supplements, she is much more likely to choose the product for pregnant women, even though it's exactly the same ingredients as the folic acid supplement positioned next to it on the shelf. If a 60-year-old man is searching for vitamins, he will be instinctively drawn to the product that mentions his age bracket, sex and particular joint pain that he recognizes as his own.

Just look at shampoo these days - the basic ingredients are the same as they have always been, but now you can buy shampoo for blonde hair, red hair, curly hair, long hair, short hair, men's hair, dry hair, greasy hair. Is it really that different? I'm not blond or curly. Will my hair be any different if I use those products? Probably not. It's usually just a way of making the customer feel special, unique and understood and *it works.*

The days of mass marketing are well and truly over, so you need to look at the products you have and find out who else would like, want, or need them. Ask yourself how they could be re-packaged, re-positioned, or re-pitched to meet the requirements of niche groups in your overall market. Who else might benefit from them?

Finding new markets is relatively low-risk because you already have the product development done - you just need to repackage or reposition it and alter the marketing message to focus on your targeted niche groups.

Both - Diversification

The third way to create new revenue streams, spread your risk, and Seek Growth is to combine product and market diversification - in other words, you create new products for new markets. As you would imagine, this is the most risky of the three types of diversification, because you need to go through the often costly product development phase and access new markets.

The best example of this type of diversification is Sir Richard Branson's Virgin companies.

His Virgin brand has diversified from music related businesses into just about anything you could think of. Though he's not personally associated with many of them anymore, they often still embody the Virgin Ethos, as well as the name. Branson has become a billionaire because of his willingness to go where others feared to tread.

Branson is known for going into industries where the customer had limited choice and the major players had become greedy and complacent. His famous entry into the airline industry resulted in a dirty-tricks campaign against Virgin by British Airways, but he was successful nonetheless. His entry into the cola market with Virgin Cola was not so successful because the customer was wedded to Coca Cola and Pepsi and didn't actually want an alternative. Still, Sir Richard is a billionaire and one of the richest men in the world because of his willingness to engage in - and his success at - diversification. There are no sacred cows at Virgin.

This type of diversification stands apart from the other three growth strategies in this model because it carries the most risk and the most potential reward. It should be the direction you move into once you have achieved success in the other three. Market penetration, product development and market development can usually be managed with the same technical, financial, and merchandising resources which currently exist in the business. However, developing new products for new markets often requires new skills, new techniques, and new facilities. It carries the most risk and will often lead to fundamental changes in the structure and direction of the business.

External Growth

Internal growth is about making more sales to more people more often, and it's executed by market penetration, product development, market development and diversification. By definition, this type of growth can be relatively slow and steady.

If you want fast growth, then you will have to consider external growth through acquisition of other, complementary businesses. If you can highlight your ideal client and identify with a company that already services a large number of clients in that demographic, then you can massively fast-track your sales and success.

If you decide that external growth is for you and you have the financial skills to pull it off, then you need to approach the venture with your eyes firmly on the outcome. There are three personal hazards you'll need to face, and you'll need the determination to clear these hurdles. External growth...

- can be all-consuming
- involves higher risk
- raises your stress levels

External Growth can be All-Consuming

Your acquisition deal will probably take over your life for a season. You will need to commit huge amounts of time and energy to the process. It helps if those around you also know what to expect and are ready for your absence from their lives.

Buying a business, especially the first time, is a full-time proposition. To contemplate it at the start of your business venture is either brave or crazy, because the time needed to get started and develop a successfully functioning business is usually considerable. To try and do that and buy another business will test even the most dedicated entrepreneur.

You will spend countless hours going over the financials, analyzing and strategizing. You will need to work out how best to proceed and incorporate the new business into the existing one for maximum impact and accelerated growth. If you don't do the appropriate due diligence and planning, then the acquisition is likely to come back and bite you. Many a good company has been destroyed by an acquisition that was poorly planned and not well executed.

Higher Risk

If you're going to buy another business, chances are you're going to need to use Other People's Money (OPM). And contrary to popular opinion, there is actually much more risk involved in borrowing money than in using your own. If you lose your own money, then it might hurt for a while, but you can start again and move forward. It's much harder to recover from the loss of OPM because you are not starting from scratch - you are starting from minus scratch.

A great story, now part of corporate legend, that tells how Donald Trump, walking along the street with his second wife Marla Maples, saw a homeless person. Trump pointed to the man and said, "That guy is worth $900 million more than me." Donald Trump was in serious financial trouble at the time and his situation was actually a whole lot worse than the homeless guy's because he had borrowed Other People's Money.

There is more risk involved in buying another business, and you have to be prepared for that. You will often need to put all that you own on the line in order to access the money you need to pursue the opportunity anyway. Lenders want to know that you too have something at risk before they will feel comfortable lending money.

You will need to get comfortable with the idea that you could lose significantly borrowing equity to finance the next move, as is an inevitable stage of growing a business. Get comfortable with it - if you're not, then don't buy the business.

External Growth can Brings Increased Stress

It's clear from my own experiences - and those of others I've met who have achieved great wealth - that external growth is no picnic.

The pressure can be enormous. So think of the most stressful time in your life and double it. If you feel able to deal with that level of stress, then you are ready for external growth. If not, then get used to running a successful business for a longer time, stick to internal growth, and get really good at that first.

External growth is a great way to take quantum leaps, but it is not for the faint-hearted, and it's always capital intensive…so it's not likely to suit all readers of this book. Occasionally you can pick up a bargain and make a good deal if the business is in trouble, but then, if the business is in trouble, you have to make sure you know what you are taking on and that the company's troubles are managable and can be capitalized on.

Other Key lessons For Seeking Growth

- The customer is not always right
- Competition - around the world, not across the street… and certainly not across the corridor
- Understand business cycles
- Understand the importance of systems

The Customer is *Not* Always Right

Traditional business and marketing training will often tell you that the customer is always right and that you should always be customer-centric. The customer *isn't* always right. Many businesses, especially at the start, are just so keen to get *any* customers that they don't take the time to figure out *whom* they want as customers.

Consequently, they waste valuable time and energy trying to keep the wrong people happy. Just as you need to be clear about your target and clear about your strategy, you also need to be clear about what your ideal customer looks like. Separate the wheat from the chaff early on and focus on getting the right kind of clients and customers: the ones you enjoy working with, the ones who pay on time, the ones who really appreciate everything you're doing for them, and the ones that don't take up endless amounts of your time on trivial issues.

Not all customers are created equal, so be a little discerning - and let your competitors deal with the difficult ones. Find out as much as you can about your customers so you can work out a profile of your best ones. Use this profile to seek out growth opportunities and find more "ideal clients" and fewer tire-kickers.

Competition - Around the World, *not* Across the Corridor

I have often said that competition can sometimes bring out the best in products and the worst in people. Did you know it was rumored for a time that Fuji's unofficial mission statement was "Kill Kodak"?

Competition shouldn't be across the desk or down the hall. Despite the undeniable fact that competition is global, too many businesses have departments or teams pitted against each other. I remember doing some consulting work with a pet food company many years ago. They ran three shifts, and each shift was measured on productivity against to the previous shift. At the end of each shift, employees would clock off and invariably make it as hard as possible for the next shift to get started effectively because they didn't want to be beaten. They were competing against each other, and management wanted to know why morale was low!

Don't pit your people against each other. Pit them against the external competition or a significant but achievable goal. Work hard to make sure that when one department wins, everyone wins. Develop incentive schemes that include everyone - not just sales - and keep everyone focused on results. If everyone is helping everyone else to succeed, then everyone in the business wins.

Understand Business Cycles

Growth comes down to a few key considerations - having a crystal-clear idea of where you want to go and an understanding of the current business climate, the business cycle, and the trends that happen to be timely.

Take the best management team and a good idea in a bad economy, and the venture might work out, particularly if the business is able to ride out the cycle. If you take an average team and idea, in an up-trending cycle, that may work out too. In an uptrending cycle there is always an opportunity for both businesses to seem strong.

However too often, people panic in a downturn and can be overly pessimistic; similarly, they're too optimistic in an up-trending market. Yet there are always opportunities in both. Often the best ideas and businesses emerge from chaos. Being the first to consolidate a new or cottage industry can bring huge rewards.

Learning to create success amidst market uncertainty will always produce untold rewards because it's during these times that there's a lot up for grabs. This situation can sometimes create a dilemma: on one hand, you have to take advantage of the downturns to seek out opportunities and growth possibilities…and yet you also have to make sure your timing is right; otherwise, it doesn't matter how good the business idea is.

People panic when things slow down. One of the biggest mistakes business leaders make is to contract from the market. They batten down the hatches and reduce costs in an effort to stay afloat. Often one of these "costs" is marketing. But sales and marketing activity should never be seen as costs. They are investments, and they should be increased, not decreased, in a down trending market. When companies withdraw, they leave opportunities for the competition that you, as a proactive, marketing-focused company, can and should capitalise on.

The Importance of Systems

The ultimate end-game for your venture should be to sell the business. Some business owners would disagree with me, and certainly you need to create value and deliver something people need and want. But your end-game should always be to cash out, especially if you're seeking major wealth and not just something to do for a few more years.

Starting with this in mind, as you build your business you will need to ensure that you pay particular attention to *how* you grow. You can't afford to grow in a haphazard, ad hoc way where individuals in the business effectively hold you hostage to the information in their heads. You need to document processes so that you retain crucial knowledge and allow efficient sharing of information when new people join the business. You don't want people wasting their time re-inventing the wheel. You need to have systems and processes in place that allow you and your team to consistently deliver high quality products or services, regardless of the comings and goings of employees.

If you want to create a saleable asset or franchise your business, these processes are imperative. If you can create a duplicable, turn-key approach to your enterprise, then you have the opportunity to franchise for exponential growth and profit. Franchising allows other people to run your business model to a consistent standard, regardless of your personal presence.

A great example of a franchise success story is Young Rembrandts. Founded in 1988 by Bette Fetter, she began the company working at home teaching kids to draw. Today the organization teaches thousands of kids in weekly classes conducted across America.

Fetter combined her unique skills in fine arts education and her understanding of child development to create a step-by-step approach to drawing. This transformed kids from doodlers into "Young Rembrandts" by utilising the fundamental skills of all visual arts. Research has indicated that there is a strong connection between the skills these budding artists are taught…and improved performance in the classroom. Perhaps it's simply due to increased confidence, but whatever the reason, Young Rembrandts is a roaring success. The system was franchised to capitalize on its initial growth and to ensure that more kids were given access to the experience and benefits the program offers.

What To Expect If You Fail To Seek Growth:

- You'll wake up one day and realize you've been treading water for 10 years!
- You'll miss growth opportunities

You'll Wake Up One Day and Realise You've been Treading Water for 10 Years!

If you choose not to follow Law 6 and Seek Growth, then you will be running just to stay in one place. The busyness of business life will take attention away from the target, and you will not actually achieve what you set out to achieve. *If significant wealth is your target you have to keep your eye on the ball and Seek Growth at every turn.*

If your goal is to create wealth, then you need to actively make that happen. It won't fall in your lap. It won't happen by itself. There are examples of people who have come up with an idea that has mushroomed on its own, but they are rare - so rare, in fact, that it does not warrent mention. The McDonald brothers had a truly innovative fast-food business model, but it wasn't until Ray Kroc saw their genius - and did the relentless grunt-work of marketing and franchising - that a worldwide business was born.

Wealth is rarely an accident - it's designed and worked for. If you don't work toward that goal, you will end up working, and what you'll discover is that you have created nothing more than a job for yourself - not a wealth creation vehicle. That may be fun, and if you're living Law 2, then what you're creating and doing will be enjoyable to you. But you still need to keep your eye on the end-game - business sale and equity in that transaction.

You'll Miss Opportunities

When you Seek Growth as an active pursuit, you'll see opportunities that you wouldn't otherwise notice. Remember the gorilla on the basketball court in our discussion of **Law 2** - Embrace the Future? If you don't focus on growth and make it your mission and your driving focus, then you'll be so busy with the activity of your business you'll miss the gorillas in your midst.

What You Can Confidently Expect If You Seek Growth:

- You'll achieve far more than you thought possible
- You'll be ahead of trends and always have options

You'll Achieve Far more than you Thought Possible

If you're focused on growth and on moving your business forward faster than mere organic growth, then you will be stretched to grow and develop faster.

That experience isn't always pleasant, and it can be confronting and scary at times, but the results are worth it. Getting through to the other side after a baptism of fire builds confidence. When you consistently do what you didn't think was possible, what becomes possible…expands. Even if you fail to meet interim milestones, stretching for the impossible means you will always travel further, faster. Aiming high and far is the key, and maintaining that commitment will yield results - it's a natural law of growth.

When you do more than you think you can, you face your fears, insecurities and move through them, then you expand as a human being. This journey that you want to embark upon is not just about the money. It's about who you become as a result of the process. You will feel more alive, more passionate, more committed, and more confident than you've ever felt in your life - and that is something money can't buy.

You'll Be Ahead of Trends and Always have Options

If you are constantly evolving, finding new uses and markets for existing products and new complementary products, then you stand a far higher chance of success. Fifty years ago companies could do one thing well and be successful. But the world has changed, and consumer demands and expectations are constantly changing.

Successful companies today are the ones that are always asking themselves, "How can we improve?" and "How can we become even more embedded into our customer's lives?" When you ask these questions as a business, you will always improve, and that innovation, open-mindedness, and willingness to pre-empt and act on opportunity will always create growth and dynamism. *Law 6 is about seeking growth at all times.* That means being constantly on the lookout for opportunities that can exponentially increase your sales.

Seeking growth is also about creating a thriving business that will increase your personal financial future too - so remember to put some of your profits into long-term investments that will accumulate over time. This is very basic: wealthy people are wealthy not just because of the businesses they create but because of *the equity producing assets they have bought* with the spoils of that business. They hold, protect, and increase that wealth through shrewd investments in other businesses, equities or property markets. Remember: *wealth is not about income, but about equity in a series of investment transactions.*

Change is Inevitable and Assured

Change will happen. It is an inevitable part of life. We can either wait to have the process forced upon us, or we can rise up to meet it.

The one unchangeable certainty is that
nothing is unchangeable or certain.
John F Kennedy

Law 6 - Seek Growth is about learning to rise up to meet change and sculpt that change into growth.

True wealth creation is about taking active and conscious control over the growth process, rather than waiting for it to arrive by accident or evolution. Once you have established yourself in a wealth creation vehicle that inspires you and gets you up early in the morning, then look for opportunities to expand as fast as possible. True progress is made only when you cultivate that progress and seek it out at every turn.

Are You Aligned to Law 6 - Do You Seek Growth?

Below there are 7 sets of two statements - 1A/1B - 7A/7B. Again, read each pair of statements and mark the one that's mostly true for you. Which one more accurately reflects your views, opinions, and experience?

As before, no one need see this. If you don't want to write in the book or want to keep your selections private, then make the selections in a separate notebook. Don't mark what you wish you were like or hope to be like in the future; answer as you are right now. If you are unsure, then ask for feedback from someone you know and trust.

	A	B
1	☐ I am always looking for ways to expand - both professionally and personally.	I know growth is important, but seriously, I'm paddling as hard as I can just to keep on top of the day-to-day. ☐
2	☐ My income is growing each year - albeit a little.	I had early success but can't seem to take the step to the next level. ☐
3	☐ I have attended development courses or professional training programs and am a voracious reader.	I don't have time. And even if I did, I think a lot of it's just a waste of time and money. ☐

4	☐ I know what's going on in my industry, and I know what my competitors are doing.	I try to keep up to date, but it's difficult with work commitments. To be honest, I don't know what my competitors are doing. ☐
5	☐ I recognize the importance of marketing and top-notch customer service.	Marketing is all very well, but it's expensive, and it's one of the first expenses to get slashed in an economic downturn. ☐
6	☐ I think if everyone gets involved in growth, then you'd be surprised at some of the good ideas that all sorts of people have.	I just want my people to do their jobs, and I'll worry about new ideas. ☐
7	☐ There are written policies and procedures in my business.	It's on my to-do list. ☐

If you have marked five or more of the statements in the A Column, then you already have a good grasp of Law 6. If you have checked five or more statements in the B Column, then we suggest you read the supplementary guidebook; ***Law6 - Seek Growth: Applications and Insights.*** This companion guide will give you further information about Law 6, together with practical techniques, ideas and insights that will enable you to successfully align yourself to this law and harness its power.

Law 7

Give Back

Don't Let Prosperity Destroy Generosity

He who is not liberal with what he now owns...does but deceive himself when he thinks he would be liberal if he had more. If there be any truer measure of a man than by what he does, it may be by what he gives. Revered are those who can give without remembering. Remembered are those who take without forgetting. Examples are few of men ruined by giving. In all you do, Give Back.

Chapter Nine
Law 7 - Give Back

WHEN PASSENGERS AND crew boarded Air Florida's Flight 90 in Washington National Airport on January 13, 1982, they expected an uneventful flight to Fort Lauderdale. Take-off clearance was received at 3:58 p.m. Within minutes of take-off, it was clear that the plane was in difficulty. Failing to gain altitude, the Boeing 737 clipped the 14th Street Bridge, killing four motorists before plunging into the icy waters of the Potomac River. Soon only the tail section, which had broken free of the fuselage, remained afloat. Six of the 79 passengers and crew survived the initial crash.

At 4.20 p.m., *Eagle 1*, a United States Park Police helicopter, arrived at the scene; on board were pilot Donald Usher and paramedic Gene Windsor. A life-line was hung from the chopper, and the first man caught the rope hooked it around his waist and was lifted to safety. On the second trip, the rope was caught by another man who immediately passed it to a fellow survivor, who was also lifted to safety. On the third trip, two-life lines were used, as the crew realized that no one would survive in the freezing water for much longer. Again the same man caught the rope and again he passed it to someone else - three more survivors were rescued.

Keen to meet the man who had so selflessly given up his opportunity to be saved, Usher and Windsor went back one last time to pick up the hero. Tragically, as they approached the wreckage, they realized he had succumbed to the cold and slipped beneath the water.

Who was this man? Why did he choose to save others instead of himself?

He was Arland D. Williams, Jr., an unassuming 46-year-old bank examiner from the Federal Reserve Bank in Atlanta. He was identified by the coroner some time after the crash because he was the only person recovered from the river who had died from drowning rather than from crash related injuries.

There were many acts of heroism on that terrible day but Arland Williams stands out because he could have saved himself - not once, but many times. He was the least injured from the crash and stood a good chance of recovery. He was the proud father of two, and although divorced, was soon to be remarried. Described by friends and family as quiet, competent, cheerful and humble, he was above all else an average man. And yet he did something remarkable when he gave up his life to save people he didn't even know on that cold January day. In fact, he was anything but average.

I remember being told this story when I was just eight years old, and it had a massive impact on me then, as it does today. Even at that young age, I was in awe of such bravery and selfless heroism, and those feelings have stayed with me all these years. Today the 14th Street Bridge is called the Arland D. Williams, Jr. Memorial Bridge in honor of his ultimate sacrifice.

It's impossible to hear that story and not be moved. And it raises uncomfortable questions for us all... We find ourselves asking, "What would I have done?"

It's a question I have asked myself often, not just in relation to this story. The truth is that you and I will probably never have to answer that question in such a dramatic and tragic way. We will probably never have to demonstrate courage and selflessness in the way Arland Williams did - but we all can do *something*.

Williams was an ordinary man who showed extraordinary compassion and care for his fellow human beings, and that is something that we can all do - regardless of the circumstances or the level of our success.

Doing Good And Making Money Are Not Mutually Exclusive

All too often, there is an unspoken assumption that if you have achieved great financial wealth, then you did so at the expense of others. The image of the "fat cat" business person is still alive and well in the 21st century. And to be fair, there is a smorgasbord of evidence to back it up. Unscrupulous investment bankers, hedge fund managers, wealthy people raking in the profits from weapons, oil, third world sweatshops, and other dubious sources of revenue...the list goes on.

No one can deny that some individuals have a poor reputation for their social conscience and willingness to find win/win solutions. But this "dog eat dog" mentality is *not* a prerequisite of business success. More and more business owners and employees are seeking an alternative. You don't have to be a bastard in business; you don't have to scrape and claw your way to the top, burning bridges as you go.

For example, it is possible to do something good for the planet and yourself - and still make money.

That's exactly what Cheung Yan did. You probably haven't heard her name before, but she is the founder of Nine Dragons, China's largest maker of container cardboard.

After her employer's business collapsed, Yan decided to start her own business. In her previous role, she had hit on the idea of trading waste paper, after helping her boss earn a tidy profit shipping waste paper from northern China to Guangdong. She recognized in the mid-80s, that as China's economy took off, demand for packaging for its growing exports would soar. Almost everything shipped, comes in a box.

Yan could see a huge problem on the horizon, because China had very limited paper resources of its own. Most of the forests had been destroyed to make way for a quarter of the world's population. The mills China did have used mostly straw pulp, which was environmentally devastating.

China's problem was environmental devastation and no paper. Over in the US, however, the problem was too much paper! So Yan brought the two together and solved them both. She brought the unwanted paper from the US back to China, where it was recycled into the all important boxes so it could begin its journey once again. This brilliantly simple solution has made Cheung Yan the richest self-made woman in the world. Her company employs thousands of people and is doing something positive for the environment at the same time.

Social Entrepreneurship and Venture Philanthropy

I'm not suggesting that Yan's reason for starting Nine Dragons was environmental rather than financial. More likely she simply saw an impending problem that she could solve and make money from. That problem also happened to solve a few other problems, and it does demonstrate that it's possible to make money and do something that's beneficial to a wider audience.

The great news is that more and more people are consciously and actively pursuing a more socially responsible approach to financial gain. It's something I am passionate about. You don't have to decimate natural resources, pollute the environment and bully your staff and suppliers to make money. Whatever you decide to do to create your money, I would strongly suggest that you adhere to the Hippocratic Oath: *First do no harm.*

This new attitude about making money and doing something meaningful and worthwhile is known as "social entrepreneurship" or "venture philanthropy."

There is a lot of debate about what the idea constitutes, but suffice it to say that it is the recognition that social responsibility and financial reward are not mutually exclusive; sooner or later we all have to adhere to **Law 7**.

Some choose to Give Back rather than profit; they turn their ingenuity and passion toward a broader social goal. Others do it with the money they make in their entrepreneurial ventures.

Make no mistake: social entrepreneurship and venture philanthropy is still business. The misconception is that classic entrepreneurs are motivated by money and social entrepreneurs, by altruism. The reality, borne out by my interviews with world's financial elite, is that entrepreneurs are rarely motivated by money alone. More often, they are motivated by the chance to pursue a vision and see their ideas come to life.

Thus, classic entrepreneurs seek to exploit opportunities that exist in a market that can afford to purchase their product or service. The entrepreneur and their investors will make a profit, and the business will develop.

The social entrepreneur seeks to address issues and problems that exist in a market that can't necessarily afford their product or service. They are not as interested in profit as in large-scale transformation, and they seek to sustain the business rather than generate (and distribute) large profits.

A really remarkable example is The Institute for One World Health, created by Victoria Hale. Hale is a pharmaceutical scientist who became disillusioned and frustrated by the status quo. Although big pharmaceutical giants had the know-how and drug patents to cure countless diseases, the drugs were never developed because the people most in need of those drugs couldn't afford them.

Driven by the need to keep shareholders happy, drug companies focused instead on creating and marketing drugs for diseases and conditions that affected the well-off, who could afford the medications.

Clearly, this is unjust (and a terrible waste of knowledge and resources), and Hale did something about it - by creating the first non-profit pharmaceutical company whose mission is to ensure that drugs targeting infectious diseases in the developing world get to the people who need them, regardless of their ability to pay. She is a social entrepreneur in the purest sense. Interestingly, programs and ideas such as this are often supported by individuals who have made their money and are now dedicating their efforts to Law 7 in Giving Back.

One of Hale's investors is The Skoll Foundation. Jeff Skoll is the co-founder of eBay (with Pierre Omidyar), and since leaving eBay, he has focused his energies on social change, creating the Skoll Foundation and the film company Participant Productions.

It is clear that whether you start your wealth creation journey as a classic entrepreneur or a social entrepreneur, you will reach a point where you must Give Back. I believe we all have to master this law - even before we have the means to do so.

How to Master Law 7 & Give Back:

- Do what you can
- Start early
- Apply law 1 - 6

Do What You Can

Whatever you do and however you've built your business and made your wealth, you must Give Back. Often this idea is associated to the religious practice of tithing - the idea that you should donate at least 10% of all you earn to the church. I was brought up in a family where we were taught that everything we have is God-given, and so it was only right that we gave something back, because that taught us there is always more than enough.

Giving back and making a contribution to others is not just a noble thing to do; it is a natural law. Law 7 is not about single-handedly changing the world. It's about doing what you can when you can.

It's easy to become overwhelmed by the world's problems - economic disruptions, poverty, environmental challenges, escalating population, and natural disasters. In the face of such overwhelming problems, it's easy to bury our heads in the sand and convince ourselves that there is nothing we can do.

It is the greatest of all mistakes to do nothing
because you can only do a little.
Do what you can.
Sydney Smith

Instead of cursing the darkness, ask yourself what candles you are lighting? When it comes to darkness, Elie Wiesel has experienced more than most. At 15, he and his family were deported to Auschwitz. His mother and younger sister perished. Elie and his father were later transported to Buchenwald, where his father died shortly before the camp was liberated in April, 1945.

In 1986, he won the Nobel Prize for Peace and soon after, he and his wife Marion established The Elie Wiesel Foundation for Humanity. Rooted in the memory of the Holocaust, the foundation was established to combat indifference, intolerance and injustice through international dialogue and youth-focused programs that promote acceptance, understanding and equality.

It would have been easy for Wiesel to escape the horrors of the Holocaust and disappear, an angry and bitter man. But he didn't - he lit his own candle and did what he could to eradicate the darkness.

The darkness didn't stop at the end of the war. In December 2008, the foundation issued a press release to say that it had lost $15.2 million at the hands of Bernie Madoff. Wiesel, then 80 years old, gave only one TV interview. He said, "For the first moment, of course, it was almost paralyzing. Then we shook ourselves up." It was the shaking up that Wiesel wanted to focus on in his interview: How do we find the resilience to "shake ourselves up" in the face of such a blow?

Wiesel went on to say, "When my life seems to be partly or wholly in ruins, I build on them... I will never allow anyone to change my life or destroy what I have done with it. Somehow, what I must keep in mind is what I think of myself."

Despite the financial blow, the Foundation did manage to meet all its commitments. Donations came flooding in from around the world, proving once again that we all have the capacity to do something.

If someone as bitterly betrayed by humanity as Elie Wiesel can Give Back, then we can all Give Back. As the builder of a successful company and the creator of wealth, you have an obligation to help others and the community you live and work in. It doesn't have to be huge - you don't have to win any "philanthropist of the year" awards. You don't need to go down in history for giving away your fortune - just do what you can. Often it is the little things that can make a big difference.

One such example can be seen in the work of practical visionary and social entrepreneur Muhammad Yunus. In 1976, Yunus loaned $27 from his own pocket to forty-two people living in a tiny village in Bangladesh. They were hard working "micro-entrepreneurs" who only needed enough credit to purchase the raw materials for their trade, but until that point could only do so from usurious moneylenders. Yunus's small loan helped them break the cycle of poverty for good and sparked an idea that would change millions of lives.

In 1983, Yunus founded the mutually owned Grameen ("Village") Bank, which later won the Nobel Prize for Peace for its contribution to eradicating poverty. By offering the poorest in the world access to credit - even a tiny amount of credit - Yunus was able to transform lives.

As of January 2010, Grameen Bank has over eight million borrowers. Since inception, the bank has provided $8.85 billion in micro-loans. Ninety-seven percent of those receiving the loans are women without any collateral.

Grameen Bank focuses on women because they are often neglected in Third-World societies. The opportunity of self-employment and self-sufficiency empowers women and gives them the opportunity to lift themselves and their families out of poverty. Studies have also shown that output is greater when loans are given to women instead of men, "as women are more likely to use their earnings to improve their living situations and to educate their children."

The micro-finance model has been used around the world, from the shanty towns of Bolivia to Nairobi slums and villages in India. The money is often used to buy livestock or start micro-businesses. What makes it such a powerful model is that it enables individuals to take the first critical step to wealth and exercise Law 1 by Gaining Control. This raises their self-esteem and motivates them even further. Not only is micro-finance giving families a way out of poverty - it does so while flying in the face of convention. According to traditional banking, the poor are a bad credit risk - and yet the repayment rate for Grameen Bank is over 96%.

Never doubt that a small group of thoughtful,
committed citizens can change the world.
Indeed, it's the only thing that ever has.
Margaret Mead

Professor Yunus is a vocal pioneer of "social business" - using the creativity and passion inherent in successful business to tackle social problems such as poverty, pollution, inadequate health care and lack of education. What he advocates is nothing short of a new, more humane form of capitalism.

Start early

Wherever you are right now, start to Give Back. It's easy to sit on your hands and decide that you'll start when you have something significant to give. Perhaps you think you will donate money to charity when you are rich. Perhaps you think you will offer your time when you are less busy. Perhaps you think you will get involved in your local community when your kids have left home.

You won't. *Unless you start giving back when you can't really afford to and feel you can't spare the time or effort, then there is no way that you will give back when you do have the time or the means.*

To be clear: Law 7 is not just about money. We can all do something that is of value and makes someone's life better, even if it's just by giving some time and encouragement to a project.

When Warren Buffet's children were growing up, he set up a foundation for each of them so that each child could give away $100,000 a year. Buffet was eager for his children to get used to the idea of philanthropy.

As the family sat around the Christmas tree in 1999, Warren and Susan Buffett told their kids they were giving each of them $35 million to donate to the causes of their choice. They were each told to "go and do good things." Since then Buffett has famously pledged to give away the bulk of his fortune to the Bill and Melinda Gates Foundation but has also committed about $1 billion worth of stock to each of his children for charitable giving.

Buffett has made no secret of the fact that he is leaving the vast majority of his wealth to good causes. His children are not poor by any stretch of the imagination, but neither are they obscenely rich - or ever likely to be, despite *his* immense personal wealth.

You may be thinking, "Well that's all very well for one of the richest men in the world," but it's all relative. If you wouldn't Give Back ten cents on the dollar now, then you won't give away $100,000 of every million either. Giving Back is something that we should all do - *right now* - regardless of what we have to give.

Find causes or projects that are close to your heart, and make a commitment to do what you can. Very few of us have the resources to encourage our children to give away $100,000, but we can encourage a caring attitude so that our children make a donation of time or money, whenever they so desire. Giving and receiving is a two-way street, and each is made more pleasurable by the other.

Apply Laws 1-6

Once you arrive at the 7th Law of Wealth, you need to apply Laws 1- 6 to your philanthropic ideas.

You can't just give money. You must apply each Law to your philanthropy, in order to make your efforts truly effective.

You need to Gain Control, decide that you need to be responsible for your own efforts, and Give Back to projects that inspire you. You have to Embrace the Future and have a clear outcome you hope to achieve by Giving Back. You have to Own a Strategy and Always Execute that strategy, come what may. You need to Create Value with your giving and Seek Growth, so that your efforts can take on a life of their own.

My own giving has changed over the years, for many reasons. Most recently I have created a foundation with my friend and CEO of my private capital, investment management company. Bob grew up an orphan and lived in several orphanages in his early years. They were not easy years, and he knows what it's like to be homeless. For several years he has gone to Mission Beach in San Diego twice a year to feed 250 of the homeless people living there.

We've put a foundation together to formalize this activity and to offer some simple workshops for those who are interested. We are certainly not there to preach or change the lives of people who don't wish to be changed, but instead to offer support and options for those who are seeking an alternative. The fact of the matter is that there are some really fantastic people at Mission Beach - real characters. They have so much to give and we always gain so much from their association and friendship.

We may not change the world, but there is always something we can do for these individuals, and I always look forward to it and know they do too.

The 7 Laws methodology is intended to bring you full circle, Law 1 requires you to take responsibility for yourself. By Law 7, we are looking for ways to extend that responsibility to others who cannot always do it for themselves.

When starting on the journey of the 7 Laws of Wealth, you Gain Control of yourself by being responsible for your actions and redirecting those actions toward a chosen goal of wealth. By the time you have mastered Law 6, you are well on your way to those objectives, and Law 7 brings you back to responsibility again - this time, for others.

By Giving Back, you give other people the opportunity to go through the 7 laws themselves and perpetuate the *virtuous cycle.* It is exactly this journey through the 7 Laws of Wealth that has made the Grameen Bank so successful. As Muhammad Yunus discovered, the people in need of help were not lazy or unskilled. Far from it: they would create beautiful intricate goods that they would then sell for a pittance. The woman that inspired Grameen Bank made bamboo stools. Bamboo is not the most pliable of materials, and the young woman *"squatted barefoot on the hard mud. Her fingers were callused, her nails black with grime."* For her efforts she made two cents profit per stool.

With micro-loans of a few dollars, she was able to buy her materials without money lenders and create a proper business. Because Yunus gave back, millions of people in poverty around the world have been able to journey through the 7 Laws of Wealth themselves and inspire many others to do the same. They may not become millionaires but they are self sufficient, and that can make all the difference in the world.

The 7 Laws create *virtuous cycles* that can change lives - both your own and other people's.

What To Expect If You Fail to Give Back:

- Fear
- Your success will eventually feel empty and pointless

Fear

A drive for wealth so that you don't have to experience poverty is a powerful motivator. Many a fortune, including my own, has been forged in difficult times. I remember vividly that I decided that I *wasn't* going to be poor when I grew up and that drive pushed me into serious action toward wealth.

I have met people who have made a great deal of money, and all that consumes them now is hanging on to it. The fear of poverty is just replaced by another type of fear - the fear of losing it all.

That's not freedom.

Avarice hoards itself poor; charity gives itself rich
German Proverb

Wealth needs movement to survive and flourish. You have to use money to make money; you have to invest it to make it work for you - it's an active transaction of give and take. Hoarding it away won't make you happy, contented or fulfilled. Money is supposed to be spread around and enjoyed by more than just *yourself*.

Success Will Eventually Feel Empty and Pointless

If all you are seeking is money, then you may achieve that objective, but it will be a hollow victory. There are only so many homes you can buy and you can only live in one at a time. There are only so many holidays you can take and beaches you can lie on before you will wonder what you are doing with your time.

Sure, it may be fun for a while, but once you've bought the cars and the yacht and spent one afternoon on it in two years, then it all might feel a little pointless. Trust me on this.

This confusion and emptiness is very often experienced by lottery winners who became obscenely wealthy overnight. Because there is no work attached to the wealth, the novelty can soon wear off, and the money becomes a curse rather than a blessing.

John McGuiness won over $15.5 million in a $61 million rollover in 1996. At the time, he was earning $230 a week and sleeping on his parents' floor after splitting up with his first wife. In a note worthy gesture, he even gave his ex-wife over a million dollars and lavished a further $4.6 million on his family. He bought the toys, too, including a Ferrari for over $4 million, as well as five other exclusive cars. He relaxed on a Caribbean cruise and bought a villa in Majorca. He spent over $300,000 getting married again to wife No.2. He even bought a soccer club which began his downfall in 2004. In February 2008, he was seeking public housing in Scotland and was $3 million in debt. Mr. McGuiness is not an exception.

Angela Kelly won $54 million on Euro Lotto and within seven weeks had split from her partner. US winner William Post scooped up $16.2 million in the Pennsylvania lottery in 1988 but now lives on Social Security. He said, "I wish it never happened. It was a total nightmare." He was sued by a former girlfriend for a share, one of his brothers was arrested for hiring someone to kill him to inherit his share, other siblings pestered him to go into business with them and lost everything, including the relationships. Within one year, he was $1 million in debt and deserted by friends and family.

In the US there is an organisation called the 'Sudden Money Institute' that helps individuals deal with windfalls and inheritance and the pressures and disappointments it can bring. Money itself is never the answer to anyone's problems. It's certainly preferable to poverty, but unless you have a purpose and meaning to your life above and beyond the money, unless you have a reason to get up in the morning and try your best in whatever it is you do, then money can make you the loneliest person on the planet.

Of those who make their money through hard work and dedication, there can also come a time when everything is questioned. Tom Monaghan had a strong work ethic that took him from the orphanages of Michigan to the creation of a fast-food giant. He grew Domino's Pizza from a single $500 store to over 6,100 franchised and company-owned stores in 64 countries, with revenues of more than one billion dollars.

Monaghan was an innovator who set the bar for other companies. He's the man behind the corrugated pizza box to keep the pie hot. He also introduced insulated bags to do the same in transport. Monaghan worked 18-hour days in the early years of his business and visited more than 300 rival pizzerias to find the best techniques. Domino's, is of course, also known for their brilliant guarantee - "Delivered to your door within 30 minutes or it's free." Innovations such as these made him a force to be reckoned with, and in 1998 Monaghan sold Domino's Pizza for a billion dollars.

Unsurprisingly, with such wealth, Thomas Monaghan was also known as a big spender. He bought the usual toys and spent lavishly on holidays. He even bought his own island, complete with its own golf course, called Pepperoni Links. He bought the Detroit Tigers baseball team and had the biggest Frank Lloyd Wright collection in the world, a multi-million-dollar array of cars, a helicopter, and several airplanes.

After selling Domino's he intended to devote the rest of his life and his money to spreading his Christian beliefs - especially in the business arena. But then he read a little book by C.S. Lewis called *Mere Christianity* and decided to Give Back in a major way. He divested most of his ostentatious possessions, including the Detroit Tigers, and stopped the construction on a huge Wright-inspired mansion that was to be his home.

According to an interview in *The New York Times*, February, 14, 1999, Monaghan said, "I don't want to take my money with me when I go, I want to die broke."

Man must have an idol and the amassing
of wealth is one of the worst species of idolatry
No idol is more debasing than the worship of money
Andrew Carnegie

Whatever Monaghan read, it was enough to make him re-think his entire life and lifestyle. The toys and baubles of wealth became meaningless to him, and he set about giving it all away.

What You Can Confidently Expect If You Give Back:

- A sense of accomplishment and pride
- The opportunity to create a lasting legacy
- Fulfilment of an innate need

A Sense of Accomplishment and Pride

In 2009 I was asked to appear in a UK television program called *The Secret Millionaire*. A millionaire goes undercover into a poor, run-down or deprived area in the hope of finding some people or projects to which they-can donate. Usually there is a pretense that the millionaire is making a documentary on locating to the area. The wealthy individual has just ten days to find out about the area and meet the locals to find people to support. In the end, the person reveals their real identity and hands over a cheque.

What I particularly enjoy is the journey - not just for the people who eventually benefit from help, but for the millionaire. Often you see the millionaires in their beautiful homes talking about what they expect. More often than not, they are looking forward to the process and are keen to help and make a difference, although often there is some understandable trepidation. What they rarely anticipate, however, is how the experience will change *their* life.

Hilary Devey built up a successful hauling business in a very male dominated industry. She lived in a magnificent Staffordshire mansion with her only son, who had by all accounts put her through the mill. She was extremely rich, but her wealth brought only loneliness and isolation.

Devey went undercover to Rochdale and ended up giving away some $200,000 of her own money - and more, since the show supported projects on the Falinge estate. One of those projects was The Back Door Music Project, set up by mum Carol Moore, who gave local kids something to do provided the opportunity to develop their musical talent and creativity instead of being bored on the street. Devey was convinced that if something like that had existed when her son was growing up, he wouldn't have ruined his life with drugs.

Another of her projects was a local hospice run by pensioner Sheila Acton. The hospice was a focal point in the community, yet it was under threat of closure. Devey said, "Returning to see how the work was going felt like going home. I've made a lot of friends, true friends. The way the people I met gave their time and money to projects for others humbled me. Seeing how I've been able to help them is overwhelming."

Nick Leslau was another individual who posed as a social worker in a deprived area of Glasgow. Estimated to be worth $300 million, Leslau made his money in property development. The extent of his wealth essentially meant that Leslau lived in a different universe from the one he was about to be plunged into - from a $20 million home in Mayfair to the uncomfortable reality of Possilpark in Glasgow.

Up to that time, he was a cocky, assured and a self confessed "ass for 48 weeks of the year!" It was amazing to watch his transformation as much as the changes in the lives of the people he helped. He says, "I found I had a fear of disability. When I see someone in a wheelchair at an airport, I am a metaphorical road-crosser. Afterwards, I thought what a twit I am for being afraid of talking to a kid with Down's syndrome. I had the best evening of my life with those kids." Leslau was clearly moved by his experience, and he was one of the most significant benefactors on the show, giving away over $600,000 of his own money.

To see how selfless others are in Giving back time and effort under difficult circumstances is humbling for many. Getting involved in helping those people to make even more of a difference is clearly deeply rewarding and fulfilling - and money alone will never give you that. Giving back doesn't just help others - it makes us better people.

The Opportunity to Create a Lasting Legacy

Most people have heard of Andrew Carnegie, the wealthy American industrialist who made his fortune in steel. He was the Bill Gates of his time.

The question is: would you know his name if all he had done was build a business and make a fortune?

Probably not. The reason Carnegie is so famous is that he dedicated the first half of his life to making a fortune and the second half to giving it away. It is because of Andrew Carnegie that the public library system works in the US today. His passion was education, and he felt that anything was possible for individuals if they had access to the right knowledge. He founded the Carnegie Corporation of New York with the mission to "promote the advancement and diffusion of knowledge and understanding." He founded the Carnegie Mellon University. He established schools and universities in the US and UK, as well as pension funds for former employees. Carnegie Hall was named after him.

There is no doubt that Tom Monaghan will be remembered for Domino's Pizza, but his legacy will be what he created by Giving back. The same is probably true of both Bill Gates and Warren Buffett. The two richest men in the world for well over a decade, they have already given away billions. It is that generosity and philanthropy that will be their true legacy, as much as Microsoft or Berkshire Hathaway.

We Fulfil a Basic Need

In Chapter 2 we talked about our basic human needs:

- to live
- to love
- to feel important
- to experience variety
- to grow
- to contribute

Giving back is perhaps the only activity we engage in that allows us to meet all six of those needs. You could argue that we don't need to Give Back to survive. But we must Give Back if we are to truly live. Survival is a poor choice to settle for. A life well lived is a life well given. We each have a moral and ethical obligation to help others, whatever religious or spiritual beliefs we may hold.

We are all connected. What we do for others we ultimately do to and for ourselves. Giving back allows us to feel connected and loved; it gives our life variety, since it often engages us in new experiences. We get to feel needed because our efforts matter and make a contribution. This allows us to grow as a human being, and we are better for the experience. This also makes us feel significant through our giving to better a cause or situation.

Wealth alone will never make you happy. However I do understand that until you achieve a certain level of wealth, you will never really believe that statement. Eventually, though, you will learn that happiness does not come from digits on a bank statement or the material possessions in your home.

Happiness comes from a sense of purpose and from doing your level best to achieve a worthwhile goal. It comes from surmounting challenges and tackling the impossible and coming out stronger and wiser for the adventure. It comes from knowing that your presence on this planet mattered - if even just to handful of people. It comes from making other people's lives easier or better in some way. It comes from giving the very things you were always so keen to acquire more of: time, money, experience, love, friendship, knowledge and laughter.

This is why giving feels so good and it's why we will often give to others even when we are in need of assistance ourselves. This innate drive was powerfully demonstrated by Project 100.

Project 100 is an idea created by Co-op Services Credit Union in Livonia, Michigan. It was designed to help local communities by encouraging their residents to focus on giving. For 100 days, Co-op Services Credit Union and Project 100 visited 100 random people all over town and gave each of them a single $100 dollar bill.

What was the catch? There wasn't one. Recipients could do whatever they wished with their money. All they were asked, was that they thought about what they could do to make the community a better place - whether it was volunteering for a community event or helping out a neighbor in need. The act itself didn't matter. It was the idea that any simple act of giving could spark a change for the better.

Project Coordinator Greg Wohler suggested that "Project 100 gained traction because it was the ideal mix of spontaneity and generosity. At the time we started, everything in Michigan felt very negative. We wanted to move the bar. The beginning of any change is a move to the positive."

Don't Let Prosperity Destroy Generosity

Our capacity to Give Back is enormous. Even when we are struggling, there is still room for generosity. Just look at the Haiti earthquake disaster of 2010. The world was still reeling from the impact of the global financial crisis, yet people all over the world dug deep and gave a financial donation to help the relief effort. Perhaps it's because when we see footage of the victims or witness the devastation caused by terrorism or natural disaster, we are reminded of how lucky we are - regardless of what we have.

Or perhaps, it's because we are reminded of our own humanity. Maybe that's why Project 100 worked so well: even in hardship, people were able to appreciate that there is always someone else with a greater need, and we can all help and make a difference.

It doesn't matter what you have right now, what you own or where you live. We all have the capacity to Give Back. And sometimes money can be the least effective method. A word of support, encouragement or even a smile costs nothing but can change the course of someone's day or even their life. So don't ever let prosperity destroy generosity - do what you can when you can. If everyone did, then the world would be a very different place.

Are You Aligned to Law 7 - Do You Give Back?

Once again I've given you seven sets of two statements. Mark the one that's mostly true for you. Which more accurately reflects your view on life and opinions?

As before, be honest. Don't check what you wish you were like or hope to be like in the future. Answer as you are right now. If you are unsure, then ask someone you know and trust to give you feedback.

	A	B
1	☐ I regularly give to charity.	I don't have spare cash to support charities regularly - I'm barely keeping my own house in order. ☐
2	☐ It can be a little overwhelming to know what to do, so I just do what I can.	There are too many causes that need help. Individuals can't make a difference; that's the role of government anyway. ☐
3	☐ I have given my time to a good cause at least twice in the last year.	I can't remember the last time I gave my time for a good cause. ☐
4	☐ I often compliment and encourage others, including complete strangers.	I don't often compliment anyone - not even loved ones. It's embarrassing. ☐
5	☐ It's awe inspiring to see how generous people are - even when they don't have that much themselves.	I think people are stupid for being so gullible - the money they give never gets to the people that need it anyway. ☐
6	☐ I remember my parents giving to charity.	I don't remember my parents ever giving to charity. ☐
7	☐ I often help clients or customers without expectation of getting anything in return. I do it because I can help.	I don't really do anything without payment or reward. I don't have time for good deeds - I'm trying to run a business/do my job. ☐

If you have marked five or more of the statements in the A Column, then you already have a good grasp of Law 7. If you have checked three or more statements in the B Column, then we suggest you read the supplementary guidebook; ***Law7 - Give Back: Applications and Insights.*** This companion guide will give you further information about Law 7, together with practical techniques, ideas and insights into how you can successfully align yourself to this law and harness its power.

Chapter 10

Final Thoughts

The only conquests which are permanent and leave no regrets are those over ourselves. The greatest achievements of man have resulted from the transmission of ideas and execution. Failure to live these laws is failure to understand them. Rewards follow accomplishment, they never precede them.

Chapter 10
Final Thoughts

WARREN BUFFET ONCE said when he addressed a group of Stanford University students: *"Everybody here has the ability absolutely to do anything I do and much beyond. Some of you will, and some of you won't. For the ones who won't, it will be because you get in your own way, not because the world doesn't allow you."*

He's right, of course - but not because the rich belong to some secret club or there is some invisible, mysterious "rich quota" which automatically stops everyone who seeks wealth once the quota has been reached, but because *the natural laws that govern wealth are often the antithesis of modern life*. In other words we often exhibit 7 flaws instead of habitually following the 7 Laws of Wealth - and then wonder why we are not rich.

The 7 Flaws

Too often we:

1. Place blame instead of Gain Control
2. Promote the past instead of Embrace the Future
3. Manage procedure instead of Own a Strategy
4. Hold back instead of Always Execute
5. Grab profit instead of Create Value
6. Maintain position instead of Seek Growth
7. Keep it all instead of Giving Back

1. Placing blame instead of gaining control

It's easy to look at our own life and come up with reasons as to why it's not turned out like you expected or hoped. It's so convenient to blame your parents or your upbringing for the flaws in your character, even though genetics and environment are by no means the only influences on the way we turn out.

It's easy to decide it's the government's fault…or to rationalize that the reason you never got off your backside and committed to anything was because you didn't have the education. For every excuse you can come up with, there is a shining example of someone who has overcome all those obstacles to become successful. It's not about the color of your skin, your gender, education, background, genetics, religion, or even where you live - success is a matter of *choice,* not chance.

Ninety nine percent of failures come from
people who have the habit of making excuses.
George Washington Carver

Placing blame is an excuse to wallow in self-pity and mediocrity. Placing blame doesn't hurt the other person - the only person that suffers is you. *Resolve to remove blame from your life TODAY.* Gain Control - take charge of your mind, and direct your action toward a goal that inspires you and brings a smile to your face and pride to your soul.

Create a compelling future for yourself and your loved ones - and make it happen. The wealth you desire is possible - but only if you master the **1st Law of Wealth - Gain Control**.

2. Dwelling on the past instead of embracing the future

Forget your history or the story that you carry around with you about why you can't do what you dream of. It's as useful as placing blame. So what if your father was a lousy father. So what if your Mum couldn't boil an egg - forget it! Just because you grew up poor doesn't mean you have to stay that way. It is not the circumstances or the events in life that shape us; it is what we decide to make them mean. If you've had a difficult past or survived a terrible experience, then don't re-live it every day and use it as justification for shrinking from the world. Instead, use it as fuel to drive you forward to a strong and powerful future.

The best revenge is massive success.
Frank Sinatra

When you get stuck in the past, you use it is a crutch or explanation for why *your* life is the way it is. It's just another form of excuse. There are innumerable examples of people who have endured terrible events and horrendous circumstances, but far from allowing those things to destroy them, they have risen above the difficulty to become stronger and more determined than ever.

Nelson Mandela could have been forgiven for being bitter. Apartheid is a stain on humanity, and he had every right to be angry. He was an active anti-apartheid leader in his youth and paid a heavy price for his dedication to the cause. Mandela was incarcerated for 27 years, most of which was spent on Robben Island. Following his release, however, he supported reconciliation and was a pivotal player in the move to multi-racial democracy in South Africa. He has received more than 250 awards, most notably the 1993 Nobel Peace Prize. Today he is one of the most respected and revered men of all time.

Never look back unless you are planning to go that way.
Henry David Thoreau

His stand changed the course of a nation because he refused to live in the past and believed in a new and better future.

Like placing blame, getting stuck in the past and using old hurts, difficult circumstances, or betrayals to limit your future doesn't make the perpetrator of those events suffer. We've all been a victim at some point - *how much of a victim and how long we stay a victim depends entirely on our strength of character and willingness to move on*. Forget about the past, it's gone. Now is all that matters. Gain Control and master **Law 2 - Embrace the Future** to make a new beginning.

3. Manage procedure instead of owning a strategy

It's easy to look busy and run around like a headless chicken. It may even make you feel superior to others or allow you to think you are making progress. Focusing too tightly on the detail without a firm plan for your future will build nothing.

You might successfully "put in your days," you may even be able to convince yourself that you gave it your best shot - but the quiet whisper deep inside you will know the truth. No one wants to Own a Strategy or take a stand because it requires courage. However just managing procedure is a sure path to failure.

Science may have found a cure for most evils; but it has found no remedy for the worst of them all - the apathy of human beings
Helen Keller

Doing stuff for the sake of doing stuff is pointless. At best it's a tragic waste of human capital. At worst, a sole destroying excuse for a life. What happens when you are sitting on your porch in your retirement? What will you have done with your life? What will you have achieved? What will you have tried? What adventures will you be able to tell your grandchildren about? Gain Control, Embrace the Future and master **Law 3 - Own a Strategy** so that you can systematically achieve your dream and be proud of a life well lived.

4. Hold back instead of always executing

Consistency is a key aspect of success, but the modern world offers us endless choices. Those choices can make us lazy and undisciplined. We may prefer to hold back and see if a better offer comes along. We enjoy sitting on the fence because that way we can hop on and off whatever side we feel most drawn to in any given moment.

Most of us are completely promiscuous when it comes to values and beliefs. We choose what feels good in the moment rather than acquire the conviction to go all out in one direction - no retreat, no excuses.

Unfortunately, modern society has taught us that commitment is optional: we can wait until the last minute and then decide. We don't even need to make concrete plans with friends anymore because we can '*wing it*', all day every day. Why should we do what we don't want to do anyway - something better may come up and just because we said we would do something doesn't mean we have to do it - *right*? We can execute occasionally or randomly, and that's OK - *right*? No. Wrong. It's a fast track to failure.

We are what we repeatedly do. Excellence, then, is not an act, but a habit.
Aristotle

Holding back is just a cop-out. It's a socially acceptable way of avoiding commitment. You can tell yourself that holding back is smart because it gives you more options, but that's not true. Success requires commitment. It requires courage and consistency and the discipline to do what needs to be done, regardless of whether you want to or not. Be assured if you Gain Control, Embrace the Future, Own a Strategy and master **Law 4 - Always Execute** - then you will reap rewards. And those rewards are huge, for the simple reason that so few people are prepared to do it. If you are, then wealth will be probable. Every noble work is at first seen as impossible or at least difficult. Then accepted, and eventually embraced as the only way. This consideration illustrates to us that a higher law beyond that of mere will regulates all results both in business and in life.

5. Grabbing profit instead of creating value

Grabbing profit doesn't work, and yet the perennial interest in "get-rich-quick" schemes would indicate that we are still reluctant to accept that fact.

Sure, you can start a business, especially in the anonymous online world, it is still possible to make fast money. But it doesn't last very long and will lack sustainability. People are not stupid. The Internet makes everything faster, so you have an opportunity to create wealth quicker, but you can also destroy a reputation faster.

If all you are interested in is the money, then you become a slave to it, and when that happens, you're lost. Grabbing profit is short-sighted and degrading - this is not how long-term wealth is created, regardless of what the media might imply.

Avarice has ruined more souls than extravagance.
Charles Caleb Colton

Grabbing profit comes from a mentality of scarcity. The implication of money-grabbing behavior is that you believe that there is only a limited supply and you must fight for as much as you can. If you have a mindset like that, you will never keep your wealth. You may create it, but it will be a constant battle to do so, and you will never keep it, because all you will be interested in is what you can get rather that what you can give. Gain Control, Embrace your Future, Own a Strategy, Always Execute that strategy at all times and master **Law 5 - Create Value.** Add as much value as you can, and if you do, then you will create significant wealth.

6. Maintain your position instead of seeking growth

We are meant to grow. Everything in life develops and evolves and grows; otherwise, it's receding and dying. That's the law of nature, and yet far too many of us are content to hang on to the status quo. We are so terrified to lose what little we have that we put all our effort into maintaining our position.

What we fail to realize, however, is that the very nature of life itself will not allow us to maintain our position. Life changes, people change, situations change. We have to rise to meet and embrace those changes - or we may be swept away by them. You and I can no more maintain position than hold back the tides. Why waste our time trying to achieve the impossible? Invest that energy and focus into seeking growth opportunities. Work with the laws of nature to harness that power.

Only put off until tomorrow what you
are willing to die having left undone.
Pablo Picasso

Fear of change is at the heart of everyone who seeks to maintain their position. It's easier, safer and more comfortable. Of all the flaws of character, however, this is perhaps the least corrosive. You can live a good life by following the first 5 Laws of Wealth, but you will not achieve significant wealth without mastering Law 6.

Wouldn't it be a shame to journey so far and then power down the engine? Seeking Growth is the 100th of a second that separates Olympic silver from Olympic gold. You've already done all the hard work, you've already Gained Control, you've Embraced the Future, Owned a Strategy and Executed that strategy come rain or shine. You've Added Value, and the finish line is in sight - all you need is to master **Law 6 and Seek Growth**.

7. Keeping it all instead of giving back

The modern world has made us greedy and impatient. We don't want to strive for things - we want then handed to us on a silver platter. We want to take as much as we can lay our hands on while giving as little as we can get away with. We think the world owes us a living just for being here. It doesn't.

Somehow we have come to feel a sense of entitlement, and it's destroying our creativity and inventiveness and our ability to find our own solutions to the challenges we will face in life. Far too many sit back waiting for handouts instead of working out what they can Give Back.

If you want to create serious wealth - or any sort of success, for that matter - get used to the idea of giving back. No one is entitled to success - each of us has to work to create it in the best way we can. Only when you have given, and given again will the wheels of "luck" click into motion so that you can reap the fruit of your effort. And so the cycle begins again - first we give, and then we receive. It's a natural law.

The big problem is not the haves and the have-nots
- it's the give-nots.
Arnold H. Glasow

The irony of giving back is that it makes you feel richer. It doesn't matter if you give money, time, effort or encouragement - you leave the exchange a better person. You have only to listen to a perennial welfare recipient to hear how bitter and angry one can become by taking without giving.

Mastering the 7th Law of Wealth is as much about spiritual and emotional health as it is about financial wealth. If you have followed the path of the 7 Laws, then you will make money, there is no question about that. It is a simple outcome of the laws cause and effect. But more importantly, if you master Law 7 and Give Back, you will become a better, more balanced and happier person.

The character flaws associated with taking and not giving don't just relate to financial wealth; they rob us of all of our potential. They are the actions and behaviors that lead to failure in every walk of life.

Instead, make a commitment to the **7 Laws**. Seek out your weaknesses and address them today. Go back to the self assessment questions at the end of each law and transfer your responses in Column A on the table over the page.

Law	Number of Results in column A
Law 1 - Gain Control	
Law 2 - Embrace the Future	
Law 3 - Own a Strategy	
Law 4 - Always Execute	
Law 5 - Create Value	
Law 6 - Seek Growth	
Law 7 - Give Back	

The lowest number indicates which Law(s) are your weakest; here is where you start in your alignment process. As I mentioned in the introduction, **The 7 Laws of Wealth** are a cumulative, all-or-nothing philosophy. It doesn't matter if you rate brilliantly on one or two; you have to master them all to truly succeed.

If you would like practical ideas and insights on how to effectively mold yourself to each of the 7 Laws, you may want to read the companion book and supplementary in depth materials for each of your weakest Laws. Sign up at www.7lawsofwealth.com for more details.

It's Never About the Money

I have been accused of being "all about the money." But if I have done my job correctly, you will now realize that this book is about far more than monetary wealth. I am really not that interested in money *per se*; I'm just not into poverty. I've tried both, and being rich is definitely better, but *it was the journey toward that wealth that has made me truly rich*. I am happier and more generous, and my passions have changed as I've been able to see how my efforts can influence and help others.

What I care about is that *you* understand what's really involved in building a successful business. That way you can decide what you truly want in life - and find the courage to go after it.

People have so many hang-ups about money. That's the reason I wrote my first book, *The New Rules of Wealth: Dispelling the 27 Myths of Personal Prosperity*. I get a sense sometimes from the individuals I meet in workshops and speaking events that people question if it's morally '*right*' to be wealthy.

So let me ask you this: Is it right to be healthy? To be knowledgeable? To be in love? How healthy should you be? As healthy as you can be. How much knowledge should you gain? As much as you can gain. How much should you love? As much as you possibly can! These things make life the adventure it is meant to be. The same applies to money. How much money should you make? As much as you can, first for yourself (Law 1), then to benefit others (Law 7).

A tree doesn't decide before it starts growing that it will grow only to a certain size. It grows to its full capacity, whatever that may be, depending on its location and access to nutrients. Life is the same.

The purpose of life is not to be happy.
It is to be useful, to be honorable, to be compassionate,
to have it make some difference that you have lived and lived well.
Ralph Waldo Emerson

Your self-worth is not dependant on your net worth. However if you increase your net worth, you can't help but positively affect your self-worth, *providing* you have done it with integrity. Take a stand, make a decision to change your life, and follow through on that personal promise. If you do, you'll be inspired, and you'll be filled with a pride you may never have experienced before.

If, after reading this book, you decide, *"Hey, I really don't think this wealth thing is for me"* - then great. That's a truly worthwhile result, because you can stop beating yourself up about not being rich and enjoy the many other things in your life that make you wealthy in different ways - good friends, your pets and hobbies, a close family and a career you enjoy.

You don't need to be mega-wealthy to live a great life. But you do have to love where you are and appreciate what you have as a starting point. Decide what you want and what price you are willing to pay - and make informed choices about what is necessary instead of living in some fairytale where money grows on trees and lottery millions are just a ticket away.

If you chose to take this journey, then do so with passion, commitment and perseverance. Embrace the fact that getting rich doesn't have to happen at the expense of others. It's the exact opposite - it's about creating wealth for everyone involved, it's about taking people with you, having fun, making a contribution, and doing good for yourself, for others and for the planet.

If you can do that, then you truly are wealthy.

Bonus Chapter

The 7 Attributes of Wealth

The gratification of wealth is not found in mere possession or in lavish expenditure, but in it's wise application. Two things are required in this; for rich men to understand how poor men live; and poor men, to understand how rich men work.

Bonus Chapter
The 7 Attributes of Wealth

One of the things I like is getting things I don't expect. Who doesn't? I remember buying a CD years ago and listening to it. After the last song had finished, there was a pause and just as I was about to turn it off, a surprise song burst from the speakers. It wasn't expected, and it wasn't mentioned on the CD, but it was there, like an extra hidden present at Christmas, or your birthday.

The 7 Attributes of Wealth are a bit like that extra present. It's something you didn't expect - a bonus chapter. I wanted to surprise you, so you won't find this chapter listed in the contents at the front of the book.

By living the 7 Laws of Wealth, your outcome will almost certainly be more money - significantly more money. But that's not all you will receive.

One of the most amazing things about setting out to achieve significant wealth are its *side effects*. When my mentor suggested to me that I should become a millionaire, I initially laughed because the idea was so far out of my frame of reference. And yet the idea grew on me, I decided to make it my goal. I put everything I had - blood, sweat and plenty of tears - behind that ambition. I became a multi-millionaire, not once but twice, in completely unrelated fields. In doing so I was tested, pushed and stretched to meet a new, higher standard.

The "self-made" men and woman we're always hearing about usually have created their own wealth. But have you considered that we are all "self made". If you set your sights on wealth, then the only way to achieve it is by adhering to its laws. If you do that, then the process you must go through *will* change you. What you have decided about your situation up to this point will be irrevocably altered, and you will never again be the same person.

What surprised me most about my own journey was that *the money was the least important part of what I achieved!* Learning to adapt yourself to the 7 Laws of Wealth doesn't just make you rich in monetary terms; it also makes you a better person. I was amazed to discover that in bending myself to the 7 Laws, I also gained what I call the 7 *Attributes* of Wealth. These are the late presents you didn't know you'd get. And they all came as a by-product of aligning with the 7 Laws methodology.

The 7 Attributes of Wealth

1. The ability to live with uncertainty
2. The ability to adapt to abrupt change
3. The ability to tell the difference between a truly threatening situation and one that just threatens our self esteem
4. The ability to delay immediate gratification
5. The ability to deal with significant financial pressure
6. The ability to follow through
7. The ability to navigate obstacles

1. The ability to live with uncertainty

Although we are programmed to seek certainty as a means of survival, the really wealthy have all mastered uncertainty as a life principle. As a high performing individual, you will have to get comfortable with uncertainty. If you don't, it will tear you apart when you try to escalate your business or investment concerns. You'll get little sleep and end up an emotional disaster.

I'm not sure anyone loves uncertainty, but once you've applied the 7 Laws and achieved your outcome, you will be able to live with it comfortably and even thrive on it.

Most people prefer to stick to what they know because it's safe. They stay in jobs they hate because "better the devil you know." They believe the education rhetoric that states if you get good exam results, you'll get a good, safe job. But there is no such thing as a good, safe job. Look at any economic downturn in history - it doesn't matter if you have an exemplary work record; you are usually just as susceptible to redundancy as the person in the next office.

We have been led to believe that working for others offers certainty and security. Even the banks consider a job "safe" and self employment or having a business "unsafe" when applying for an overdraft protection or a loan.

The real opportunity lives outside safety and certainty. If you master Law 1 and Gain Control, then you, not your employer, are in charge of your destiny. You will make it happen, and accept uncertainty as a the other side of opportunity.

2. Ability to adapt to abrupt change

One hundred and fifty years ago, we couldn't communicate by telephone; now almost everyone has a mobile phone. If you wanted to tell someone something, you had to send a letter or a telegram; now you can send an email to the other side of the globe in seconds. As a result of these technological advances, things can and *do* change very fast.

In the days before computers, stock markets were controlled by pieces of paper passed back and forth. Now everything is computerized, and markets can tank in seconds. Billions in market capitalization can be wiped out faster than it takes you to phone your broker and scream, "Sell!"

That speed of transaction has meant that we live in a constantly evolving, constantly changing environment. Seriously wealthy individuals accept that and relish the opportunity that it can bring.

Countless companies have gone to the wall because they were unwilling to see the writing on it. On September 15, 2008, the prestigious financial services firm Lehman Brothers filed for what was to be the largest bankruptcy in US history. The firm incurred unprecedented losses as a result of the continuing subprime mortgage crisis - losses that were reported to be a result of holding on to large positions too long. Although it's not clear if that was a conscious choice or the result of an inability to sell, it was however, pivotal in the collapse.

Lehman got really greedy and took huge risks in the subprime market. Its collapse caused a meltdown in already distressed global markets. What followed was what many have called the "perfect storm" of economic distress factors, which eventually necessitated a $700 billion bailout in the US and huge government support in the UK and Europe.

Other famous near misses include Ford Motor Company, in which Henry Ford endangered the company by hanging on to the iconic Model T and refusing to acknowledge changing consumer requirements. Having given the masses a car, he couldn't believe they wanted choice.

Over at General Motors, Alfred P. Sloan acknowledged a growing consumer desire for variety. He split the car buying population into market segments and targeted his Chevrolet, Oldsmobile, Pontiac, Buick and Cadillac to particular segments. Customers could climb the ladder of success with increasingly expensive and prestigious GM car brands.

Sloan also introduced the annual model change. The idea of cars as constantly changing fashion goods transformed the industry and assured GM's leadership for decades. Sloan recognized that change was coming and he went to meet it.

More recently, technology giant Motorola has committed a couple of strategic missteps that nearly wiped them off the business map.

In addition to ploughing billions into Iridium, which we discussed in Law 3, Motorola also refused to accept the impending impact of digital technology and kept all its eggs in the analog basket. At its height Motorola enjoyed a US market share of 60%, but the refusal to see the digital opportunity decimated that market share, and the company fell 34%.

Change is a constant and swift part of everyday life. As you come to live the 7 Laws of Wealth, you will appreciate and be ready to change direction and adapt to whatever comes your way. You will understand that you must adapt or be left behind. It's that simple.

3. Ability to tell the difference between a truly threatening situation and one that threatens our self esteem

I remember reading a terrible story in the newspapers in 2008 about Kevin Tripp, who was killed in his local supermarket in southwest London because another customer thought he had cut in front of him in line. Even if he had, cutting in may be irritating, but it's not a valid motive for murder.

Similarly, the man who killed this father and devastated so many lives in the process clearly didn't know the difference between a physically threatening situation and one that threatened his self esteem.

Although there are obviously extreme examples like this, we can see this confusion all around us. Too many people get worked up over the strangest little things - things that don't threaten their survival or safety in any way but that simply bruise a fragile ego.

Not all wealthy people know the difference between these situations. However in most cases the journey toward wealth is sufficiently difficult, with enough highs and lows, to teach this valuable lesson. As a high achiever, you will be able to easily differentiate between something that is genuinely threatening and things that may simply offend your ego.

You will learn not to take things personally. You will be able to step back from situations and events and take an objective approach.

The psychologist Dr. Martin Seligman has done some interesting research into what he calls "explanatory style." How do we explain the things that happen to us?

Those with a more naturally optimistic outlook on life don't take things personally. If they miss a train, they will go about trying to find a solution to their immediate challenge. It is seen in isolation, nothing more than a temporary setback on the way to their objective.

Pessimists, on the other hand, will attribute poor results or that missed train to some personal defect or other. Each of these events or circumstances will be stacked one on top of the other to create a sense of some permanent personal failing that will plague them for their entire lives. They thus develop "learned helplessness".

Almost without exception, the really successful people I've met have an explanatory style which supports them in achieving their objectives. They couldn't care less what others think of them, and they are able to separate what is important from what might bruise their ego but cause no long-term damage.

4. Ability to delay immediate gratification

This ability is of *huge* importance. In many ways it is the most important of the 7 attributes. Sadly, this ability is on the decline and represents the absolute antithesis of modern society.

In your grandparents' day, if they wanted something, they had to save up and buy it. That was the way of the world. An innovative banker called John Biggins changed all that. Biggins worked at the Flatbush National Bank, in New York, and in 1947 he set up a local community credit plan called "Charg-It" that covered a two-square-block patch surrounding his bank.

It was a huge success, and two years later, Diners Club launched their credit card. Within one year, Diners had signed up 285 establishments and 35,000 cardholders - each paying $3 per year for the privilege. Today credit cards are a gigantic business, consumer debt is astronomical, and the idea of delayed gratification is seen as arcane and out-dated.

According the US Federal Reserve statistics for September, 2009 Americans owe $917 billion on revolving credit lines and $69 billion is past due. In 1968, consumers' total credit debt was equivalent to only $8 billion in today's dollars. Over two million American homes carry more than $20,000 on credit cards. With average interest rates at 19%, that's a serious problem.

And the UK is no better. According to the Credit Action figures for February 2010, the average consumer debt owed by every UK adult is £30,252 (including mortgages) - that's over $46,000, 129% of average earnings. Clearly, delayed gratification is not a concept understood by most people. The total credit card debt in December 2009 was £54.5bn (over $84 billion). The UK collective credit limit on credit cards is £158bn ($244 billion), which is an average credit card limit of £5,129 (or almost $8,000) per person. The average interest rate on credit card lending is currently 17.79%, which is 17.29% above base rate (0.5%). It's not surprising that in the UK, one person declares bankruptcy every 3.72 minutes.

Even those involved in the credit card industry realize how dangerous they can be to financial prosperity. In 2003 Barclays then-chief executive, Matt Barrett, gave evidence at the Commons' Treasury select committee investigating credit card charges. He said, "I do not borrow on credit cards. It is too expensive. I have four children. I give them advice not to pile up debts on their credit cards."

Nowadays people can be divided into three classes -
the haves the have-nots and the have-not-paid-for-what-they-haves.
Politician Earl Wilson

When it comes to delayed gratification, I am not talking about money. I'm talking about time, effort, energy - everything. Everything worth having in life requires a period of effort and focus where results are not obvious. When you sow seeds in a garden, nothing appears to happen for a long time until the shoots burst through the soil. Even then you can't keep pulling up the shoots to see how the roots are doing. The same is true of any endeavor. As you master the 7 Laws of Wealth, you will appreciate the necessity and importance of delayed gratification.

All the wealthy people I know have experienced times when they felt as though they were going backwards...when they had to give up certain things and miss out on certain experiences while keeping the eye on the prize. They were able to delay gratification in order to secure the long term goal because they knew the rewards far outweighed the sacrifice.

5. Ability to deal with significant financial pressure

Those who have achieved significant wealth are able to do so because they are comfortable with significant financial pressure. This was a huge lesson for me on my journey. There were times where I felt physically sick at the commitments I had taken on. Unless you are feeling nauseous from time to time, you are not stretching yourself and will not make significant progress.

One caveat to this idea is that "progress" doesn't always come in the size and shape you hoped for. *Progress doesn't always come when things work out - but when they don't, and you survive anyway.*

As a high achiever, you will have to make some hard financial decisions that could destroy you or make you. They are not comfortable decisions. But if you want to step up financially, you will have to learn how to deal with amplified financial pressure. It's not something that happens overnight; it's a gradual process, as you become the sort of person who can comfortably deal with the uncomfortable.

6. Ability to follow through

The sixth attribute of the super-wealthy is their ability to do what needs to be done, regardless of whether they feel like it or not.

The journey toward serious wealth is not always easy. You will be called to make hard choices and follow through on what you set out to do. There will be times when you don't want to do that, when you would rather do just about anything than make the call or write that report. Without exception, the truly rich are those people who make the call and do what needs to be done regardless of how they feel. This principle is the heart of Law1.

If you want to become seriously wealthy, then you have to learn how to be hard on yourself in the tough moments. You must follow through on your strategy and plans, regardless of what you feel like doing or whether or not a better offer or more enjoyable possibility presents itself.

We all have two choices in life - *hard/easy* or *easy/hard.* If you do the hard work now, you will have an easier time later. If you take the easy route now, your future will probably be hard later on, the choice is yours. If you do the things you are supposed to do, when you are supposed to do them, there will come a time when you can do the things you want to do, when you want to do them.

7. Ability to navigate obstacles

One of the common denominators of successful people is their inability to accept the word "no." When they are told they can't do something or someone won't assist them in their plight, they don't see this as the end but as a call to action to be more creative. They simply find a different approach and try again. They see obstacles and challenges not as the death knell of the idea, but as a test of their resourcefulness. Sometimes you will have to simply change your approach, rather than change the objective.

Developing the 7 Attributes

I remember when I had achieved a significant level of success in business, I wondered if all significant wealth had hallmarks, if there were common threads in the experience for all those who had started with nothing and made a fortune. The same will happen for you as you travel toward your goal.

The 7 Laws of Wealth is not only your road map for becoming wealthy; but the side effects of such an adventure mean that you will develop the 7 Attributes of Wealth and become a stronger, more competent and productive person. If you are not quite there yet - don't worry. Just act as if you are and foster these attributes consciously, because they create a wealth mindset - regardless of whether you have the money to back it up.

Index

BEN BENSON IS recognized as one of businesses top minds. He has dedicated his life to helping individuals build better businesses through understanding and applying the Natural Laws that govern sustainable growth, both in business and in life.

Ben started with nothing – twice. After building up a multi-million-pound training consultancy, selling up and losing everything, he started again, working around-the-clock on a multi-million pound property empire. His private and commercial property portfolio now sits alongside finance, publishing and venture-capital interests. He is the architect of the '7Laws series' of books and training programs and presents to senior managers and business owners throughout the world. His first book The New Rules of Wealth – Dispelling the Myths of Personal Prosperity' sold out in the United States, United Kingdom and on Amazon.com in 3 days.

From this entrepreneurial melting pot of personal drive and collective expertise, Ben has interviewed over 200 of the 'Times Rich List' to find out how they tick. He has emerged as a dynamic speaker who has presented at over 2000 conference events worldwide. He's also consulted with senior managers at companies such as Bank of America, Cisco, Federal Express, Hallmark, BMW, Kodak, Kimberly Clark, Ford and American Airlines.

His 7Laws of Wealth methodology and training program have been conducted to over 180,000 individuals in businesses, colleges and schools around the world. Ben's mission is to educate individuals to realise a commitment to the 'life of business and the business of life', Ben is also passionately committed to assisting entrepreneurs and struggling businesses find restructuring solutions that identify hidden value for sustainable long-term growth. Ben also privately mentors individuals on a year long, one-to-one basis in the 7 Laws Methodology.

For more information on Ben Benson and the 7Laws of Wealth visit; 7lawsofwealth.com